NOW YOU KNOW

The Story of the Four Freshmen

By Founding Freshman
Ross Barbour

Balboa Books
A DIVISION OF TIARE PUBLICATIONS

Book design: John C. Herkimer,
Next Wave Graphics, Caledonia, NY

Cover design: Peter S. Janzen Art and Design,
Fontana, WI

Cover photo: Capitol Records

Published by Balboa Books, a division of
Tiare Publications, P.O. Box 493, Lake Geneva,WI 53147

ISBN: 0-936653-83-3
Printed in the United States of America

Library of Congress Cataloging-in-Publication Data

Barbour, Ross, 1928-
    Now you know : the story of the Four Freshmen / by Ross Barbour. -
- Golden anniversary ed.
        p.   cm.
    ISBN 0-936653-83-3
    1. Four Freshmen (Musical group)   2. Musicians--United States-
-Biography.   I. Title.
ML421.F68B37   1998
782.42164'092'2--dc21
[B]   98-29601
                                                                      CIP
                                                                       MN

This book is dedicated to my wife, Sue, who consistently did more than humanly possible during the road years. And to the memory of Stan Kenton, the greatest leader of men I've ever met.

CONTENTS

ACKNOWLEDGEMENTS

May I, by mentioning you people here, have the effect of personally shaking your hand and thanking you every time you open the book to this page.

John Bangs and the Four Freshmen Society made the manuscript happen by underwriting the cost of its production. Chick Trafford, editor of *Fresh News* and Nikki Gary, our booking agent for nearly a decade, were of special help as well. Besides my Sue, several of the Freshmen helped me fill in the blanks, especially from the years after my retirement. Thanks to Bob Flanigan, Ken Albers, Mike Beisner and Greg Stegeman for their informative interviews. And I appreciate Greg and Dottie Woolridge, who put me up in their lovely home in Las Vegas during the interview process.

For their painstaking help in writing the manuscript I extend my thanks to Peter and Marilyn Gillquist, and to forever fans Babs and Wayne Frederich who edited the final draft. Jamie Stuart did a special read-through for us, too. And thanks also go to Syd Knowlton for his artistic assistance.

I appreciate so much the encouragement of our high school friends, Bill and June Hoeltke, who typed some of the original draft. Ginger Gillquist typed the early chapters of the book and Terri Beth Speier ran the entire manuscript through her word processor more times than I'd care to admit. Thanks, ladies!

And a big thank you goes to Bobby Troup, our "Honorary Freshman."

FOREWORD

By Bobby Troup

I first heard the Four Freshmen in 1950. They were appearing at a club in Beverly Hills near La Cienega Boulevard, on Los Angeles' famous "Restaurant Row." As I entered the lounge I saw the Freshmen for the first time - Ross Barbour on drums, his brother Don on guitar, their cousin Bob Flanigan on bass and trombone and Hal Kratzsch was singing a song I had written in the Marine Corps in 1943, "Baby, Baby All the Time."

By the time I sat down at my table and ordered something to drink I heard that wonderfully warm sound of the four guys together singing their hearts out. It was a sound I'll never forget as long as I live.

I've always been infatuated with close harmony groups - the Boswell Sisters and the trio in Jimmy Lunceford's Orchestra: Sy Oliver, Joe Thomas and Willie Smith, and later Trummy Young. And who can forget the Pied Pipers, the Modernaires and the Pastels? But for me, the Four Freshmen eclipsed them all. I'll never tire of hearing their unique and easily identifiable sound.

If I could put together my very favorite Freshmen album, I would want to include Don Barbour's tenderly moving "Old Folks," that swinging song everyone predicted would be a hit, "Whistle Me Some Blues," Dick Reynolds' a cappella arrangement of "I'm Always Chasing Rainbows," and, I guess immodestly, I'd have to include a song I wrote with Neal Hefti, with a beautifully sensitive arrangement by Ken Albers, "Girl Talk."

Now, thanks to Ross Barbour, we can read about these four gentlemen and the many more who fitted into the group over the years. The story is entitled "Now You Know," which is also the title of the first of my songs the Freshmen recorded.*

Enjoy!

Bobby Troup

*Other Bobby Troup songs recorded by the Four Freshmen include "Please Remember," "Their Hearts Were Full of Spring," "Lonely Night in Paris," "Julie Is Her Name," "Route 66," "It Happened Once Before," "This October," and "Lemon Twist."

PLEASE REMEMBER

"And here they are, ladies and gentlemen! Let's give a rip-roaring, Nittany Lion welcome to the fabulous Four Freshmen!"

The Penn State basketball arena thundered with wild applause 'till it nearly rained in there! It was a full house of college students, many of whom had come more than an hour early to catch the Freshmen. Before the applause began to fade we were into our opener, "Somebody Loves Me."

That Penn State performance in the spring of 1957 was one of about 200 college concerts we did each year from the mid-fifties to the mid-seventies. Each one of them was a blast. College students were young enough to be excitable and old enough to know their own minds. These people had heard our records and those who wanted to hear our kind of music were ready for us. And we were ready for them because we were specializing in college concerts, a brand new segment of show business. After we played at a school they were spoiled. We entertained them beyond their highest expectations.

As usual, while we were setting up the instruments on stage at Penn State, we asked the stage crew a few questions: "What is the most notorious local bar? What do you call your lover's lane? Who is the one teacher all the students know?

Name your rival school. Who's the football coach, the band director? It took only a few minutes to put the local names into our gags (I wrote them on my drumhead) so later on I could say, "This tune was written by (the band director)," and Bob could tell them, "Later, I'll meet you at (the notorious local dive). They loved these localized jokes.

While the applause for the first tune was still going strong we jumped right into our second song, "Please Remember." The first two chords were in a different key and without instrumental accompaniment. It was one of the dreamy love songs they had played on their jukeboxes, so it was greeted with still more applause.

Because our harmony seemed so very different and complicated people marveled that we could "pull our notes out of thin air." They didn't realize that, with the instruments in our hands, we were getting the new key while they were still applauding. We were starting the song long before they were expecting anything to happen.

That Penn State concert was recorded and released a short time later by the Penn State Jazz Club, solely for their members. It was our first "live" album.

But more than that, the whole scene that evening - the gymnasium, the crowd of coeds and their dates, the Freshmen and the songs themselves - made this concert a prime example of our work in those years when collegiate America was the center of our existence. If the people weren't already Freshmen fans they were by the time we sang our closing theme. The durability of their devotion to our sound is the thing that's kept the group going for half a century.

On a Roll

Somehow, our momentum was surging. After three or four early years of low-lit lounges, cars that wouldn't run and checks that sometimes wouldn't clear the bank, we were finally on a roll. "It's A Blue World" was out and was already a Freshmen classic. Ditto "The Day Isn't Long Enough," "Day by Day" and the more recently recorded, "In This Whole Wide World." Heck, we even had a movie under our belts! Our repertoire of love songs, and the harmonies we used, seemed to melt right in with the optimistic feeling of that decade after World War II. It seemed we just couldn't miss.

And we certainly didn't miss that night at Penn State! After "Please Remember," I took the mike as emcee and introduced Bob, Ken Albers, brother Don and myself - though Flanigan insisted to the delight of everyone that he was sure we had already met! Then, I segued into introducing one of my few solos. "Ready?" I asked the crowd. "I'll count to three and each of us will choose his own favorite song and we'll be set to go! One, two, three..." and off we were into "My Heart Stood Still," "Angel Eyes," "There Will Never Be Another You," "Old Folks," "Day By Day" (where they broke in with spontaneous applause), "Stormy Weather" and the ever popular "Graduation Day." Then, "After You've Gone," "In This Whole Wide World," "How Can I Tell Her," and "Circus," followed by my funny-voiced "Leroy" solo, "Sweet Lorraine."

Bob interrupted my chatter with what came to be a surefire routine. "We came here tonight via the University of Pittsburgh," he blurted out.

"Oh-oh," I responded with orchestrated shock as the student body broke into an immediate and spontaneous, "Hisssssssssss." Bob loved it and shouted off mike, "This building has a leak in it, you notice that?" The place went wild.

It was a relatively new thing for concert entertainers of our era to play back and forth with the crowd. When the laughter subsided, Bob had another line ready. Knowing they'd paid at the door to hear us sing, he quipped, "All this may not be very entertaining, but it sure kills a lot of time!"

That was my cue: "He thinks he can say anything. He's got Blue Cross!" They howled some more.

I turned back to the mike to introduce our next song. "This is a number from our new album, *The Four Freshmen and Five Trumpets*. It's called 'Good-bye.' This isn't the final piece of the program - you can leave if you want to - but there will be more after this. We always lose a few customers because they think it's our closing song."

"Yeah, well I'm leaving after this," Bob would offer, to a whole new round of giggling and applause. We were hitting a magic combination of music and chatter. The kids knew it and we knew it. The rest of the fare that night included Bob's "special" part of the program with his "Li'l Christmas Song," followed by "Blue World" and closing out with "Street of Dreams," our farewell number for 15 years before "And So It's Over" came along.

The Joy Factor

From the opening year of the Freshmen to this very day, with the lively new ensemble of Greg Stegeman, Brian Eichenberger, Kevin Stout, and Bob Ferreira, joy has always been the ultimate goal of everything we did as a vocal quartet. The more effort we made to be musically good, the more joy it held for us.

I must admit there were times we gave a total effort on something, like an arrangement that took longer than common sense dictated, and thus cut down on our joy. But at least the effort was there the whole time. We were always working to do our very best.

Other groups sang in tune; we felt we had to do better than that. Having a strong rehearsal or even an effective performance was an upper, but it was never enough. No matter what we did, we seemed driven to do more. And that sort of dissatisfaction with the status quo can often bring with it great frustration. Our challenge became to keep the goals out of reach, and at the same time to stay content with each other while we were falling short of perfection. Hopefully we transferred some of that to our listeners.

The Story

We've often been asked to tell our story, right from the start. When did you first get together? How did you find your sound? What were your disappointments over the years? What kept you going? These are the questions our listeners have asked repeatedly over the years and I'll do my best to answer them. To do so I want to go beyond just dates and places into the real heart and soul of who we are, the behind-the-scenes development of the Freshmen.

So besides the fun, celeb stuff, I want to deal with the discovery of new-sounding chord progressions, how we kept our unison sound, our instrumental back-up technique and a basketful of heretofore unpublished episodes that were life changing for us.

To start out, we'll go down home to Columbus, Greencastle and Warsaw, Indiana. I'll invite you on campus at Arthur Jordan Conservatory of Music in our freshman year. We'll journey through those crazy times at Elks Clubs, church bazaars, spring proms and crummy bars - wondering with Sartre if there would ever be an exit from the human dilemma. And then you'll climb aboard the fast track with us to Hollywood, New York City, the recording studios and lots of places like Penn State. By the end of the book, I want you to know the Freshmen as they are today after 50 years - still singing those great chords that were the hallmark of the original group, while adding some new zest with their own personalities.

So come along with me and get to know my favorite group in the whole wide world - the Four Freshmen!

FRESHMEN YEAR

Bob Flanigan was born and raised in Greencastle, in west central Indiana. Bob is a first cousin to Don and me; his mother, Nellie, and my mother, Maude, were sisters in the Fodrea family. Bob's father, Lee, was a truck driver based out of nearby Terre Haute.

Music permeated both our families. Maxine, Bob's sister, became a concert level pianist. Growing up, Bob was a stunning "boy tenor" in church and school programs.

At the Harold Barbour house on Route 3, Columbus, about 40 miles south of Indianapolis, we actually had a vocal quartet. Don and I played ukulele and trumpet, Daddy played piano and Mother had a natural ear for harmony. We spent many evenings together around the piano in our rural farmhouse. By day, Daddy raised corn and soybeans, sold insurance, and drove a school bus.

One of my favorite childhood memories is of us Barbours driving over the two lane country highways up to Greencastle after church one Sunday morning for a Fodrea family reunion. Before the meal, the 40 or 50 of us paused to sing "The Doxology." I can remember thinking, "I can't believe the beauty and depth of four-part harmony. What a wonderful sound!"

Bob, who was a couple of years our senior, was also a prankster. After dinner he got Don and me into smoking cigarettes behind the garage while the adults were busy visiting under the shade tree in the side yard. "You've gotta watch that Flanigan boy," Daddy chided us on the way home.

In high school, besides being pivot man on the varsity basketball team (his big feet earned him the nickname "Snowshoe"), Bob did solos in the annual Christmas program and sang with a five-part vocal group his senior year. He also played lead trombone in the high school band. He performed so well, in fact, that the DePauw University band "borrowed" him on occasion to fill out their trombone section at local concerts.

After graduation from high school in 1944 Bob enlisted in the Army and was stationed with the infantry in Bremen, Germany. Word got out they needed a bass player with experience to play in the Army band on base. Private Flanigan stepped up to volunteer. He had never played the bass a day in his life, but he picked up on the instrument in no time and began touring with the band to other military bases and playing USO shows. The prankster had ducked the infantry! Later, he switched back to trombone. Bob came out of the Army as good on the bass as he was on the trombone. He had also developed a feel for the big bands and their sounds.

Don was 20 months older than me and two years ahead of me in school. He was quiet, thoughtful and physically very strong. Both of us were involved in music, as well as a host of other school activities. Like Bob, Don joined the service immediately after graduation, while I completed my last two years at Columbus High. As a senior, my yearbook reminds me, I was class vice president, and Nancy Sue Carson's steady boyfriend.

Off to College

Arthur Jordan Conservatory was connected with Butler University in Indianapolis, and my high school band teacher, Russ Goucher, encouraged me to go there. I graduated at the same time Don finished his two years in the Army and returned from overseas duty. To my delight he decided to enroll as a freshman with me at Arthur Jordan in 1947. It was a warm, sunny, September morning when we finished packing and headed an hour north to "Nap Town" to register.

They assigned us and ten other freshman boys to a dorm of sorts. Actually it was a huge old 1880s style three story home at 2142 N. Delaware, run by a lady named Mrs. Stam. She and her family lived on the third floor, we boys were on the second, and other tenants rented out the first floor. The place was a typical Midwestern center city home, with an expansive porch all the way across the front, punctuated by four massive white wood pillars. It was decked with a wooden planked floor that talked back to you as you walked across it on cold winter nights.

Usually we went back home to Columbus on weekends to work in local bands. During the week we studied, kept a low profile and tried our best to be somewhat normal college freshmen.

First Effort

I met Hal Kratzsch that October. He was a Burt Lancaster type, with a dimple in his chin, a lot of brown curly hair, and a smile full of bright white teeth. The girls were absolutely knocked out with Hal, especially when they saw him drive up in his proud '41 Packard convertible. It was a gorgeous item! Hal was from Warsaw, Indiana, and had transferred from Indiana University in Bloomington, where he had begun his studies in music. He arrived at Arthur Jordan a month late.

One day after our music theory class he walked up to me. "We ought to get something together, like a quartet," he said out of the blue. "Do you know anyone else who can sing?"

"Heck yes," I said, "My brother Don has a perfect voice for a quartet. He's here at school and I'll bet he'd jump at the chance to sing."

We would still need a fourth voice to sing the high harmony part. There was a girl named Marilyn in our theory class. She was pretty, dark haired, and had a good, clear singing voice. The three of us began rehearsing with Marilyn in mid-November, whenever she had free time. She took hold of the top part and did quite well. We thought, "This quartet of ours could sing at a few dances, make a few bucks and have a few kicks."

But a couple weeks later Marilyn informed us she would no longer be available to sing. What a letdown! We were supposed to go down to Bedford, Indiana, to work a night job that would last until one or two in the morning and not have us back until three or four. Marilyn said her mother wouldn't permit her to do that. This, after all those rehearsals!

"Marilyn, what in the world are you doing to us?" Hal asked. "Why do you think we rehearsed together all this time? Look, quartets perform at night, not at noon!" We lightened up because we knew she meant well. But when it got right down to it, she couldn't continue as a member of the group. We decided to cover our bases by asking more questions of our next top-voice candidate. (Bob, where were you when we needed you!)

A Place at the Top

There was a guy named Marvin Pruitt at our dorm. He was a natural barbershop high part singer. Marvin was, as we said back then, groovy - a fun kind of guy. He was brought up on a farm near Rensselaer, Indiana, near Lafayette. Marvin got by our initial interrogation and we discovered he sang the top part very well. That meant Don was still on the lead singing melody. I'd been a baritone from the beginning, and Hal, beautiful low-voiced Hal, sang the fourth part.

When you name the bass guys in a group - any group in any era, you've got to name Hal Kratzsch as one of the great low voices of all time. The funny thing was, when Hal did a solo he always wanted to sing it up in the second tenor range. He never wanted to do it down low. I guess that's the way it is - tenors want to be basses, basses try to be tenors, singers want to be dancers, and on you go.

Hal moved into our dorm and parked that big Packard outside on the street. I remember it was in December, the night of the Joe Louis/Jersey Joe Walcott fight. Nat King Cole's "The Christmas Song" was on top of the charts. And remember? We were all out looking at those new Kaiser-Frazer automobiles in the local showrooms.

We didn't really have a name for this a cappella quartet so we decided on "Hal's Harmonizers." Most of the jobs we did called for barbershop songs, but the musical motif we were anxious to build wasn't barbershop. We were in the early stages of getting bitten by a musical bug called modern harmony

One Group, Two Sounds

During the 1940s the popular big bands had vocal groups like the Modernaires, the Mel-Tones and the Pastels. They did this new, close harmony, where you really had to listen to hear the parts and even then you still weren't sure you had it. They usually featured five voices, with a female voice on top doing the melody. We took a cue from these groups and learned "White Christmas," "Moonglow," "Dream," "Talk of the Town," and "The Christmas Song," and did them all in this close, tight, modern harmony. Sometimes my girlfriend, Nancy Sue Carson, sang at our rehearsals.

But publicly we kept singing the barbershop songs. That's what most people wanted. And Marvin was really much more into barbershop than modern. So at that point we were a far better barbershop quartet than we were a modern quartet. We sang "Daddy, Get Your Baby Out of Jail," a barbershop song that really pleased the crowd. We would often close our set with "Coney Island Baby" or "Dry Bones." We worked some of the local places around town, including the Indianapolis Athletic Club.

The second week in December we piled into Hal's Packard convertible and drove down Highway 37 to Indiana University in Bloomington to work with a band headed by Gordon Platt. Hal knew Gordon when they were students at IU the year before. Gordon had wanted to add a vocal group and we were supposed to rehearse with them but we never did. We just winged it.

We met Gordon at an event called the "Powder Puff Ball" on campus at IU. I believe they held it every year. On this winter night, while the band was taking an intermission, our group was to get up and sing the modern stuff. Platt knew we would never fly as Hal's Harmonizers. His band was called the Top Hatters so he spontaneously dubbed us the Toppers. We did two 15 minute segments and some of the kids listened, some didn't. We got some wrong notes mixed in with the right ones, but we sang with wild enthusiasm. It was some kind of evening for us, a real confidence builder.

A bit of tradition found its way into our young career. When we sang modern we'd go on as the Toppers and wear sweaters or coats and ties. As Hal's Harmonizers we wore barbershop outfits - black slacks, white shirts, white bartender aprons, bright arm garters, phony mustaches and black derby hats. We'd come out at the Elks Club or a church bazaar and sing "Daddy, Get Your Baby Out of Jail," "Aura Lee," and end that package with "Dry Bones," which was a huge number back then.

Mind you, none of this music was written out! We'd sit together in the car or in the rehearsal room on campus and sing one after another.

"To spend one night with you...Let's see, on 'to spend' - make that unison - on 'one' - let's spread into a trio, and on 'night,' we'll have four notes on 'night'." We would sing straight through until "rendezvous" and we'd try some extra special harmony on that word. We'd go over it again and again. Then, somebody would say, "Next time let's try it a note higher so we can get the bass to go an octave down on that last note. We'll spread that chord out a little bit." It was as though we were looking for another sound. We didn't enjoy singing sounds the other groups had done.

The more we rehearsed the more we were becoming diehard fans of the Mel-Tones, the five-voice group Mel Torme had put together with the Artie Shaw band. We also listened carefully to the Pastels. Stan Kenton had organized them to sing with his band. The Mel-Tones did "What Is This Thing Called Love?" and the Pastels sang "After You" on a new record with the Kenton band. They were five singers with a female on the lead

We copied some of the quartets, too. We had the Pied Pipers' records and we learned to sound just about like them - close up and together. Later we did "Kate," the rendition by the Town Criers, who traveled with the Tommy Dorsey band. We copied these groups as a strong tribute to them and to their music. We were their fans.

But when we merely sang the arrangements of these groups there was no thrill in it for us. It seemed we were but an echo of somebody else; there was no real fulfillment in doing it. But, at that time that's who we were - four guys trying to make an illusive sound, and being ignored. Even so, those were still good days!

It's odd. All four of us played instruments but it never dawned on us to play them while we sang. Hal's Harmonizers were strictly vocal; sometimes a friend did play bass behind the Toppers. Don and I were both in the music education course, preparing to be music teachers. I was a trumpet major. Don played guitar, but his major was voice. Hal was a trumpet player and Marvin was a trombone major.

Campus Unrest

Each day we walked the ten blocks to campus, down a series of tree-lined streets with endless two and three-story frame houses. We were beginning to get bored with our classes. In the music theory class, for instance, we waited for a number of freshman theory students to catch up. Maybe they had never even read a note of music, but they had shown "promise" somewhere. The class could only move as fast as its slowest members, so there was growing impatience. Each student took piano lessons and secondary brass and reed instruments as well.

Adding to our frustration was the reality that our number one interest had become the quartet, not our classes. We were into those chords, the harmonic progressions, the vocal sounds. The curriculum, on the other hand, prepared people for chamber orchestras, composition, teaching, conducting. What we were interested in, we were learning on our own.

Further, there wasn't much activity on campus. Arthur Jordan was a small school of only 700 or 800 students, some of whom came for only one lesson a week. The campus consisted of just two brick buildings plus two World War II Quonset huts. That was it! The Quonset huts were divided into rooms, probably nine feet square. Each had a piano, maybe two. A few even had organs. We were each assigned a rehearsal room at the beginning of the fall quarter.

Talk about wild, confusing, cacophony, this was it in spades! You would walk down the center hall and be overcome with a mix of some soprano doing scales, a beginning piano student playing both hands for the first time in his life, and a trombonist doing his pedal tones loud enough to drown out the girl on clarinet in the next room over!

Mostly, I concentrated on the piano. Not as an academic pursuit, or even for pleasure, but with four fingers - two on each hand - chording, inventing - searching for ways a vocal quartet could sing. Sometimes I would write out arrangements, but mostly I was a memorizer and always will be. When it comes to sight reading or really knowing how to write out music, I honestly have never been a whiz at it. Part of me wished I could be. If I heard the music I could play it, or I could sing it and memorize it.

It was that way with all of us. While I was picking my notes out Hal would be working on an arrangement or two and Don and Marvin would come up with other new ideas, some written down, most of them not. We would gather to rehearse and it was, "You sing hum, you, mmm, you sing hum."

We continued going home on weekends - Don to play guitar with the Reeder McDonald Band, I to keep my trumpet job with the Delmos Holmes Quintet. We were disappointed with school but very pleased with the quartet.

The Liberty Bell

After class, after rehearsal, after everything, we'd go to the Liberty Bell Cafe, a dairy bar on 22nd and Meridian, around the corner from school.

We'd go in, drink a malt, put salt in the sugar bowl, and serenade the waitress. (I think when the world gives thanks we ought to give special thanks for patient waitresses!) She put up with all kinds of nonsense from the college kids, most of it from us. If we had half an arrangement nailed down we'd sing it to her and have to quit right in the middle. The Liberty Bell became a pivotal place for us in the early days of the quartet.

On December 18th we had an audition with a man named Barney Barnett of the Burton Theatrical Agency, a booking agent who was going to get us "all kinds of promising jobs." We brought along Don Lehnen, a bass player, so we could sing the modern things.

If we had known what Barney was thinking of that day we wouldn't have bothered to get Lehnen out of bed. Barney wanted the barbershop stuff. That was what sold to the variety shows and the conventions. We even cleared some money - maybe $12 or $15 per show.

It was a strange time for vocal music. One by one the famous big bands stopped carrying vocal groups. They seemed to be part of a dying era in the world of popular music. It was becoming out of style to build new groups, but we didn't care, we did it anyway. Frankly, we've been out of step all along; whenever we had the chance to be in step, we stayed out!

The fall term at school came to an end with the Christmas break. The four of us headed home to enjoy some of mom's cooking and celebrate the holidays - Hal to Warsaw, Marvin back to Rensselaer, and Don and I to Columbus.

Don and I got the surprise of our lives when we returned to campus after the break. Hal had decided to drop out of school! We were very relieved to learn he had no intention of quitting the quartet! Fact is, his main interest had become the quartet. He found a daytime job as an adding machine repairman.

In January we did our first radio show as the Toppers with the Reeder McDonald Band, live on WCSI in Columbus. We sang "That's My Desire," "Dream" and "Moonglow."

The LVL

Just before Valentine's Day we met a man at the Liberty Bell who invited us to audition at the LVL Club south of town. (LVL stood for Liberal View League.) The place was run by two wonderful old reprobates. It was a rural nightclub that stayed open after hours and usually booked acts from Chicago, Cincinnati or Cleveland. The place had been raided a time or two in recent months. We went out there one evening with mixed feelings and asked for the boss.

"Well, all right, sing a few things for me," he muttered.

We began with the modern package but that didn't seem to impress him. He picked up a bit on the barbershop routine and hired us for three nights a week at $60, to be split four ways. But they let us sing for tips so in between sets we would cruise the tables and do requests.

"OK, guys, sing 'Sweet Adeline,'" somebody called out on our first night. We blew the pitch pipe and away we went. Nat King Cole's new big hit was "Nature Boy," and a few nights later a man flashed a $20 bill at us and asked for the song. Fortunately, Don knew the words to almost every song ever written, and the rest of us bluffed our way through three part back-up harmony.

On April Fool's Day we picked out our first Toppers outfit. Get this - white wool cardigan letter sweaters with "Toppers" in red chenille letters on the sides, black slacks, white shirts, with red and white knit ties in horizontal (not angled), stripes. Were we the cat's pajamas!

Since we worked the LVL three nights a week, there was little time left for much else besides school. Billed as the Toppers, we were doing more and more of the modern songs and less and less barbershop. It was becoming apparent that we were still looking for our permanent high voice lead, although little was said.

By the time school was out in late May, Marvin was out of the group. We parted friends, grateful for a tremendous first year at school. Our time was also up at the LVL Club. We said good-bye to our landlady Mrs. Stam, and headed home to Columbus. Don and I took summer jobs as tree trimmers. We had to find a new lead voice.

THE SUMMER OF '48

"Ross, let's give Bob Flanigan a call before we go to work," Don said as we finished breakfast. It was early summer and Bob was working on a Railway Express loading dock in Florida. "Maybe he's sick of Florida by now. It's an hour time difference - if we hurry we can catch him before he leaves the house."

"Who is this?" Bob yelled after we had said hello. "Man, have we got an idea for you," I told my cousin. Don and I took turns on the phone, telling him about meeting Hal at school, starting the quartet and developing a respectable repertoire.

"Sounds like it sure could beat loading big fruit trucks," Bob quipped, as we told him of our need for a lead voice in the group. "What does it pay?"

"Bob, we're all in the same boat," Don responded. "We can't offer you a guaranteed career. But if you're willing to work on the side and rehearse with us, I'll bet we can build it into something good."

Two days later, Bob called back. "I'm on my way," he announced.

Finding the Sound

"Guys, these notes are *high*," complained our new top voice after less than an hour of singing around the piano in the Barbour living room. "I may need surgery to do some of these songs!"

Truth is, Bob Flanigan took to the music like a duck to water. We knew at this first rehearsal with Bob on June 13th that we had found our lead voice and we were on our way. This was the summer we would turn the corner in finding our sound. It would take some time to perfect it, but we were beginning the process. That summer we began to discover several key components that would be the hallmark of the "Freshmen sound" through all the years that followed.

The Top Voice Lead.

Our early prototypes, the famous modern harmony groups, featured a female lead as the high voice, generally with three or four male voices doing the close-chorded parts to fill out the sound. Bob's range was such that he could easily handle the high melody line, and as far as we can tell, we were the first male modern quartet to assign the lead, the melody, to the top voice. This was one of the significant elements of the Freshmen sound.

As the years went by, other factors came into play with this high-voice-on-melody approach. Bob used his voice more and more like an instrument, a lead trombone, rather than simply as a predictable first tenor. You can hear it in his slides to a particular note, and occasionally in his blaring sound on a note or phrase. In fact, his voice had an almost piercing quality on top, as did Hal's on the bottom. By contrast, Don and I, who handled the second and third parts, had more of a mellow sound, to color the middle area of the chord. Though we all used roughly the same volume as we sang, it was Bob and Hal whose voices were usually discernible. Don and I were more difficult to hear and follow.

As time went on other groups picked up on this high lead voice technique. Jim Pike, the original high part and organizer of the three-voice Lettermen, told me years ago how hearing the Freshmen sing for the first time was a pivotal experience in his concept of their own sound. Though the Lettermen sound didn't mandate a top voice lead on all their songs, nonetheless the clear high voice lead certainly became a component of their music. A quick listen to their rendition of "White Christmas" is a case in point.

Similarly, Gene Puerling and the Hi-Los employed the high voice lead, as did many arrangements of the Beach Boys in the 60s. If you ever get the opportunity, compare the Beach Boys' "Graduation Day" to ours. They're quick to tell their public they ran with our arrangement, and honestly it's difficult to decide whether the record is the Beach Boys or the Freshmen.

Our Trademark Unison.

Don and I, being brothers, had many of the same vocal qualities, nearly identical word pronunciations and that special family blend. So, rather than all four of us doing the unison parts, usually it was just the two of us who handled it. The unison portions of our songs served to give Bob a break from his high register work, and it provided a pensive and restful contrast to the aggressive full sound of our four-part blend. We picked up on this early in our vocal development, as evidenced in our arrangements of "Blue World," "The Day Isn't Long Enough," and "It Happened Once Before."

The Peg Chord

Late in the spring of 1948, just before Bob Flanigan came on board, we made a crucial discovery that has stayed with us through our career. We must have been getting ready for Mother's Day because we were rehearsing "M Is For the Million Things She Gave Me." It was then that we adopted what we called our peg chord.

I remember hearing Cab Calloway say in an interview, "Everybody has to have their own peg to hang their hat on, a thing that is especially theirs, something that identifies them and sets them apart."

If you're a student of music, it is not that difficult to communicate. We had the fifth of the chord in the top voice, the ninth in the second, the major seventh in the third part and the third of the chord in the low part. There wasn't a song we sang that didn't use that peg chord.

Not that this is the only sound we tied ourselves to. When the two middle parts of the peg chord go down a whole step you've arrived at another distinctive Freshmen sound, an inverted sixth. Also, we used the major sevenths more than other groups did. We loved that sound!

The spread voicing, the moving harmony parts while the melody stays in one place, that's very much ours, too. Some groups claimed the augmented eleventh, some groups claimed the sixth - the Crew Cuts sang the sixth on every song they did. Ours was the Freshmen peg chord. You can hear it on the final chord in "Time Was."

The Open Sound

We've talked about the close harmony of the vocal groups with the big bands. Often all four or five parts were arranged to be sung within one octave. We grew to love the chords but not the sound. It seemed too tight for us.

At Arthur Jordan we had experimented off and on with taking a tight sixth or diminished sixth chord and dropping one of the middle notes down an octave and assigning it to Hal. But over the summer of 1948, with Bob on board, we made a concerted effort to use that technique more consistently. We were trying to sing sounds we hadn't heard a quartet do before.

If we were arranging by ear and came upon a chord that sounded like the Pied Pipers we'd say, "Let's change that. You drop down a third and I'll take the ninth." We tried to open the chord up an octave and a half or more - whatever would surprise us.

We weren't especially trying to make musical history. Instead we were attempting to entertain ourselves, to do things that hadn't been done before. We loved it at once and yearned to perfect it in all of our arrangements. There were times, especially on the big endings of our songs, that we'd actually cover the better part of two octaves. The sound was revolutionary and our fans grew to love it.

The Moving Middle Parts

Remember the second verse of "Blue World," right after the unison? It went, "It's a throo-oo-oo wo-or-or-orld for me!" There were three chords we wanted to use in that phrase but there's no way to sing but one, unless you move the parts around to cover all three in the progression. So we moved our voices together through all three chords. This strategy, which had been used for years in the brass sections of the big bands, soon became a Freshmen signature in so many of our songs. It sounded gutsy and complicated, but with practice it was quite easy.

The Density and Intensity of Vocal Delivery

Four guys could get together around somebody's piano and learn a Freshmen song but it wouldn't automatically sound like the Four Freshmen. Why? We tried to always apply pressure to the listener with the chords, to put enough energy into the chords that it would be transmitted to the listener. In short, we sang loud! Our love songs pleaded with the audience to experience the fullness of romance, our good-bye songs carried an aggressive lament over lost love. There was an urgency, a passion in our sound. We sang each note as though it was our last, and we'd do the next note the same way. Let me underscore this: while the practice sessions during the summer of '48 brought us to discover the new elements of our sound, the employment of them took months, even years to fully achieve.

Going Public

Just three days after Bob's first practice session with us we appeared as the Toppers on June 16th at the Elk's Club in

Bloomington. It was a real landmark in our fledgling career. The Elks had wanted a barbershop performance but we were charged up to do the modern sound. That night we did far more of the modern stuff than we did barbershop. It was our first night out of the blocks with what we really wanted to do. Bob was such a natural for this new sound; it was his lead voice that made the difference.

Hal finished with the adding machine repair company and came to Columbus on the 25th just to sing with us. Bob drove in from Greencastle. For the next formative years it was Bob on top, then Don, then me on baritone and Hal on the low part.

I played piano on our instrumental numbers, though I could only play in C and F (and struggled with F!). Hal played trumpet, Bob played bass and Don played guitar. Then we'd move into another song where Hal would play bass and Bob would play trombone. When we sang nobody played instruments at all; we just sang unaccompanied 'cause, heck, who would have thought of playing an instrumental background while singing?

There was a place just west of Columbus called The Umbrella. It had tables and chairs around a concrete dance floor and an umbrella in the center of each table. Up front there was a tiny band shell just big enough for a piano and for us to stand around it and sing. We worked the Umbrella as the Toppers on July 1st. They took up a collection and, I don't know, I think we got $3.25 for the night's work.

We played other spots the rest of the summer, occasionally working with the Reeder McDonald Band, now renamed the Rhythm Macs. As we had the year before Don and I worked our tails off trimming trees in and around Columbus and on the campus at Indiana University. Hal had various pick-up jobs and Bob was enrolled in summer school as a freshman at Arthur Jordan.

On July 21st we drove to Greencastle, where Bob had gotten us a job at the V.F.W. We played a little, sang a little, and succeeded in not impressing very many people. The

28th found us at Bridgie's in Seymour, Indiana. For that night we invented what we called the "trampsaphone" - a single cymbal mounted on a coat hanger wire with one drum brush attached to a spring, activated by a foot pedal. When I pushed down on the pedal, the brush would strike the cymbal. It was easy enough to play because I had both feet free. Or the guy on bass could play it because he had both feet free. It didn't make much noise but it was better than not having any drum at all. That night at Bridges was the beginning of our use of a background drum brush sound.

On July 29th we started a series of fifteen minute shows called Topper Time on WCSI-FM in Columbus. Hal finally got a job, at the Standard station on Eighth and Washington in Columbus. We would rehearse there when Hal wasn't pumping gas.

The rest of the summer we worked the Rainbow Girls dance, the local V.F.W., and a Moose Club opening. Some feedback indicated that the audience didn't always like the modern numbers. We were too "far out" for their ears. But we went over well on WCSI radio, and were a major part of their celebration show on their first birthday. At least somebody had taste!

Going Pro

By September 7th we had made a major decision. We had dates that night and broke the news to our girlfriends: we were going to Chicago to get an agent and go professional! Don was dating a neighbor girl and I was dating Nancy Sue Carson. They were not at all happy that we were going on the road, so it was one of those really tearful evenings. On September 11th, after Don and I had spent the day helping Dad build a chicken coop, Hal, Don and I drove to Greencastle to pick up Bob and we went on to Chicago.

This sleepy bunch of guys hit the outer drive at morning rush hour. The other guys had seen big towns when they were in the service but they had never driven in such heavy traffic before. By this time Hal had traded his convertible and bought a green, four door '41 Packard, a classic beauty.

We came to a hotel called the Planters and it looked like a place we could afford. After we checked in, Hal and I took the car out to the north side and parked it on a street where there was no time limit on parking; we couldn't afford the hotel parking lot! We took the elevated train back into town.

Hal had seen Chicago before, but as a wide eyed kid of 19, I never had. Don was 21, Bob was 22, and Hal was 24, the old man of the bunch.

The next morning we got out the yellow pages and looked under "A" for agent and "B" for booking agent. We called a lot of them but met with little success. We walked from one agency to another, office building to office building. They just looked at us with sidelong glances and said, "Next." But there was one guy, Dick Sheldon, at the McConkey Office. Their specialty was booking inexpensive acts. Sheldon said he would take us. I guess we looked inexpensive! We signed a short term agreement and took the "El" back out to Hal's car. All the way home we rehearsed "The Night We Called It a Day," a song we eventually recorded.

We figured that if we were going to be booked we had to have union cards. So after a day's rest at home we boarded the bus to Indianapolis to sign up with the union. We got there only to find the office was closed, so we had to take the bus back home. The next day Hal drove us to Indy in his car and the three of us divided up the cost of the gas. We all joined Local 3, and we continued through the years as active members there.

Booked

On Monday, September 15th, Hal called Dick Sheldon, who said he had a steady job lined up for us, starting on the 20th. We were in! We packed up a bunch of things we figured we would need on the road and made up a list of songs we did and the keys we did them in. I took my driver's license and smudged my date of birth so it would appear I was 21, because working in a nightclub at 19 was a problem. My fake ID did little good because I looked like 17. Any fool could see I wasn't 21.

On September 17th we recorded our last Topper Time radio show. On the 19th Don and I said good-bye to our folks and our girls. As soon as we picked up Bob in Greencastle, we started singing "Summertime," a Topper's arrangement that we kept for several years. We finally got to Warsaw at 2am and sat around at the Chat and Chew Restaurant downtown and sang for everyone.

Tomorrow was to be the first day of the rest of our lives!

IS THERE LIFE AFTER THE 113 CLUB?

On September 20, 1948, we opened a week long stint at the 113 Club in Ft. Wayne, Indiana. We'd been paid modest cash for some appearances in the past but now, under the watchful oversight of an agent - with circles on the calendar and contracts in hand - we became professional musicians! Or so we thought! We had driven as far as Warsaw, Indiana, the day before and spent the night at Hal Kratzsch's home. We arrived in Ft. Wayne about noon the next day and checked into the hotel at Washington and Webster. A classy place, it even had a pay radio in the room!

The modest 113 Club was only a couple of blocks away, at 113 Washington Boulevard. It was a double store-front in a row of brown brick buildings set maybe eight feet back from the curb. It had a lengthy front window, partially painted over so passersby couldn't see in. The dimly lit main room had tables and chairs on the right and a dance floor on the left, with a waist high stage against the left wall.

We arrived at 8pm and tuned up. For our opening night we simply gathered at the mike, sang a few songs and then played few more. The boss, a Mr. Walsh, called Dick Sheldon immediately. "These guys stink!" he shouted into the phone. He was right. We were awful, as ghastly as we had ever been. We knew it, the boss knew it and the customers knew it. Sheldon talked him into keeping us one more night and promised he'd drive down from Chicago to hear us.

Re-groupings

Later that night we sat in our hotel room and tried to figure out what we had done wrong. We decided we needed a master of ceremonies (up to this point we had just done one song after another). Next, we decided we would do a 45 minute set, then sing a snappy closer, take a break and then do a second set. This would give the show a little more class.

I was the emcee on our second night. We sang our special ending: "With your permission, we would like to take an intermission," ending on our peg chord. Ta da! We were improved!

We later discovered there was more to the boss having tried to fire us the first night. His daughter, Paula, liked us and became an instant member of Hal's fan club. Hal had a way of just being there, with the girls falling all over themselves for him and apparently Walsh didn't like that. Besides Sheldon's influence, Paula talked her dad into keeping us, so that's why we worked the second night, the third and the fourth!

Dick Sheldon came to hear us on Thursday. Let's face it, he knew when he signed us that we weren't professionals. But I don't think he had any idea how unprofessional we were until he sat through a couple of shows. Sheldon was a dapper guy, with a sort of Alan Ladd look - sleek, neat and efficient. He called us together at a side table after the evening ended.

"Guys I've got some suggestions that, if you follow, I guarantee I'll have you working some of the best nightclubs in the Midwest." That was the enticement he used to get us to make the necessary changes.

"Ross, you're okay as emcee but stop playing piano and get yourself a drum or sock cymbal. Don, you be the guitar player. Bob and Hal, you trade off playing bass. And (here came the kicker) I want you to accompany yourselves while you sing." Wow! How do you play an instrument while you sing?

That first week netted us $325. It turned out to be $81.25 each, minus the agent's 10%, and the hotel bill, the union, our food, and gas for that big Packard. We realized then and there that our prime motive had to be having fun because we weren't clearing any money.

September 27th - I've got it in my diary - Bob and Hal got angry at each other. That was the first time I realized they were two very different guys. As time went on it was bound to happen again. We were only seven days into our professional careers and already having our first crisis!

The next day we had our first professional pictures taken, wearing tuxedos and looking off to the side. We were four misty-eyed, dewy-lipped kids.

Kenton Comes to Town

We were back home on October 1st and Stan Kenton was coming to Indianapolis! The guys were saying, "We ought to take the gals and go see the Kenton band, but it's $3 a ticket!" Let's see, four guys, four girls at $3 each is $24, plus we are going to have to stop at a restaurant afterwards. I drew $30 out of my bank account and we went to see the Kenton band.

That night opened up a whole new vista of musical ideas for us. We heard a band play things that we hadn't dreamed about in our wildest imaginings. You probably felt it the first time you heard Stan Kenton - zowie! Can this be? We went home changed people. There were other days that changed our lives, but that first Kenton concert impacted us musically more than anything else ever has.

It was as though our music happened in a jungle clearing. We found some boundary lines and stayed inside them. But here was Stan Kenton clearing out the whole jungle, taking away the confinement, opening up almost infinite space. He was bold, loud and pleasantly dissonant -

two trumpets sounded out above the rest, just a half step apart. Furthermore, the Kenton band looked good. Stan's magnetic presence literally sold the group to the people.

We came home from that concert totally convinced there were a million unsung sounds out there, sounds yet to be made - and we were the guys who were going to make them!

Off to Illinois

On October 3rd we said good-bye to our girlfriends and loaded instruments and amps on a wooden car-top carrier we had built. Marvin Pruitt was there that day and I rode back to Indianapolis with him. From there, Hal and I headed to Warsaw for the night. The next day I met Dave Hibben, a friend of Hal's who owned a drum set. Sheldon had said I needed a sock cymbal so I invested $10 and bought Dave's. A sock cymbal is two cymbals which face each other on a stand and are opened and closed by a foot pedal. I also bought some brushes. I had never played drums before, but I figured it couldn't be that hard. If you can keep time there's not much you can do wrong!

We took this rig back to Hal's house and began practicing. Bill and Vicki Wagner were there. They became very close friends and great fans. Later Bill would become our manager.

Illinois had a lot of laws that most lounges didn't adhere to, and I don't mean just one or two nightclubs here and there - I mean all across the state. There was Calumet City on the northeast, Rock Island on the west, and East St. Louis to the south - the Illinois entertainment zone. This area offered whatever you wanted to find, and a lot you didn't want to find! In LaSalle we were booked at a place on the edge of town called the Stables. It was an old barn with the downstairs converted into a nightclub. We performed at knee high level on a stage ten feet square.

The first night was a struggle. I didn't know anything about playing the sock cymbal. Don provided our background chords on his guitar while Bob and Hal switched off on bass. It was grim! So we figured the next day we'd better rehearse. There was a banquet room with a piano in the upstairs of this barn so we hauled our instruments up there. That's where we learned "Poinciana," and did our initial work on "Moonglow" and a half dozen others.

The 6th of October was the first day I ever performed as "Leroy," the little voice that did "Sweet Lorraine." When you sing 40 minutes on and 20 off from nine at night to four in the morning your voice wears out, so you look for any way to rest your voice. Leroy rested everybody else for three minutes or so. He became a permanent part of the group. The next day we went out and bought white bow ties to wear with our used black tuxedos which didn't match. We were a beautiful bunch!

Dick Sheldon called from Chicago. "Hello you guys," he said as we crowded around the phone. "Look, we've got too many groups called something like the Toppers. There are the Tophatters, Topnotchers, Tiptoppers, the Corn Toppers - do you see what I mean? We're going to change your name to the 'Freshmen Four.'"

The only groups called the "Something Four" were rhythm hymn quartets who sang "Church in the Wildwood," clapping on the first and third beats. We said okay, but we weren't hot for it at all. Somehow, this new name seemed misleading.

Mayhem in Muncie

On October 17th we checked into the Kirby Hotel in Muncie, Indiana, and prepared to open the next night at Camel's Oasis. They had a picture of a camel outlined in pink neon lights on top of the place. It blinked on and off. Impressed?

By now, I was standing up playing sock cymbal instead of piano and was also the emcee. Hal and Bob were trading off playing bass, trumpet and trombone and Don was on guitar. We thought we sounded good. But while we were playing our first set, Mr. Camel was on the phone calling Sheldon. "Get these guys out of here! They're terrible! Awful!" (We were trying to sing over his phone conversation.) "This is the last thing I am ever going to buy from McConkey!"

We got all kinds of calls from Dick Sheldon the next day. In the afternoon we went back to see if we could reverse Camel's decision. He said he wanted piano music and no more kidding around on the P.A. system. We decided Hal would be the master of ceremonies. He was the oldest and a little more serious minded. So the second night Hal was emcee and Bob did a drunk act. I wish I had it on video tape. He pulled a hat clear down over his head so that his ears stuck out. Then he yanked one sleeve of his coat clear off his shoulder so it covered his hand. A broken cigarette hung from his lip while he sang, "A good man is hard to find...hic...you always get the other kind!" People fell out of their chairs laughing. This was kind of a forerunner to our pantomimes and everything else we did on stage later on. Bob really saved it for us in Muncie.

We were nutty about Stan Kenton, but a close second for us was Woody Herman. Woody's band came to Muncie and we got to talk with bass player Chubby Jackson and drummer Don Lamond. After a stunning show we went around back to the stage door. "When Woody comes out," we told each other "we'll introduce ourselves to him. He'll say, 'Hey, let me hear you sing.' And we'll sing and knock him out, and right then we'll get our big break. We'll sign on as the vocal group with Woody Herman. It'll be a rocket to stardom from that moment on."

When Woody came out there were three guys with him and they were walking fast. Woody had this way of wearing a cloud around himself that just automatically told anybody planning on a "Hi, Woody," that they better not do it, because Woody doesn't want to hear it. None of us stepped forward, none of us said, "Hey Woody" or anything like it. He just walked right on past us, got in the car and took off.

We looked at each other like, "Why didn't you?..." "I thought you..." The Freshmen Four looked like the Four Stooges. We did everything except pop each other on the head with newspapers!

Our week in Muncie netted us $100 a man. And while that looked encouraging, the bad news was there was nothing scheduled for the next couple of weeks.

Back to Route 3

We spent a week or two back in Columbus, with all four of us at our place, seeing the family and our girls, and learning new songs. Late one night, after the folks had gone to bed, we were sitting around the kitchen table, singing. Somebody had a pack of cigarettes. Now my father was against cigarette smoking, very against it, on both a moral and a health basis. He hated the smell. Bob's father, Uncle Lee, used to come down to our house and deliberately light up, just to see Daddy sputter and fuss. But that night we decided, "Heck, we'll open the kitchen windows, close the doors to the rest of the house, and seal the kitchen off from where the folks are sleeping." The four of us soon created a giant cloud of smoke.

Suddenly, Daddy was in the kitchen! Harold Barbour always took charge. He grabbed a tin cup off our wood burning cookstove, went over to the faucet, filled the cup half full of water, and then held it over the kitchen table. Four cigarettes were in that cup instantly! Daddy took the cup over to the sink, poured the water off, threw the cigarettes in the wastebasket and went back to bed, having said not a word. That broke up our rehearsal, but it was midnight anyhow and we had to leave early in the morning.

At 6:30 on the morning of October 27th we headed to Savannah, Georgia, where we first heard "Street of Dreams" and decided to learn it. During November and December we played spots in Milwaukee, Sheboygan, and Camden, Arkansas. In Sheboygan Hal met Betty Wehrwien, and they were married ten months later. Hal and Bob had another falling out and ended up firing each other! Camden was the one place in our career where the club canceled our contract after hearing us. The upside was that we got to go home for Christmas.

My One and Only One

Don and I pulled up to Sue's aunt's house on Christmas afternoon. Sue had seen us drive up and came running out, crunching through the frozen crusted snow, and jumped into my arms. I think that moment settled our future. We wanted to get married. A life together was more important than even the quartet! Years later, Ken Albers and I put our memories to music and wrote "First Affair."

> Though we're young, our search for love is done;
> We made our first affair our one and only one.

Christmas at home was wonderful, but Sue and I both dreaded the thought of separation again. She was fearful and lonely when I was gone. And she was sure I would fall in love with someone else out on the road. I was sure I would never love anyone else. We both wanted to put our worries about the future to rest. So, like young people sometimes do, we sneaked off (to Covington, Kentucky) and got married on New Year's Eve, 1948 (my 20th birthday). I say "sneaked off" because she was only 17 and a senior in high school. In those years a girl would not have been permitted to stay in school if she were married. And our folks, especially hers, would have never approved.

There was no way to have a honeymoon, so we had "dates" each night I was home. During the day we rehearsed and worked on a beautiful black '36 four door Ford Don and I had purchased together just after Christmas. On January 6, 1949, we sang at a convocation at Columbus High School - the big college guys coming home after a couple of years to wow the high school kids. We loved it!

Showing Improvement

A few days later we were off to Green Bay, Wisconsin. Dick Sheldon came to hear us a second time and, hey, he had never heard music like this from us before! We had choreographed ourselves to play our instruments while we sang, standing around a single mike, belting out "Basin Street Blues," "My Kind of Love," "Slow Boat to China" and "Kate."

We begged Sheldon to turn our name around, so from this point on we were billed as "The Four Freshmen." And we were developing. We were working "some of the best supper clubs in the Midwest!" In Green Bay we introduced Don's rendition of "Stormy Weather." Dick Sheldon was impressed.

After nearly six weeks we drove back to Columbus for a few days, which allowed Sue and me to see each other briefly. Then we headed all the way back up to Kenosha, Wisconsin, where we cut our first radio commercial, a singing spot for Stern's Men's Clothing Store. Other stops included Austin, Minnesota, and Oglesby, Illinois, where we heard "Fools Rush In" and became permanently hooked on the number. In Lansing, Michigan, we debuted "After You," and Hal traded his Packard for a sleek 1941 Cadillac.

The Pla-Bowl

Believe it or not one of the most important spots in our whole career was a bowling alley lounge - the Pla-Bowl in Calumet City, Illinois. We worked three nights in May, and came back to spend the summer there through the middle of August. Those first three nights started something for us. We proved the Freshmen sound was what they needed. Before the summer was out were pulling in three to four hundred people a night on weekends. We established ourselves as a quality group which took its music and its listeners very seriously.

We began watching television on our free nights. Those early TV sets were great big things, four feet cubed, with a little round seven inch screen and a snowy black and white picture. Friends invited neighbors over to watch Uncle Miltie. TV was a brand new way for people to be entertained, and it forced groups like ours to do a quality job. After all, we could now be compared with the top flight talent on national network shows.

Don met Dolores Anderson in Calumet City and they fell hopelessly in love. As soon as Sue graduated, we went public and announced our marriage and had it solemnized in a Christian ceremony in Hammond. Hal married pretty blue-eyed Betty on August 24 in Sheboygan.

Before fall, I bought a fancy snare drum and Don and I traded the '36 Ford for a 1941 model. On a lark, Hal added a '31 Chevy to his Cadillac and Bob picked out a huge black '36 Nash. We were a five-car, two-wife family.

Cut to The Chase

On September 5th we opened at the Silver Congo back in LaSalle, Illinois. Dolores had joined us for a few days, riding with Don in Hal's old Chevrolet. Bob was following them in his big four door Nash. They were on a country road, coming to see us and the Kratzschs at the apartment we shared. Suddenly the spare tire fell off the back of the Chevy. Bob swerved to avoid hitting it, then slowed up and made a U-turn. Don didn't hear the tire fall off, but he looked in his rearview mirror and saw Bob turn around.

A guy who had been drinking quite a bit was watching all this from his front porch. He came lurching off the porch yelling, "Stop thief! That tire didn't fall off of your car. I'm not going to let you steal that man's spare tire."

A policeman also saw Bob make the U-turn so he pulled up to the scene. "You in the '36 Nash that made that U-turn! That's illegal."

Bob is saying, "Yeah, but..." and the drunk says, "This man is a thief. Arrest him. He's stealing this spare tire." And Bob is saying, "Yeah, but...but."

Don came back to see what was going on with the flashing lights and the squad car. In the '31 Chev, Dolores was sitting there with Don's new "toy" - a .22 caliber revolver he used for target practice on boring afternoons. Meanwhile, the policeman had detained Bob and the drunk is waving his arms.

Dolores suddenly realized, "Yikes! I've got a gun in my hand." So she tossed it under the front seat. It was like a Laurel and Hardy comedy routine. Don assured the officer he had lost the tire, and Bob was not a thief. When all the dust settled Bob got a ticket for the U-turn. By the time they arrived at our place their eyes were red from laughing over a neighborly drunk protecting Don's tire from light-fingered Bob.

In October we arrived in Dayton, Ohio, to work at the Esquire Lounge. That's where we first sang "Cherokee," and Don introduced "Circus." Sue and I bought a used 14 foot aluminum house trailer. It had no toilet, no air conditioning and was warmed by a kerosene heater. We loved it. I had a trailer hitch put on the '41 Ford. We moved in two days later and the Freshmen gave us a trailer-warming party.

In Dayton we entertained one evening at a state mental hospital. They had an auditorium and the people sat on benches or in wheelchairs. Some of the people really got into the music but others got up and wandered around. One man was chasing butterflies, another decided to lie down at the end of the row of benches, still listening to the music.

I don't know if we did them any good, but they certainly helped us because at times we worried that the future might bring more problems than we could handle. Seeing these people confined in this place made us realize we were not so bad off after all. They gave us heart to keep going.

It's Arthur Godfrey Time

A call came from our agency in Chicago. We had been cleared to audition for the Arthur Godfrey Talent Show! The only problem was that we had to have some kind of work lined up in New York or we would starve. The New York agent, Lloyd LaBree, promised, "There's work out here. All you have to do is come east and I'll have more work than you can handle."

It meant pulling the house trailer. And the wives would be further from home. I remember we had some long and hard arguments about whether we should or shouldn't. But ambition won out and we decided we had to do it.

The Godfrey show was a "talent scout" thing on network television. Each week he would present people he had discovered. The winner would be picked based on the amount of applause received. If you won once you would play again the next week. After the third show you would retire as an undefeated winner. We figured if we could win it would give us a lot of national exposure.

Sue and I were expecting! Golly, kids on the road! Sue had morning sickness and couldn't stand the smell of grease or smoke or a lot of other odors. She wasn't anxious to head east. Sue and Betty had become great friends so Sue could count on her help. We left Dayton on the 20th, with that '41 Ford and the house trailer.

A few miles out we had a flat. The next day the Ford overheated, which put us late into Pittsburgh. Though a beautiful city today, the smoke-laden air from the steel mills almost did Sue in. We made a wrong turn, corrected it after going more miles than I want to admit, drove through Harrisburg and Allentown and parked the trailer in

Hackettstown, New Jersey, 50 miles from New York City. On October 25th we auditioned for the Godfrey show and passed with flying colors! "Come back for your second audition in one week," the man told us.

"What do you mean, 'second audition'?" we asked.

"There are so many contestants that we have to screen each act several times. There may be two or three auditions before we can put you on the show."

Some other hopefuls were sitting in the lobby. "We've been here for five auditions," they moaned. "We passed every one and we're still not on the show." We decided then and there that it was the end of the Godfrey show for the Four Freshmen.

"Hello, Lloyd?" Hal said the next morning to our agent. "We're here in New York and ready to go to work. What's on the docket?"

"Let me call you back," he said.

A day passed. He phoned and sent us to Tony's Tavern somewhere in Jersey. It was a wild goose chase. They had nothing. Lloyd had nothing either, except a hotel in Asbury Park with free rooms, two meals a day and no pay. But the restaurant closed early most nights so we usually missed our evening meal. We were flat broke. I'd spent all but the two nickels in my penny loafers.

Sue and I went walking hand-in-hand on the boardwalk one evening and came upon a candy stand. "Pralines - 10 cents" the sign said. (A praline is a cookie-shaped confection of brown sugar, butter and nuts - and oh so good!) "Let's get one," she said. I took the nickels out of my shoes. "One praline please," I told the lady.

"That'll be 11 cents," she said.

"But the sign says 10," I offered.

"Tax," she answered.

I took back my 10 cents, and we walked away, half laughing, half crying. We closed three days later on the 30th. Betty wired her folks for gas money.

Toll Bridge Trauma

Don rode in Bob's Nash. They had no money and just enough gas to get them to the next job in Pottsville, Pennsylvania. We wouldn't eat en route, but in Pottsville we would get an advance.

They had carefully planned the trip to avoid all toll roads and bridges. They'd found a smooth alternate route and they were making excellent time when up ahead was a toll bridge that wasn't shown on the map. Traffic can pile up quickly at a toll bridge, especially when the two guys in the black Nash tell the guard they are sorry but they have no money.

The guard said, "You can't go through."

Don looked at Bob. "Wait a minute. I've got some pennies in a sock in one of my suitcases in the trunk."

"There can't be any problem then." Bob said to the guard. The traffic was backing up and people were starting to honk their horns.

Bob and Don got out of the car and opened the trunk. By this time the guard was standing with his hands on his hips, beginning to sweat. Cars were already lined up all the way back to the last curve. Bob removed a couple of suitcases after Don grabbed the loose items piled on top of them. Finally Don found the suitcase where the pennies were packed. Motorists were yelling. The guard said, "Go on, Go on. I'll put in your 25 cents."

But Don and Bob were indignant. "No, no, we are paying our debt to society," Bob explained.

The guard kept saying, "Go on, Go on." He was beside himself, watching the steadily-growing line of congestion. By this time Bob had found the sack of pennies. He started counting, "One, two, three, four," and he dropped one. "Don, get that. . . five."

"Go on, - please!" begged the guard.

A few minutes later they got the toll paid and drove off with their moral victory.

The was no trailer park in Pottsville so we parked in a parking lot across the street from the railroad station. The station had a restroom and we carried water in buckets from there so we could wash. By this time Sue was quite pregnant and had to use the bathroom often. She made good use of her house slippers and robe, using the ladies' room at the station all the while we were there.

The first evening we went to get our advance but the manager was out. We had one can of spaghetti and a couple of eggs in the refrigerator. Hal had stopped along the way and bought a sack of malted milk balls. So all of us congregated at our trailer and Don fixed dinner, pretending to be a great chef. He put the two eggs into the spaghetti, stirred it all up, and heated it on our stove. We had the malted milk balls for dessert.

Milestones

On the evening of November 8th we pulled into the driveway at the home of Sue's folks. It was countdown time to the birth of our first baby. We were to sing again in Calumet City on November 22nd. I sneaked home on the 28th, but still no baby. Don and Dolores were getting married in Calumet City the next day and I was best man. Sue's water broke as I was leaving. I took her to the hospital on my way out of town, made it to the wedding by 6pm and found a telegram waiting for me. Kent Edwin Barbour entered the world at 4:05pm. We worked the Pla-Bowl again the next week, I could hardly wait until the job was finished on December 4th so I could see my new boy and my Sue.

Kent, Sue and I returned to Calumet City and closed on New Year's Day. Kent and Sue joined me and the Freshmen for a stint on Chicago's South Side in January. Woody Herman came to hear us one night, and this time we talked with him about the possibility of going with his band.

In March Hal traded his '41 Cadillac for a seven passenger 1940 Packard, even bigger than the green one we started with on the road.

We were busy learning "I'll Remember April."

COAST TO COAST

Stan Kenton was to be at Memorial Hall in Dayton, Ohio on March 20, 1950. We bugged our boss at the Esquire Lounge to change our night off so we could go and hear the band. This was the big Innovations in Modern Music Orchestra, with strings. It was a momentous occasion! The boss, George Vaval, was kind, but not so kind as to give up his drawing card. We worked, and missed the concert. But all our customers went to hear Stan so we didn't have a crowd until later that evening.

Kenton Comes to Call

That night we spent our first intermission at the restaurant next door. Bob came in and said, "Hey guys, Stan Kenton's here! Stan Kenton has come to hear us!" Don rocked back in his chair and challenged the King of Prank. "Sure Bob, sure! Tell us another."

"No really!" Bob insisted. When we saw the size of Bob's eyes we realized he was telling the truth. Stan had come to hear the Four Freshmen after his show because two local disc jockey friends of his, Gene Barry and Sid Garris, had said, "Let's go hear the Freshmen."

Stan arrived at the Esquire about ten. By the time we got back on the stage we were so nervous we were barely able to perform. It was as though God was there! We felt we would have to sing better than we ever had sung before. But we were so keyed up we couldn't breathe deeply, and our voices trembled. We fumbled through "After You," "Laura" and "You Can Depend on Me."

During the next intermission we sat with Stan Kenton. He was very friendly, and honestly interested in what we were doing. We told him we had met Woody Herman and that he had suggested we sing with his band. Stan said, "I probably will be gone by the time you finish your next set, but here is my address. Write me." We did the next set, and he stayed to the end.

"You know what?" Stan said after the show. "You guys shouldn't try to sing with Woody's band or my band or any band. What you ought to do is get yourselves a recording contract and make a career for yourselves. I'll call Capitol Records and make plans with them so they can hear you. I'll do my best to talk the executives there into signing you, to give you a chance to make some records."

His offer fell upon confused ears. We always had thought the biggest thing we could do would be to sing as a quartet with Woody or Stan. But now Stan had set a higher goal for us. We had never dreamed of anything that big. Before the evening was over we had Stan Kenton's address, his phone number and his promise to call Capitol. But would it ever happen?

George Vaval told us later, "If I'd have known Stan Kenton was that kind of man, I would have closed my place and all of us would have gone to hear his band!"

Two weeks later Stan called. Everything was set. We were to come to New York and cut some things for Capitol. Pete Rugolo would be there, and he would supervise the recording session. Pete Rugolo! Wow! The pride we felt having these names even mentioned in our presence was enough to stop our hearts.

By the way, at no time did Stan Kenton ever take as much as a single percent of what we earned; he never required anything of us. His help was unconditional. He became our father, our inspiration, our coach. In future years, if we would be down in the dumps, Stan would come around, and say, "You've got to succeed, you can't fail. You're part of my ego!"

The high standard Stan set for us is what makes the whole Four Freshmen story possible. This daring dream Stan put before us gave us the drive to make it and to make it last, no matter what. We knew we had to succeed, if not for ourselves, for Stan Kenton.

And while we are talking about Kenton I should say one other thing. He was the greatest leader of men we ever met. The astute vision and creative originality of this man was a deeper inspiration to us than he would ever know. He heard in us that night in Dayton what we could be. His ability to see our potential was so much greater than our own vision. Words are inadequate.

We were full of a new dream. There was no thought of failure or of defeat. Nothing was going to stop us!

The Audition

We closed Dayton on March 26th and headed for Green Bay and the Picadilly. We stopped in Sheboygan to see Betty, who was now expecting a baby and having trouble traveling. We worked April 9th at the Picadilly, stayed up all night, and caught the 7:10 train to Chicago. Then it was on to New York. The boss in Green Bay, Bob Harrill, gave us a couple of days off. We checked into the Dixie Hotel in Times Square on the 11th and got an hour and a half of sleep.

At noon we went to meet Pete Rugolo in the dressing room at the Paramount Theater. Billy Eckstine was the star there and Rugolo had the orchestra behind "Mr. B," featuring Kai Winding and Eddie Safranski, both ex-Kenton players. We sang for Pete in the dressing room. He was pleased but kind of surprised. He was not sure why we came to sing for him because he knew the next day we were going to do the record. Our fault. We thought when you met somebody under those circumstances you were supposed to sing for them. That night the Freshmen went to Bop City. George Shearing was there with Denzil Best, the drummer, and he always knocked me out. Shearing was alternating with the Lionel Hampton Orchestra.

The morning of the 12th we practiced in the room to make sure we had our voices. We were ready. We met Pete and Stan Kenton in Pete's dressing room, along with Bob Allison, who was managing the Kenton band then. Allison paid us for our train tickets. Evidently this was money out of Stan's own pocket. At the time we thought it came from Capitol Records.

We went to the WMGM Studio and recorded from nine in the evening until one in the morning. Out of that session came "Baltimore Oriole," "Dry Bones," "What Is This Thing Called Love?," "Laura," "Basin Street Blues," "Room Full of Roses," "Circus," and "Without A Song." We got them all recorded and sent them off to Capitol to convince them that we were going to be the biggest thing since the phonograph.

After we finished we thought, "Here is New York City at our feet! We're not just going to go to bed." So we went out to Bop City again. Sarah Vaughn and Woody Herman were the star attractions that night. "We've met with Stan," we told Woody after the show. "Stan is trying to get us a contract of our own. Thank you for offering to consider us, but we can't go with your band. We've got to try this other dream."

On the 13th we went back to Grand Central Station in New York, caught the train to Chicago and up to Green Bay. Did we have stories to tell? We spent all day telling our wives and our boss about the big things that happened in New York City.

In the middle of April Hal bought a mellophone. It's a horn curved much like a French horn, which is what everybody thought it was. A mellophone has the same size pipe throughout and has a piercing sound, whereas the French horn has pipe that increases in size as it progresses toward the bell and makes a blending sound. This mellophone was corroded and dented but that didn't matter. Hal painted it chartreuse - it was our "chartreusophone." He used a trumpet mouthpiece and played solos with it on "My Heart Stood Still" and "Mr. B's Blues."

The only thing we would argue about was music. Let somebody drag the beat, or play an instrument out of tune, or sing the wrong note on an arrangement and there was a fierce battle. We all cared about quality with a passion and at various times each of us would get angry with the others. Through this we grew, and somehow we all kept coming back for more. We put the Freshmen sound to two songs that spring: "I May Be Wrong" and "Somebody Loves Me," both of which were recorded.

On Thursday night June 8th, after work in Springfield, Ohio, we drove with Bob to Covington, Kentucky, and stood before a justice of the peace with Bob and his bride, Margaret Carpenter. The ceremony lasted only about a minute - "I do!" "I do!" Then we hurried back to work in Springfield. Peggy had a son, Steve, whom Bob adopted.

Cars, Cars and More Cars

On the 27th of June, while we were playing Sheboygan, Don showed up with a '39 LaSalle, a car produced by Cadillac. It was an expensive, powerful automobile, a classic. It had a beautiful interior and rode like a dream.

On July 16th Hal and Betty's first son, Nathan, was born. Our Freshmen family was growing! Two days later we opened at the Pla-Bowl again. Mac McGraw, the owner, evidently thought we needed to spiff up a bit because he gave us $500 to spend on new clothes. Mac McGraw was a big bear of a man, a rough looking guy, but everyone should have such a friend. We bought gray suits, white shirts and ties, and matched to a tee!

In August Bob went off the deep end. His old Nash needed a new everything by now so he bought a maroon 1948 Chrysler Imperial. Our trailer had developed a strange scent. Sue was pregnant again and the smell in the trailer really upset her. So I told her I'd wax the floors and the wooden walls and wash down the blinds. I took Sue and Kent home for a week and did the clean up. Meanwhile, Hal sold his Packard and bought a 1941 Lincoln Zephyr. It was gray and it had - get this - 12 cylinders! We were car crazy!

After we got the trailer fixed up Sue and I decided to sell it. Our California trip was coming soon, and we didn't want to tow it all that way. On the way home to Columbus in late August the rear main bearings of my car started leaking oil onto the clutch. We had to keep adding oil, but we got the car and trailer to Columbus. I felt low. We didn't have the cash to buy another car and we had to get to California. We couldn't sell the car in its condition. We tried to sell the trailer, but nobody is going to walk up the first day and buy a trailer. Trailers take a while to sell.

If you can call a maroon '47 Kaiser a car, that's what I bought for $700. The only way I could get it was to have somebody co-sign the loan. Sue's father came through, bless his heart.

If You Plan to Motor West

It's the 29th of August and Sue and I and son Kent are heading west! We met the others at the foot of the bridge on Main Street in Rock Island, Illinois, and formed our caravan about two in the morning. Bob had his '48 Chrysler, Hal his '41 Lincoln Zephyr and Don was in that '39 LaSalle.

We hadn't driven far before the cold and sinus infection Don had picked up got really bad. We stopped to get him a shot of penicillin. It turned out that he was allergic to it and his arm swelled up until it looked like two gigantic sausages, with the link at his elbow. Because of his fever and drowsiness Dolores had to do a lot of the driving. We hit Rawlins, Wyoming, at daybreak on September 1st and decided to sleep in a park in Green River. The park had a large tree near a creek so we stretched out in its shade, some of us on car seats, some on blankets. Of course, the shade moved as we slept. When Bob woke up his bare feet had been in the hot sun for quite a while. They were so sunburned he couldn't lace up his shoes!

We continued to Rock Springs, then down through Utah. A detour lead to another detour. My Kaiser had leaky valves, poor carburetion and not very much power, especially at this high altitude. Inevitably, there came a hill I just couldn't make. We were overloaded and the car coasted back down to a level area. The other guys stopped and we huddled in the bright moonlight, wondering what to do. We decided Don and Dolores would go ahead to see if there were any steeper hills beyond this one. Why bother here if it's worse up ahead?

Bob's wife, Peggy, woke up, and when she didn't see Don's car she feared that he had gone over the side. Delores and Sue, both pregnant, wondered how in the world we ever got ourselves into this predicament. We were a hundred miles from anywhere, with no gas station around and nobody else on this road. The silence was deafening.

Don returned and said, "Yeah, after you pass this steep hill, it's all downhill. There is even a settlement down there with a filling station and a store. All we have to do is get you over this hill." So everybody pushed! I was flooring it and the wheels were spinning in the gravel. Finally I pulled away and made it over the crest. When we got to the filling station they were all talking about "the accident." A few minutes earlier a car with four or five people in it had blown a tire on a narrow bridge and skidded into another car, also loaded with people. Nobody lived. We figured that the time we had lost on that hill saved us from being right in the middle of that accident.

We hit Baker, California, about dawn and checked into a motel, then got to Barstow the next midnight. Was it hot!

City of Angels

We pulled into Los Angeles at 4am September 4th and opened at the York Club the next day. Stan Kenton had found us the job. It didn't pay much, but it was a good place for Stan's friends and the Capitol people to come see us. Bob Allison and Gene Howard were managing Kenton and they came in with Pete Rugolo and Stan.

On our second anniversary, September 20, 1950, we looked back and counted our blessings. We had worked most of the Midwest and weathered the East. We had decided not to do the Godfrey show, and we had met Stan Kenton, who got us with Capitol. It looked like the sky was the limit.

On the 2nd of October we opened at the Studio Club, Jerry Wald's place at Sunset and Vine. It was a tiny nightclub, but more of the important people saw us at Jerry Wald's club than at any other place in our whole career. The very first week we played to Ray Anthony, who was working at the Palladium across the street. Carlos Gastel, Nat King Cole's manager, came in one night, plus Raymond Burr, Steve Allen, Mike Gould, the guy who published "Blue World," Dan Dailey and Harry James. And they all seemed genuinely interested in what we were doing.

We had been working in the gray suits Mac McGraw bought us in Calumet City. Now, we went to Berman's House of Style and bought clothes that were more California. Expensive stuff! We chose blue suits, cream colored sport coats with chocolate flecks in them, chocolate brown pants and thick soled brown shoes. These are the uniforms you see on the cover of *Voices in Modern*.

Capitol had a magazine they called *Capitol News*, a little promotional publication distributed through record stores. They ran a picture of us with a brief article.

On October 13, 1950, we recorded our first cuts for
Capitol - "Mr. B's Blues," "Pick Up Your Tears" and "I Want to
Go Where You Go." Then we worked that evening at the
Studio Club. We sang all day and sang all night. And in
between we went over and did Steve Allen's radio show at
KNX. Steve was developing a following in California, and was
already known as the best in the business - a master of the
quick comment. In those days he didn't really have a format;
he just lined up a guest or two, and would do give and take
with people in the audience.

Blue World

October 26th was a landmark day for us. That afternoon we were rehearsing at Jerry Wald's, as usual. The
Bourne Music Publishing Company was right next door and
the secretaries there would often come over for a Coke or
coffee during their breaks.

That afternoon one of them handed us the lead sheet
of a song. "This has been done by 15 or 20 people," she said,
"but so far, nobody's got it right." The piece was called "It's a
Blue World." We worked on it the rest of the day, improvising
the introduction and the harmony. By the time we had 12
bars nailed down we were giddy and light-hearted. This song
worked! We had found the right song and we knew it. Mike
Gould, who published the song, and Ray Anthony, who
became our devoted friend and fan, stopped by the club that
night. We sang them what we'd done so far and they were
enthused.

By early November we were also working on "After
You've Gone," which we included with the *Five Trumpets*
album in 1955. And on November 13th Bobby Troup came
in to hear us sing and gave us "Now You Know." (The title of
this book is not mine - it comes from Bobby's great song.)
The Freshmen repertoire was really starting to grow! But just
to let you know we hadn't yet arrived, I must confess that on
the 16th we did a supermarket opening in broad daylight out
on the parking lot!

Back On Campus

We did a free show at L.A. City College on November 22nd and right off the bat we realized this was something that would be very important to our future. Somehow, we seemed to really go over with college kids. L.A. City College was one of the very first college concerts anyone had ever done. Bands were playing college dances, but doing a concert was unusual. Louis Armstrong, Dave Brubeck and the Freshmen pioneered the college concert business. That same week we were voted "Most Interesting Quartet" at USC!

On the 25th we did the Steve Allen Show again and got to be regulars, doing two days a week for a month. Steve began talking about taking us with him to New York to do his television debut with CBS. His idea was to take the staff he had worked with at KNX radio and the Freshmen.

Gene Puerling, a friend of ours from Milwaukee, had a fine vocal quartet. He brought them to the Halifax Hotel in Los Angeles where we stayed. I don't know what he called the group then, but he was rehearsing what turned out to be the Hi-Los.

On December 1st we worked a USC pep rally at the L.A. Coliseum. It was held in the curved end of the facility and they set up a stage near the goal posts. Mickey Rooney was the star and we did about 20 minutes of music. Even though the audience was some distance away we could feel the chemistry from the crowd. We started thinking about working colleges and universities as our prime activity. USC beat Notre Dame the next day so that rally must have worked!

Steve Allen

Steve Allen closed his radio show on December 6th. On his closing show we did "I Want To Go Where You Go." Was that prophetic? He was such a success that people were turning off their TVs to listen to him. Two days later we had a surprise from Bob Allison and Gene Howard. We were going to New York City together. Steve had it all set up with CBS. We'd do the theme song with Steve, jam behind the guest star, and do a special number along with some "bit" things.

We figured we wouldn't need the cars in New York so we could sell our two cars and buy airline tickets. I sold my Kaiser for $500 and Don sold his LaSalle. Hal and Bob decided to keep theirs. We had enough money to fly our wives and kids to the Midwest and get ourselves to New York on the road.

After we closed the Studio Club on December 16th we loaded up Bob's big-nosed Chrysler and the next day headed east in two cars. We would spend a few days in Indiana and say good-bye to our families before taking the train to New York City. On December 22nd we checked in at the Dixie Hotel in New York.

We went to the Statler Hotel on Christmas Eve day. The Ray Anthony band was playing there, having a Christmas party. They invited four lonesome Freshmen to stay and have Christmas dinner. I remember we were full of hope and fear at the same time. On Christmas Day we moved to the President Hotel because it was closer to the Maxine Elliot Theatre, where we were to do the Steve Allen Show.

That afternoon we taped the debut. The Freshmen sang and played "After You've Gone." I did a "walk on" part as a Western Union boy with a crazy telegram from somebody. When we finished we cleared out our stuff and the Gary Moore Show came in for the next session. Eydie Gorme was the female singer on the show. That night we went to Birdland and caught Ella Fitzgerald. Was this all too good to be true? We taped two more shows on the 27th, and Dolores came to New York to be with us for a couple of days.

Disorganized Labor

The next day we received a harsh awakening. The union refused to let us play on the show! Their rules made it very clear: if a show is sponsored and the sponsor wants Steve Allen and the Four Freshmen, that's all right. But this was a sustaining program - CBS was paying the cost, and union rules said local New York musicians must work the show. We could only do a few special numbers as guests.

By the 29th the union had decided to nix us altogether. We weren't to be allowed on the show at all. Stan Kenton came up from Philadelphia and Steve interrupted his day's business for a big council of war. Both of them went to the union to plead our case, but to no avail. They came out of the meeting saying, "Sorry, Freshmen, we'll just have to get you a settlement on your pay." We were back in the world of the unemployed.

We figured, "We can't just sit around looking at four walls." So we took in the Statue of Liberty, went to the top of the Empire State Building and to Central Park Zoo. What an end to 1950!

On January 2, 1951, Stan Kenton came to our hotel. While we were in California we'd been offered a part in a movie but had to turn it down because of the New York trip. Stan tried to call Bob Allison in Los Angeles and tell him to call MGM - maybe they still wanted us to do the spot in "Rich, Young, and Pretty." The chances were slim to none. We were never able to get through to Los Angeles from our hotel.

CBS and the union finally arrived at an agreement. CBS would pay us for what work we had done. That was the good news. The bad news was that check had been mailed to L.A. We had a hotel bill to pay and we were broke! We finally got our checks late in the afternoon on the 5th. I think it was $688 a man. But we couldn't cash them at that hour so we had to stay over yet another night - at New York hotel rates!

We discussed a dozen different ideas, but it all came down to Stan saying, "There is nothing for you guys to do but to go home. Go back to Indiana and get out of this town." MGM and the Steve Allen Show were both history.

FIRST FLICK, FIRST HIT

The evening of January 8, 1951, Bob Flanigan called us in Columbus with the news: MGM was on again! They hadn't found another group they wanted to do the song in "Rich, Young and Pretty," so they had planned to cut the whole sequence. But then they heard that the Freshmen could do it so they put it back in.

To go from losing a network TV show in New York City to landing an MGM contract in Los Angeles in a matter of days seemed impossible. It still seems impossible! Sue, Kent and I flew to L.A. We had shipped some of our belongings to Indiana and some to New York City, so our things were scattered from coast to coast.

I went to Bob Allison's office and picked up a dub of "Pick Up Your Tears" and "Now You Know." Capitol was going to release those numbers back-to-back and I couldn't even play the record - Don had our phonograph in his car, probably somewhere in Arizona.

Rich, Young and Pretty

We were expected at MGM on Friday the 12th. They gave us the lead sheet on "How Do You Like Your Eggs In the Morning" and we went home and rehearsed. It was a cute, light-hearted song. The next day we went through the song and the situation on the movie set, then to lunch at the famous MGM commissary. In walked Dick Powell, Ezio Pinza and Spencer Tracy! I'm having lunch with Spencer Tracy? Hey, Mom, get a load of me!

We worked with Nick Castle, the dance director in charge of staging the number. Nick was a perky little guy who reminded me of Jimmy Durante - but with Fred Astaire's feet, and the heart of a saint. Earl Brent, who wrote "Angel Eyes," was the rehearsal piano player and there were two stand-ins for Vic Damone and Jane Powell.

On the 16th we were measured for our costumes - chef's caps and aprons. Jane was very pregnant and feeling badly. Day after day we would all show up to film this scene and Jane would be missing or she would arrive and begin to feel sick and the limousine would take her right back home. If we couldn't film, there wasn't much we could do but rehearse the number. Every time we went through it Nick had a dozen ideas on how to make it better and we would tighten it up a little more.

The scene goes like this: Vic and Jane are dating in Paris. They go to a late-night restaurant where the Freshmen are entertaining. The place has a neat gimmick: customers pick up their bacon and eggs just inside the door and fix their own breakfasts on a hotplate at their table. We were in chef's costumes, entertaining among the tables.

The scene was planned so that when Vic and Jane came in we would flirt with her, singing to her, never to him. One or two of us would get in Vic's way and the other two would be at Jane's elbow. Then Vic would take Jane away from them. But the other two of us were ready to move in and make friendly passes, which made Vic more and more irritated.

The second line of the song, "How Do You Like Your Eggs In the Morning" was, "I like mine with a kiss." We sang the question, Jane or Vic sang the answer. One day, after rehearsing the first chorus, I went into the second bridge with my Leroy voice, just for fun. Nick liked it, so Leroy sang

"I've got to have my love in the A.M." and Jane mimicked me with "or the rest of my day is positively mayhem." Then Vic came between us with "I'm a regular monster!" We spent two weeks and one day on that sequence, and it lasted only a minute and 55 seconds.

For about ten seconds the world saw me on the screen, almost cheek to cheek with Jane Powell. What a thrill! We had such a ball doing the movie we would have done it all for free - but it was even better getting the check!

Our part of the movie was finished on January 25th. After I got home that day, Sue and I went out and bought a black '49 Ford. We had wheels again!

A few days later MGM had us do a show at Camp Cook, a military base up the California coast. They chartered a DC3 to fly us there. The show included Vic Damone, Adele Mara, the Freshmen, a couple of dancers and a Latin quintet, with Nick Castle as master of ceremonies. One of their own GIs was on the show, too - Andre Previn. He was as unhappy as he could be. He wanted to be doing music and they had him doing push-ups.

Fack's

Our next job was at Fack's in San Francisco. Sue and Delores were both pregnant and were going to an obstetrician in LA, but they wanted to go with us. Our employer, George Andros, promised to have a doctor ready for us when we arrived.

Don and Dolores found a great place for us to stay - a big San Francisco-type house at 2219 California Street. The landlady lived upstairs and the two Barbour families had the whole main floor. Bob and Peggy Flanigan stayed with us for a night or two until they found a place.

Our second son, Gary Carson Barbour, entered the world on February 9, 1951, the night we opened at Fack's.

Fack's got its name in a strange way. When George Andros leased this place it was called "Jack's." There was a nice big neon sign out front and rather than replace it, George had the sign man put a little thing across the "J" to make it an "F". That was the only reason for the name. Through the years George opened Fack's II and Fack's III. Fack's became a household word in the Bay area.

One night there were five or six sailors in the place, and a lone marine. The navy made a few disparaging remarks about his branch of the service and the marine said a few unkind things about them. Suddenly fists started to fly. We didn't have bright lights in our eyes so we could see this marine cream a couple of the sailors, which brought the rest of them down on him. One sailor grabbed the marine and pitched him along the bar into about 50 glasses that had been placed upside down on a towel to dry. Then, somebody threw a chair. And all while we were on stage, trying to finish a romantic ballad!

George Andros finally got between them and said, "Look, I don't care if you fight, but go outside. You can fight all you want out there."

There wasn't much point in our doing more songs - the place had emptied. We got off the stage and helped the waiters straighten up. There were tables and chairs turned over and broken glass everywhere. The head waiter kept reassuring everyone that "This isn't that kind of place!"

In late February Dolores' mother, Grace, came to help. Dolores was expecting and wasn't feeling good. We had a brand new baby in our family and Kent was only 15 months old. It was a handful for Sue and Dolores. Betty was expecting, too. So Grace did the cooking, mending and grocery shopping for us all. San Francisco became a good town for us. The crowds continued strong through March and into April.

Ooops, Measles

Don had come down with a bad fever. He worked April 9th but he was punchy. Everybody gets a fever once in a while but you can't call in sick when you're a member of a quartet. This was the night President Harry Truman fired General MacArthur and the whole world caught its breath. Two days later we called the doctor about Don. "This man has the measles," came the diagnosis. Measles! We've exposed everybody in San Francisco to the measles!

By now Don was delirious; he hardly knew who he was. The Les Brown band had been in town, waiting to start a job at the end of the next week. We and Don Trenner, the piano player with Les, had become friends. With Don so sick we needed somebody to do our background chords, so we got Trenner to do a one night stand as a Freshmen. He played the piano chords and Bob, Hal and I did three-part music. A quartet with a voice missing doesn't really sound very good. The next night George Andros got another band to fill in for us.

"Whowee, I'm going to have the baby!" Delores cried out early on the morning of the 14th. Sue and I took her to the hospital on Geary Street. Don was so sick he didn't know she was gone! He still didn't even know who he was. That afternoon, Donalyn Barbour was born. Don was better by the 17th and we brought Donalyn and Dolores home. By the time Don could go back to work, though, George had hired another group. So we headed back to Hollywood.

Then it was my turn. On the 24th I broke out with the measles! It wasn't nearly as bad as Don's case, but I had rubber knees and couldn't think very well. That same day we clinched a job for a week at the Bakersfield Inn and opened on the 26th. I bought a cheap pair of sunglasses (you're supposed avoid bright light when you have the measles). I could barely stand up that night. The next evening they provided a bar stool to prop me up while I played the drums.

We didn't tell anybody I had measles. Heck no! We couldn't afford that. So I've got an apology to make to the fine people of Bakersfield and Kern County. I exposed you to the measles, and I'm sorry. It's a wonder you didn't have an epidemic after we left!

On the Run

On May 9th we got word that we'd open in Tucson the next day! It's a 14 hour drive to Tucson! We packed fast (and when you're traveling with a family that's a big job). We made it by 6pm and were on stage at 7:30. Bob had gotten there earlier and laid down to take a nap. Hal, too. They both overslept. Hal didn't arrive until nine.

More bad news: we were out of money. The next day, though, the mail contained a tax refund for $102.35! Remember me saying how something good would come without explanation? Call it God's mercy, call it grace - that check allowed us to eat that week.

After Tucson we drove on to Los Angeles but there was no job waiting for us. We were getting more and more anxious to be free of McConkey. We needed bookings and an agency that could get them for us. We hadn't gotten the full three weeks in Tucson McConkey had promised us and that did it. We were released from our contract and we went with General Artists Corporation.

We opened at the Chi Chi in Palm Springs on June 10th. Shortly before we went on a bug crawled into Bob's ear. He waited three days before going to the doctor, who said, "There's no bug in there now." But the bug was still in there, buzzing right against his eardrum, and Bob was about to go crazy. He went to a different doctor who found the bug and got it out. Ahhh!

Red Letter Days

On June 29, 1951, we recorded "Blue World," along with "Intermission Riff" and "Tuxedo Junction." These were ambitious records. Nobody was doing the over-dub thing, where you'd put down a rhythm track, add voices, and then add more voices on top of that. We used that technique with "Intermission Riff" and "Tuxedo Junction." Stan Kenton was there in the studio; he had mapped out the skeleton of the arrangements.

We were sure we had something when we recorded "Blue World," which came out back-to-back with "Tuxedo Junction." It took 14 months for "Blue World" to be released! ("Intermission Riff" never was released.) We started rehearsing the Gene Roland song "Holiday" later in the month. Don sang it and the rest of us played a Latin tempo behind him. "Holiday" became one of our workhorse songs in those years. More and more we were adding songs specifically arranged for us, replacing numbers we had played as jazz choruses to fill up time.

Capitol Records had their big outdoor picnic on August 18th. I remember we talked with the Four Knights there. It was also Sue's birthday. My child bride, with two kids and thousands of miles behind her, was 20 - almost old enough to vote!

The night of August 24th we worked the Studio Club again. The Jordanaires came in, a group that later became the well known background voices for Elvis Presley. At that time, they were a rhythm hymn and gospel quartet. Don had been in the service with their baritone, Hoyt Hilton Hawkins. We closed at the Studio Club and drove up to San Francisco on the 28th

At Fack's, they had the clippings and posters on "Rich, Young and Pretty." We were kind of gloating when we saw the picture of the Freshmen with Jane and Vic in the window out front. "Rich, Young and Pretty" had already been released in the Midwest and we got the word that our relatives had seen it. We finally caught the movie and, when our part came on, Kent, now almost two, bounced up and down yelling, "Daddy - movie! Daddy - movie!" He had me pegged, especially when we got to the part with Leroy!

We were rehearsing "My Heart Stood Still" and "Circus," both good songs for us. The big hits of the day were "Too Young," sung by Nat King Cole and "Because Of You," by Tony Bennett. Nicky David Kratzsch was born on October 18th. Another red letter day came on the 6th of November in Los Angeles, when we started rehearsing "The Day Isn't Long Enough." All four of us liked the song the moment we heard it.

We were in El Paso on December 8th and Don tried out a new idea. The first string on his guitar, the high E, had snapped and he had no replacement. So he put on a third string where the first one belonged and tuned it an octave lower. This gave the guitar a mellow, inverted chord sound. We played Biggs Air Force Base that night and, frankly, the guitar sounded better with the mellow sound behind us. He liked this innovation so well he used it in the group from then on and it became another part of the Freshmen sound.

If you saw the Freshmen play and sing in the 1950s you'll remember I had a drum dolly contraption that held my drum, sock cymbal and a larger cymbal, together with a trumpet and trombone, all on one stand. I started putting that invention together in Dayton, Ohio, over Christmas that year. This dolly became sort of a trademark stage prop for us.

Happy New Year

We closed out 1951 and began 1952 in Cleveland at a place called Moe's Main Street, out on Euclid Ave. Moe had been bringing in name entertainment for years, and he made us feel really important. When we arrived Johnnie Ray was finishing a week there. This was just before Johnnie's famous appearance on the Ed Sullivan Show and his records had not yet become the big hits they were going to be. But everybody who heard him in Cleveland knew he was going to make it big. We opened with Johnnie on December 31st.

Johnnie was something else. He played piano then and sang "The Little White Cloud That Cried," "Cry" and others. When he got into his act he would start pounding on the top of the piano, pulling the stage curtains down and practically tearing off his clothes. He would just wreck the place, and he sent people into a screaming frenzy. It was something we had never seen anybody do. There was no way anybody could go on after Johnnie Ray! We did our set first, then cleared the stage for him to take over.

That New Year's Eve, just before midnight, Johnnie finished his show and began the countdown. As the clock struck 12, the four of us - two on each side of Johnnie with arms around each other's shoulders - sang "Auld Lang Syne" while everyone in the audience blew party horns. It was a bright New Year beginning for Johnnie because from there he went to the Ed Sullivan Show. We felt a "new beginning" thing going for us, too!

In those days Cleveland was the place where the big hits were made. If you wanted your record to go to the top, you would put it into the hands of Cleveland disc jockeys. One of our favorites was Soupy Hines, who later became much better known as Soupy Sales on network TV in the early 1950s.

The 1950s were becoming the decade of quartets. I've mentioned the Four Knights, but other new groups like the Four Lads, the Crew Cuts and the Four Aces were also coming on. The Aces came to hear us at Moe's. We hadn't met them before and we got to spend the evening together. They seemed to like our music. While their harmony wasn't nearly as involved as ours, they put their melody on the third voice and developed a real free and easy sound. Fortunately, we crossed paths often and became good friends. We even did some shows together in later years.

But lest I make us sound too successful, there were nights at Moe's which were mighty spartan. One evening Mac McGraw and his family from Calumet City took a few days off from the Pla-Bowl to come hear us. This was a week-night and there were only five other people in the audience! We had our wives along, so maybe they were part of the five. The point is, you don't go from zero to 60 overnight. These were our building years, that time of our lives when we often had to decide just how much we really wanted to be the Four Freshmen.

From Cleveland we moved on to the Old Mill in Akron. It became kind of a home base for us. It actually was an old mill with the inside redone into a nightclub. The morning after we opened we went out to a place called Studio Films to do a telescription. We sang "Poinciana," "Now You Know," "Sweet Lorraine" and "That's My Desire."

The afternoon of January 20th we did a show with Johnnie Ray at the Akron Armory. His record of "Cry" had hit big, especially in Cleveland and Akron. I don't know of a more stunning hit during that period. Somebody had rented the Armory and got Johnnie Ray and the Freshmen and a couple of other acts, including (how's this for memory lane?) Mandrake the Magician! We only sang about five tunes and Johnnie's crowd liked what we did. There was special applause for "Mr. B's Blues" and "Blue World." We got paid $18.75 each for the Armory show. Getting rich fast! The Armory show ended about eight, in time to get over to the Old Mill to start work there. Johnnie came out to the Old Mill that night and sang "Cry," and we did the background the Four Lads had done on Johnnie's record.

I bought a one-wheeled trailer in Akron to give us more space to carry things on the road. Don already had one. We figured we didn't need to get bigger cars, just a bigger freight area!

Windsor, Ontario, was cold and gray when we played the Commodore in February. Bob Murphy and some of the other disc jockeys from Detroit were coming over to catch the show, which brightened up our lives a bit. We told Murphy that Capitol had decided not to release "Blue World" and "Tuxedo Junction." Capitol, in fact, was even talking about letting our contract expire! Murphy had the idea that if he could get a dub of that record, and play it enough, it would be a hit. He had places in Detroit he wanted us to work, but we needed a record going for us. Meanwhile, we were moving on to Toronto and starting to rehearse "It Happened Once Before," that haunting Bobby Troup song that has been so good to us.

In mid-March we had a break in our schedule and headed back to Columbus, Indiana. One night Don and I got to playing a few of our early unreleased singles for our folks. When we first got into the quartet business, the folks weren't very enthused. They felt we were doing this to get out of having "real" jobs, though they never said that. It was suggested that being the Four Freshmen wasn't really a valid profession like, say, banking. But as time went on, they became real fans. Mother kept clippings and Daddy kept track of everywhere we went. They were proud of the records we had going. We soft pedaled the probability that we weren't going to continue with Capitol.

Stan Comes Through Again

On the 7th of April we went to Chicago to meet Stan Kenton. We had a lot of things to talk about. We were in Stan's hotel room and he called Capitol Records' President Glenn Wallichs. Stan was a Capitol stockholder. "Say, now," Stan began, "You're not planning to release that Freshmen record of 'Blue World' and 'Tuxedo Junction,' are you?"

Wallichs said, "No."

"If you're not going to release it, why don't you let the Freshmen get a dub or two so they can use it to promote themselves where they work?"

Glenn couldn't say no to Stan, so he said yes. They would send us the two vinyl dubs. That was a victory of sorts because even if they weren't going to be released we could at least kick up a little dust wherever we went.

Stan was free that evening and we had dinner at the Empire Room. Kay Thompson and the Williams Brothers were the show, and Andy Williams was one of the brothers! Afterwards, we went back to Sheboygan and told our wives the things Stan had done for us.

On April 17th we went back to Chicago and played a one-nighter with the Kenton band at the Blue Note. It was an experiment that certainly worked because we headlined the

Blue Note later on. The next morning we went to a Chicago studio and recorded an American Van Lines commercial: "American takes you where you want to go for the lowest fare." Then it was back to work in Sheboygan.

The dubs from Capitol arrived on Don's 25th birthday, April 19th. We took them into one of the little booths in the record department of Prange's Department Store and listened to our new treasure and a few days later wrapped and mailed them to Bob Murphy.

By the time we opened at the Crest in Detroit on May 6th Bob had copied our dubs, and sent them to Bud Davies, Sid Garris, Don McCloud, Ed McKenzie, and Robin Seymour - all the hit-making disc jockeys in Detroit. They were the only ones in the world who had them, and they were spinning them like crazy. You could hardly listen to the radio for 15 minutes without catching "Blue World."

We sang to a full house on opening night - a Tuesday, no less! That didn't just happen! The Crest was a large neighborhood bowling alley and we were in the lounge. The place hadn't had much entertainment, except for a few local groups on weekends. They featured the Freshmen all week long because Bob Murphy had talked them into it! We had full houses night after night, with a line of people outside, waiting to get in. There would be 50 people waiting in line when we came in to work at nine and they knew they wouldn't get in until after the first show. So we started early and played hard and fast, singing "Blue World" almost every show.

The Crest asked us to extend our contract into July. Why not? The record is getting played every day on the air, there's still a line outside. Business was great. Dee Gee records called and wanted to sign us. There was a Mercury Records man there who wanted us, too. Woody Herman came through town and said he wanted us. The Midwest knew the Freshmen had a hit with "Blue World" but nobody could buy the record!

On Sunday, June 8th we met Stan again in Detroit. He decided to call Alan Livingston at Capitol to let him know that "Blue World" was a hit in Motown and they needed to get the record out. We got word that Capitol would release "Blue World" by July 30, 1952!

Mike Maitland, the Capitol man in Detroit, had already told Capitol that "Blue World" was a big record, but that didn't cut much ice in Hollywood. Stan Kenton's call did the job. Were it not for him, Capitol would not have re-signed us and there would never have been that long line of Four Freshmen albums on Capitol. Who knows, maybe the Freshmen might never have made it.

To add to our joy, Debbie Flanigan was born on June 19th in Dayton, Ohio, joining older brother Steve. This ended a string that began in March, 1949, of one or more of our wives always being pregnant. That night Mike Maitland and Max Callison, Capitol's man in the Midwest, came in to get the Freshmen's lapsed recording contract re-signed.

Mel Torme stopped by on June 20th. Besides writing "The Christmas Song," his main claim to fame in our eyes was the Mel-Tones, the vocal group on Artie Shaw's records. We flipped to think he would come to hear us. In late June the Ray Anthony band was in to hear us. Dick Reynolds, who later became a primo arranger for the Freshmen, was in that band.

A month later we were in a coffee shop in Akron and discovered "Blue World" on the jukebox! The Four Freshmen era had really begun!

CHANGES

With the signing of the Capitol contract on September 7, 1952, our professional career seemed to enter into a new orbit. Though we continued to play many of the same places, especially in the Midwest, recording sessions and campus appearances increased. Of course, we couldn't forsake the Pla-Bowl in Calumet City, Illinois.

Freshman fan Bud Hooper came in to listen to us almost every night. He still tells the story of the auto accident he had during our stay at the Pla-Bowl that fall. When he finally regained consciousness, he couldn't remember who he was, where he lived or anything. The doctors feared for his life. At first all he could remember was hearing the Four Freshmen! The thing that helped him most in regaining his memory was playing our records. The sound brought back the memories. Of all our fans I suppose Bud has the deepest appreciation for the Four Freshmen!

Freshmen fan clubs had started up in 1951, using handwritten membership cards at first. By the next fall there were so many fans and so many clubs that we switched to printed cards, which were distributed all across the country. On September 29th we had a recording session at Universal Studios, with Bill Putnam at the dials. We did "Stormy Weather" and "The Day Isn't Long Enough." They came out as singles and later showed up on albums.

October found us back at the Crest in Detroit. There was a new weekly program on WXYZ-TV - the Betty Clooney Show. Betty (Rosemary's sister) had Speedway Gasoline as her sponsor and we began doing the show with her every week. For a while it looked like it could become a steady thing. We were becoming a household word in Detroit and we alternated between the TV show and performing at the Crest each evening.

Back in Chicago less than a month later, we recorded "I'll Be Seeing You," "Holiday," "Poinciana" and "Baltimore Oriole." While we were inside the studio somebody broke into our car and stole our overcoats. We probably needed new ones anyhow.

How We Chose Songs

In the early years it was usually Don who selected our songs, simply because he knew so many of them by heart. But still, there was a pattern to the numbers we chose.

First, the songs had to fit the Freshmen sound. "Poinciana" was a tune the big bands played and it was an absolute natural for us. We arranged it to begin with the trademark Freshmen spread of notes, and there were those great long phrases and tones that we could milk and sustain. By contrast, a song we liked but never performed was "Love Letters." The melody was such that we could not sing it and make it ours.

Second, we watched for songs that drew pictures for the listener; numbers like "Circus," "Time Was," and "Their Hearts Were Full of Spring." People like words that stir up memories.

We chose some numbers I call "message songs;" tunes that said things we felt or that revealed who we were. The empty feeling of lost romance in our youthful years (and everyone has been there) was so beautifully and poetically captured in "Angel Eyes." And if we were ever meant to sing any song, it would have to be "Graduation Day." But for our fast songs, our prime concern was not what they said but how they swung!

Finally, there were some great Freshmen songs that were simply handed to us. You already know that was true of "Blue World." Two other such winners were "Please Remember," which someone at Capitol Records handed us, and "How Can I Tell Her," from the movie, "Lucy Gallant."

Back to the Heartland

Our record of "Stormy Weather" and "The Day Isn't Long Enough" was released in November.

We worked the Coral Gables in East Lansing for the first time. They had a rope stretching from the bandstand to the front door, and underage people had to stay on the east side. We worked out on the dance floor and knocked them dead. Right before Thanksgiving we opened at the Palm Garden in Columbus, Ohio, right across from the Ohio State campus. We sure could draw college people. Maybe they had only $7 in their pocket, but they'd leave all of it at the door to get to hear the Freshmen.

On December 3rd we did an afternoon show at the Ohio State student union, then three shows at the Palm Garden. (It's a wonder we didn't kill ourselves working.) One night Stan Kenton and half the band came in, followed by the Ray Anthony band. There was hardly room for the OSU kids!

We closed in Columbus on December 7th, drove up to Cleveland, put our families in a motel and went downtown to promote. We set up the equipment in Moe's Main Street and opened that night, having had no sleep. In between those shows we did a local TV appearance, then hurried back for the second show. Then we did a radio show downtown before the third show at Moe's. We finally got to bed at 4am. Whew!

Being an entertainer may seem like a glamorous life, but don't believe it. The people who try the hardest go the farthest, and we were trying very hard! Our records were

getting to the DJs and we were winning many of them as
friends. It served to build a firm foundation for a durable
success.

One Saturday afternoon we were asked to judge a
Cleveland TV talent show. Competing in the contest was a
broad shouldered, stocky accordionist playing "Lady of
Spain." He wore a blue serge suit, and he had forgotten to
zip his fly. That chrome-plated zipper glowed like neon on
the monitor screen! The open zipper got us laughing. We
kept trying to signal the cameraman to take a close-up of the
guy's face and get the lens off the zipper! The poor accordionist didn't win, and I suppose his neighbors and family
clued him in later about the zipper. It's always funny when it
happens to someone else!

I celebrated my 24th birthday at the Yankee Inn in
Akron. It had been a very important year in our story. We
were listed on the charts with "Blue World" and" The Day
Isn't Long Enough." Working hard was paying off. 1952
established the way we were going to be, the sound we would
repeat and the hectic pace we were going to keep. The year
ended with a boom, but 1953 began with a bust.

Downer

Hal Kratzsch was becoming a man with mixed emo-
tions and understandably split loyalties. He wanted to be
with his wife and sons, but Betty had back problems and
couldn't handle long trips. She was staying pretty much at
home in Warsaw. Hal loved the work, but the pace of our
success was unnerving to him. He was unhappy being a
Freshman and unhappy at the idea of not being a Freshman.

On January 3rd Hal told us he was going to leave as
soon as we could find a replacement. His quartet had run
away with him. It was tough for all of us, being caught in this
dilemma. I guess it was more difficult because we had never
replaced a Freshman before. We didn't even know if it could
be done! I mean, how in the world could we keep this quartet going without Hal, but how could we let it break up?

Hal's staying wasn't doing him any good. Nor was it doing Bob, Don and me any good. Hal had lost his characteristic Four Freshmen eagerness to succeed.

We still had our lighter moments. One night at the Yankee Inn we sang our closing theme and got down off the stage. A customer turned to us and said "I'll pay you one thousand dollars if you go back up there and sing 'The Day Isn't Long Enough.'" We said, "Thanks, but we're through. The place is closing." He repeated his offer, louder and with more conviction. Well, every man has his price; we got back up on stage and did the tune. But the guy skipped out during the last four bars and we never saw him again. We learned our lesson.

We worked Pittsburgh for the first time on January 18th, arriving right at the late afternoon rush hour. It was awful, trying to get to the Copa on that main street, where one side of town is built at a 45 degree angle to the other side. We could see the sign but we had to drive around the block a half dozen times before we figured out how to get to the front of the place. The club was downstairs. The owner, Lenny Litman, called it "my upholstered sewer." Lenny had a knack of picking out people on their way up, and he picked us.

It was in Pittsburgh that we first got mobbed by teenagers. Between Copa shows we did an appearance at a teen dance and were swarmed. It's a frightening feeling when overly emotional teenage kids get out of control. They tore at our hair and pulled buttons off our shirts. We were totally unprepared for any of it. Maybe this was why the major hotels offer those little sewing kits!

Hal was fighting pneumonia and was late to work on the 24th. Danny Crystal, the emcee and comic, stretched his jokes as long as he could and finally brought us on. We did "How Do You Like Your Eggs In The Morning" before Hal showed up. Our days as the original Four Freshmen were winding down.

We did a week in Peoria, then opened at the Forest Park Hotel in St. Louis. Our rooms were upstairs and the Circus Room was at street level. What a nice room to work. On Saturday afternoons we did "Saturday at the Chase," a CBS network radio show. (The Forest Park and Chase Hotels were owned by the same people.) George Shearing came in to hear us on February 19th, "Baltimore Oriole" was released on March 3rd and we received our first royalty check from Capitol Records. I got $41!

With June Christy

We went from St. Louis to Detroit and then to the Yankee Inn in Akron. On March 23rd June Christy came in to star for the weekend and we played her backgrounds. She handed us a few tattered pieces of music, explaining that the band at her previous job didn't hand in all their charts. We made her smile when we said, "You sing the song and we'll make up the backgrounds." Before her three days were over she was getting vocal and instrumental support her arrangers had never thought of!

On June's closing night Bob Flanigan cut back through the kitchen on the way out to his car. A fellow followed him, yelling "Hey, you! You've been getting in my hair. I've been trying to get next to June Christy and every time I do, you're talking with her." (June had stayed close to us, just to avoid guys like this.) Then, without warning - pow! Bob staggered back against the oven and slid down to the floor. The tussle in the kitchen aroused the burly bartender, who was usually looking to punch someone out anyway.

The back door of the kitchen opened out on a cement landing four feet square, with eight or nine concrete steps which led down to the parking lot. The bartender grabbed the guy, who I imagine was a little sorry he had started the trouble, popped him good, and sent him reeling out the door, across the landing and down the steps. Nobody saw him after that. I'm not sure we ever told June about her would-be suitor.

The Tau Kappa Epsilon fraternity at the University of Akron asked us to become honorary members, probably because Stan Kenton was a TKE. We went to the house for a formal initiation (without hazing!) and we have always treasured our status as TKEs.

We drove back to East Lansing to appear at the Coral Gables, and then went to Chicago. We talked about future recordings with Lee Gillette of Capitol, and went over to see the Kenton band at the Blue Note. Afterward, the man who ran the Blue Note threw a big party for the band. That was the night we met Frank DiOrio, Stan's band boy, who made sure all the luggage and instruments were on the bus. He was a hard working kid who was totally devoted to Stan. He adopted the Freshmen as part of the Kenton family, and we treasure his friendship to this day.

The Freshmen and Jack Teagarden alternated at the Blue Note the next week. Jack was so good to us. He liked the way Bob played trombone and one evening gave Bob a new mouthpiece. "Son, I make these at home, and I'd like for you to try one." It became one of Bob's most prized possessions and he used it for years, until it was stolen in Kansas City.

June Christy came by the Blue Note and we got her up to sing the songs we had done together in Akron. The audience loved it. I wish we had it on record.

In mid-April we opened in New York at the famous Birdland on 52nd and Broadway, alternating with the Kenton band. That was a thrill for us but also very hard work - 8:30pm to 3:30am each night. Almost every evening some of the music was broadcast on ABC radio. Ella Fitzgerald celebrated her birthday with us that week.

The long hours were really wearing out both us and the Kenton band. The trumpet players would line up in front of a tall narrow mirror backstage to inspect the inside of their lips. That would have made a great photo for *downbeat* magazine: guys pulling their faces out of shape.

From Birdland we went to Coney Island in Cincinnati. It was the first time we met Bob Braun, who was just starting out in radio, and was also a lifeguard at Coney's swimming pool. From there we went to Columbus, Ohio, and discovered we'd left the bass in Cincinnati! Some of us went back the next day and got it.

Finding Hal's Replacement

On May 31st we made a tape of us singing all the things we knew. We positioned Hal closest to the mike so whoever we got to sing the low part would have the tape to guide him.

By June our voices were all used up. Bob couldn't sing at all. So we took four nights off, during which Bob did not make one sound, not even a whisper. That's what it took. Then, on June 5th, we were right back at it.

The next day Bob, Don and I met Ken Errair in Detroit. Sammy Carlissi, a songwriter friend of ours, sent him over. Ken had been doing vocal solos and playing trumpet with a "society band" at night. During the day he worked as a skilled tool and die maker. He had never sung with a vocal group, but he was sure he could.

We signed him based on the way he had handled himself. He had proved he could do anything he set his mind to. Ken grew up near Detroit and graduated from Redford Township High School. He was a few months older than me but he seemed younger, probably because he was still single. I've never known anyone like him. We liked him the moment we saw him. Everybody did.

We didn't realize that Ken Errair was going to be as big a hit with the ladies as Hal had been. Lonely ladies would practically line up and wait their turn for his attention. Hal met Ken on June 10th when we rehearsed together at the Crest. Interior design people were at the Crest building the "Freshmen Room," designed to hold about 50 people. There was a mural on the back wall - a six by 12 foot enlargement of our publicity picture, with the sheet music of "Blue World" in the background. We rehearsed upstairs over the construction sounds.

On June 11th Ken started learning the bass violin. He'd never played one, but it wasn't long before he was able. We would also need to find a mellophone for him. New uniforms and photos were also in order. About this time Bob bought a Bach trombone. If we can credit any instrument with adding to Bob's identifiable trombone sound, that small-bell Bach was the horn. You hear its crispness on the Freshmen records from the mid-50s on.

We performed with Hal at night and rehearsed with Ken in the afternoons. No wonder we had voice trouble again. On June 23rd Ken Errair worked his first night with us. Hal was there too so we had five Freshmen on the job!

Don was recording some solo things for Dee Gee Records, Dizzy Gillespie's label, that are still in their unreleased file. Dave Usher, who ran the label, was a fan of Don's. Honestly, we had some doubt about the future of the Freshmen. Ken was trying hard, and he was good, but we didn't yet know how much we could accomplish without Hal. The fact that Don was doing solo recordings indicated that he knew anything might happen, and he wanted his bases covered. We closed at the Crest on June 28, 1953, the last night Hal Kratzsch ever sang with the Four Freshmen. Ken and Hal each worked with us that night, alternating sets.

Group Two

The next night we started a week at the Blue Crystal in Girard, near Youngstown, Ohio. We didn't have a horn rack for Ken's trumpet so he laid it down behind us by the guitar amp. When we finished the show we would step back and bow and, you. guessed it - about the fourth night I got both my heels caught on Ken's trumpet. Crunch! Ken bent it back and made it work. We purchased a horn stand shortly after that.

We went on to Erie, Pennsylvania, to the Spa Athletic Club. The Stuarts were working a half mile away - Ken Albers, Bill Comstock, Louise Stuart and Willard Scott (not the weatherman!). We got together to sing and play golf. We didn't know then, of course, what an important part they'd later play in the Four Freshmen story.

In mid-July we traveled to New York City to sign a new contract with Capitol - they needed Ken Errair's name on the dotted line. On the 15th we recorded "It Happened Once Before" and "Holiday" at Fulton Studios on West 40th Street. In Philadelphia we did an interview with a friendly young DJ named Dick Clark who really impressed us. Dick took over TV's "Bandstand" a short time later; he still looks like a kid! We got more pictures taken in New York City and went to see Duke Ellington and Georgia Carr at Birdland. At a nearby studio, Steve Allen was filling in for Gary Moore on "What's My Line." We were in the audience and he had us stand and take a bow.

We were part of the Michigan State Fair in August. They brought in everybody! The Kirby Stone Four, the Dominoes, Danny Crystal, Louis Armstrong, the Harmonicats, Teresa Brewer, Charlie Ventura, and Eddie Fisher were all there. Daddy and Mother Barbour came to see us at the fair and we introduced them to the Harmonicats and Louis, and then took them to see the Freshmen Room at the Crest. It was all finished by then, complete with the mural. Our parents were so proud.

At our rehearsals we were learning "I Can't Believe That You're In Love With Me" for Ken Errair, and Don was rehearsing "Malaya." Together we learned "Seems Like Old Times," Arthur Godfrey's theme song. On September 25th we opened at the Blue Note in Chicago. We were pleased with the great job General Artists Corporation was doing on our behalf.

In October we played Columbus, Ohio, for a week or two and then drove north to Ohio Wesleyan University in

Delaware, Ohio. We entertained both college and high school kids in the chapel. It wasn't 'till after the show was over that I discovered that my fly had been open during the whole show! I was mortified, and couldn't help remembering that poor accordion player in Cleveland! On the 29th we did *1952* a show at Bexley High School in Columbus and then on to Capital University, followed by two shows at Denison University. Those kids are today's Freshmen fans. Next it was back to Dayton to do the Esquire. One evening before the show we went to say hello to Stan Kenton who was working at another spot, in a package with Slim Gaillard and Dizzy Gillespie. The Kenton band bus had just had an accident and quite a few of his musicians were still suffering from injuries.

Winning Ways

We went from Dayton to East Lansing and the Coral Gables. Later, at the Crest in Detroit, we were notified that we had won *downbeat* magazine's readers poll, which was as high a mark as we could reach. November 29th was our son Kent's fourth birthday and Don's fourth anniversary. Sue and my boys flew in to help us celebrate.

After work in Detroit one night we flew to Chicago to record "I'll Be Seeing You" and "Malaya" with the Kenton band at Universal Studios. They recorded "Tenderly" as a follow-up to their quite successful "September Song." On these numbers the band sang a whole chorus in unison. The guys were still getting over the bus accident, and someone's mother had just died, so everybody was feeling low. After the session, Stan listened to "Tenderly" and decided it didn't have enough vocal density. So Stan got the Freshmen, Gene Howard (who had sung with the band years before), Buddy Childers and himself around a couple of mikes, and sang it again and again, placing our voices on top of the unison the band had sung. You'll hear it if you've got the disc.

We flew back to Detroit and landed just in time to go straight to the Crest. I called Sue at the intermission to tell her we were back in town. Bless her heart. For the last couple of days she had been sitting at the hotel with the boys, wondering about us. And she had been taking driving lessons because there had been many times like that past weekend when she needed to be able to drive.

We never could seem to get out of the car business! Bob now had a light blue '52 Cadillac four door. Don had his maroon '52 Buick Roadmaster and Errair had a blue '53 Olds 88. My black '49 Ford was the oldest in the bunch, but by far the best looking. I bought a '53 Lincoln demo, a factory executive's car. That was the best car I've ever owned. It was gorgeous - light green with white leather seats. We were all very happy about our choice until it came time to leave the Ford behind in the lot. Sue, the boys and I all cried as we drove away and left it sitting there. Sue had taken her driving lessons in it.

Bob Murphy, ("tall boy, third row," he called himself on his WJBK disc jockey show), who had copied the dubs of "Blue World" and helped make that record a hit, came to the Crest on December 22nd and made an official presentation to us - the *downbeat* plaque. We presented the plaque to Ted and Frank who ran the Crest. They displayed it proudly on the wall, and later at Pier 500, their new place. We were also given December 22-24 off for Christmas, which enabled us to take the families home to the grandparents.

On Christmas the Crest gave us presents - Benrus Citation wristwatches - gold with gold expansion bands. On the back was inscribed "Christmas 1953 from the Crest." I still have mine. We gave them a radio because they always had the Tigers and Lions games on during the daytime, using an old beat up radio fed through a microphone on the PA system so the customers could listen.

One afternoon we all went to Ken Errair's folks' house in Detroit. The neighbor's teenage kids had a quartet and they sang a carbon copy of our stuff. We realized then that our music was influencing people wherever "Blue World" had been heard. High school and college kids were singing our sound, just like we had tried to sing the Pied Pipers' sound on "Dream" a few years earlier.

A recording ban was set to go into effect on December 31st. The musicians union denied any performer the right to record until some sort of dispute was settled. On December 30th, in Detroit, we recorded "Over The Rainbow," "Circus," "Crazy Bones" and "Seems Like Old Times," so we would have something to release during the ban.

Things had been very touch and go, financially, from 1948 to 1953, Most of the time we barely made it. But now as we looked forward to the New Year, it seemed like a dream was beginning to come true and we would actually be able to pay things off!

Can you see the dreams in our eyes? The original Four Freshmen, September, 1948. Clockwise from the top - Bob Flanigan, Ross and Don Barbour and Hal Kratzsch - in the first Freshmen publicity photo ever taken.

Upper left, Ross and Don in 1936 at about 7 and 9, and don't you like those knickers!

Upper right, Don Barbour in cap and gown at his high school graduation with Ross in his band uniform, June, 1945.

Below, Don, second from left, Bob Flanigan and Ross, right, at a family outing on Grandpa Fodrea's farm, 1937.

Above, here's the original boyhood home of Don and Ross from about 1930 to 1938 in Burnsville, Indiana. Note "H.L. Barbour" on the mailbox.

Below, the two-room schoolhouse in Burnsville where Don and Ross started out was built in 1834.

*Above, the Barbour Family in 1936, clockwise from the top,
Don, Harold, Ross, and Maude.*

*Left, the Flanigans on a
bright summer day, clockwise
from the top, Lee, Nellie,
Maxine and Bob, 1937.*

Above, Ross at 17, on the farm, Rt. 3, Columbus, 1946.

Above, Ross and Nancy Sue Carson, summer 1947, already in love!

Right, Bob and Don both home on furlough, November 6, 1945.

Toppers

Before we were the Freshmen we were the Toppers. Dig that insignia we had sewn on our matching sweaters! The picture at right is Hal, left, and Marvin Pruitt, right with some fans at the "LVL" winter 1947-48.

Below, we were named the Freshmen Four by the time we played in Savannah, Georgia, in early November, 1948. Bob Flanigan was our new lead voice, replacing Marvin the previous summer. (Southern Photo Service)

Dear folks.

We are selling like mad. If the stables will give us, we open at Muncie next Mon. for a week at $400. Then to Dayton O. for a steady place we hope for $400.

We are now the "Freshman Tour"! We bought sport uniforms today. Tell you more later

Love Ross

Mon, Oct 11, 48

Mr + Mrs H.L. Barbour
R 3 Columbus
Indiana

Above, Ross wrote this postcard home from La Salle, Illinois, in October, 1948.

Below, Hal Kratzsch met Betty Wehrwien in Sheboygan, Wisconsin while we were appearing at Steinert's Tap in December, 1948. At this point in our development Ross had a sock cymbal but no drums!

Above, how we loved our cars! Hal shows off his "new" 1941 Cadillac and Don his 1936 Ford during an afternoon off in Lansing, Michigan in early 1949. Lansing is where we first sang "After You."

Below, this telegram proves that dreams do come true!

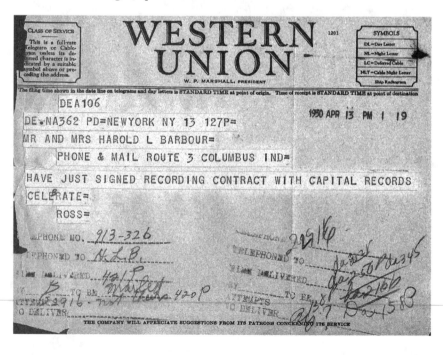

Above, the 1951 poster promoting the MGM musical "Rich, Young and Pretty" starring Vic Damone and Jane Powell, with the Four Freshmen singing "How Do You Like Your Eggs in the Morning."

Below, Bob Murphy, the Detroit disk jockey who made "Blue World" a hit, presents us with the winner's plaque for the downbeat Reader's Poll on December 22, 1953, at the Crest in Detroit. Ken Errair, second from right, had replaced Hal Kratzsch in May, 1953. (Weber Assoc. Inc.)

The Freshmen - Don, Ross, Ken and Bob - at a Purdue fraternity-sorority dance in 1955. (Phillip McArthy)

Right, the indispensable Dick Reynolds, flanked by Bob and Don. (Capitol Photo Archives)

Below, Nat King Cole came to Columbus, IN, to sing with Ted Heath and the Freshmen, April 19, 1956.

Center Right, Ken Errair and Jane Withers, October, 1955.

Below right, Bob Flanigan with the matchless Pete Rugolo. (Capitol Records Photo Archives)

Above, Ken Albers, right, replaced Ken Errair by the time we appeared with the Jerry Gray Band on television in 1956. (Universal Pictures Co. Inc.)

Below, in Fall of 1956, we were regulars on the Ray Anthony Show on ABC network TV. We rode in this new 1957 Plymouth in the Hollywood Santa Claus Parade at Thanksgiving time. The car died after the parade ended, and we couldn't get it started again!

THOSE FABULOUS YEARS WITH KEN ERRAIR

Ken Errair must have gotten caught in some bad company on New Year's Eve, 1953. He was late to work on January 1st and came in looking like death warmed over. The Crest's manager, Ted Lelek, who always kidded Ken said, "Hey, Hal, it's about time you got here!" If there was anything Errair didn't want to hear it was "Hal." Hal Kratzsch was a lot of great things, but punctual he was not. Errair didn't want to think of himself as the tardy guy. I don't think Ken was ever late after that.

New Year, New Songs

On January 8, 1954, we were to work in Muncie, Indiana. Sue and I and Sue's sister, Martha, were driving from Columbus and were almost to Muncie when I realized I hadn't put the drums in the car. That was when I found out what a sure-footed rascal that '53 Lincoln was. We turned around and drove like crazy back home and got back with the drums in time. Had the Lincoln been less a car I'd have probably been late. We did four shows at Ball State that night.

After a few other jobs in the heartland we loaded up the families and headed out to the beautiful West. This time we worked at the El Rancho in Las Vegas. We had band arrangements written for our songs and planned to just knock Vegas right on its ear. Big deal! Our part on the main show got trimmed to just two fast songs, "How Do You Like Your Eggs In The Morning?" and "Mr. B's Blues." We felt slighted, but the show was easy to do. We also worked a couple of shows in the lounge each night. In the afternoons we were rehearsing "Mood Indigo" and "Love Turns Winter to Spring." Ken Errair turned 26 on January 26th.

On January 30th Billy May came in and we reminded him that he was supposed to write a vocal arrangement for us. Fred Benson managed both Billy and us and had set this up. Billy had been indulging in a bit of procrastination. Later that night he brought in the most beat up, scribbled and scrawled on piece of music you've ever seen. He said he had drawn the lines with a straightedge, but he must have laid the page on a pillow when he did it. Some of the notes didn't even have stems or flags. We didn't know what to do with it!

We had begun rehearsing with Don Robertson, whose job it was to speed up our rehearsals by playing our parts and background chords on the piano. He figured out what Billy meant and wrote the score out legibly. If you've heard our record of "We'll Be Together Again" on *Voices In Modern* - that's what Billy meant! Does he write pretty things or what?

One night before work all the entertainers in town were invited over to the Sahara for a closing night party for Donald O'Connor. While we were there the man who ran the El Rancho was in a high stakes card game in which he lost a bundle of money. Even worse, when he returned to the El Rancho he found that a notorious high roller had won a lot of money from him there. He absolutely "lost it." He fired every card dealer as well as half the waitresses right on the spot. Then he fired the bandleader - and the Freshmen! He shoved a paycheck at me for the time we had worked. Then, still in a rage, he quickly told the cashiers not to cash the check. I tried them all. No chance!

We remembered that the next cashier shift came in at 6am. So we went to the motel and packed up our families. At six sharp, Bob pulled into the El Rancho parking lot and kept the engine running while I came whistling up to the cashier's cage. I smiled, handed them the check and they cashed it immediately. I thanked them, hurried back to the car and we were outta there like a shot! The Four Freshmen were but a speck on the horizon when the boss commanded the morning shift cashiers not to cash our check. We never worked for the man again.

We saw Nelson Riddle in Los Angeles. "Fred Benson wants me to write you an arrangement," he said "What tune?"

"Just pick your favorite song," we told him, "and write the prettiest notes you can think of." He chose "Indian Summer" and we recorded the notes he wrote - except we took out a few of them so there'd be places for us to breathe! What a number! On February 10th we recorded "Please Remember" and "Love Turns Winter to Spring," with Nelson Riddle's Orchestra at Capitol's Melrose studios in Los Angeles.

Gene Howard took pictures of us for the *Voices In Modern* album. Later we took our wives to Pete Rugolo's house and he fixed us a big, delicious dinner. Pete is a whale of a cook! June Christy used to kid him, "Pete, you're going to make a great wife for some woman!"

The 19th was memorable because we recorded "We'll Be Together Again," "My Heart Stood Still," "Street Of Dreams" and "The Nearness Of You." We were preparing to fill that first album with all our best stuff. Soon we were off again, back to the Midwest - Champaign, Illinois, Kalamazoo, Michigan and London, Ontario, where we spent a week at Campbell's. The Stuarts were over at the Brass Rail. It was as though the two groups were magnetized, we got together so often. Ken Albers and Bill Comstock were still members of the Stuarts. On March 11th Peter Potter's Jukebox Jury radio show picked our "Crazy Bones" to be a hit.

By now all of us except Ken had one-wheel trailers. We loaded up and went to Detroit. Sue and I rented a real house, a two story brick home at 18317 Greenfield. One day I was working on the car and listening to a Tigers game. It was a super hot spring day. Three year old Gary was playing nearby when a little lump of cloud moved in front of the sun and things got cooler. Gary looked up at the cloud and said, "That's fine, God. Keep it that way!"

"Please Remember" was released in early April. We were promoting the group by doing all the DJ shows we could. Everywhere we sang the song, people loved it. We finished the spring on college campuses, doing all our romantic stuff.

The summer was spent in Wildwood, New Jersey, at the Beachcomber, a nightspot with continuous all-night entertainment. Freddy Bell and the Bell Boys, the Treniers and the Freshmen performed one after the other 'till the wee small hours. We were booked through Labor Day, seven nights a week, plus Sunday afternoon shows. The Treniers were great guys and favorites at the Beachcomber. They had a loud, upbeat sound. Later, the world would call their style "rock and roll." The Treniers were doing that stuff years before Elvis and Bill Haley.

Our First Album

Voices In Modern was released August 2, 1954. Imagine, a Four Freshmen album! It changed our lives. Meanwhile, we were rehearsing "Indian Summer" and "This Love Of Mine." On August 30th Fred Benson called to say *Voices In Modern* was already number 14 on the best-selling charts, less than a month after its release!

By mid-August we were beginning to sag. The long nights were hot and our spirits were low. The Treniers showed us how a real group does places like Wildwood. They came on in spanking new uniforms and charged with energy. They were professionals; we felt like novices. We gained energy from them and we were better for it.

On September 21st we started a week at Caparella's in Buffalo. People listened intently and loved what we did. Every night Mama Caparella fixed us her wonderful Italian food. She saw how skinny we were after the hard summer in Wildwood.

The next night we sang at an outdoor ballroom in Canton, Ohio. The dressing room was below the stage. It had just rained and there was half an inch of water on the floor. We laid a few boards on the floor to stand on. I'll bet you've never tried to put on tux pants while standing with one foot on a board!

We worked Lou Posey's Frolics in Columbus, Ohio, and Woody Herman came in. By this time he and the Freshmen were "road buddies." We went on to a day in Evansville and a night in Kalamazoo. The college kids of that era would sit on the gym floor with their shoes off. Next came one-nighters in Detroit and Lansing - the biggest night there we ever had. Momentum was building. Then we took a ferry across Lake Michigan to Milwaukee and the White Pub. We were rehearsing "Mood Indigo" and "I'm Always Chasing Rainbows."

One day we went from Milwaukee to Chicago to do an afternoon TV show with Stan Kenton and Johnny Desmond. We rode back to Milwaukee with our friend Jim Hanlon. He wanted us to do "There's No One But You," so we learned a whole chorus in his car. Over the next few weeks we finished it and recorded it. Jim was dying of an incurable disease, and his fondest wish was to hear a record of the tune before he died. We prevailed upon the good people at Capitol to run off a dub and send it to him. The record reached him in time. I never hear "There's No One But You" without thinking of Jim Hanlon.

We were back at Campbell's in London, Ontario, for a week when Ken Errair decided he wanted to learn to fly. He took lessons in the morning and afternoon, and soloed before the week was out. He holds the Canadian record for completing training faster than anyone else.

Back at the Crest in Detroit we enjoyed a big Thanksgiving feast at the home of Ken Errair's parents. We had Mondays off and you'd think we would rest. But the Monday after Thanksgiving we flew to Cleveland to do TV and radio shows. Then it was on to Kalamazoo for an afternoon record shop appearance and an evening show at the civic auditorium. My diary says a few days later we went Christmas shopping with our wives and left the kids with Ken Errair in our apartment at the Clifford Hotel.

On Sunday, December 19th, the other Freshmen surprised me with a "Ross Barbour Appreciation Day." I had been knocking myself out with the fan clubs and corresponding with DJs. After work at the Crest we all got together with a bunch of good friends. They gave me a briefcase, like every true businessman should have. In it were wires from Stan and Woody and Ray Anthony and a dozen others. We headed home for Christmas with our parents. On December 31st I turned 26 at the Coral Gables in East Lansing.

Westward Ho

The Freshmen drove to California (families and all) as 1955 began. "Love Turns Winter To Spring" was our most recent single. We went to see Bobby Troup at the Celebrity Room in Los Angeles, and he got us up to sing. Afterward we went to Julie London's house and talked and sang 'till 5:30 in the morning. Bobby and Julie were dating at that time. On January 8th Dick Reynolds, Don Robertson and the Freshmen went over the "How Can I Tell Her" arrangement Dick had done for us. On the 9th we built that big ending on "This Love Of Mine." That evening, we were invited to Sammy Davis Jr.'s house.

Sammy liked cowboy guns, especially Colt Peacemakers, and he had a pair of Ned Buntline models that have barrels four or five inches longer than regular guns. His home up in the Hollywood Hills had attracted a bunch of party crashers that night. So he went upstairs, strapped on his guns and came down the stairs waving one of them. In his loud voice he said, "All right, everybody I don't know, get out!" I was surprised at how many people left.

Two days later we went out to Paramount and recorded "How Can I Tell Her" for the "Lucy Gallant" movie soundtrack. The instrumental background had already been recorded so all we did was add the voices. The song was used in the scene where Charlton Heston comes back from the service and meets his old girlfriend, Jane Wyman. We rehearsed "It Never Occurred To Me" and "This Love Of Mine" later in the afternoon. Three days later we recorded "How Can I Tell Her" and "There's No One But You" with Dick Reynolds and the orchestra. We also did "This Love Of Mine" and "It Never Occurred To Me," with a Dennis Farnon background.

Julie London threw a party on January 16th. Everybody sang or played something at these parties and Johnny Mercer did "Midnight Sun." Also at the party was a lovely actress named Jane Withers, who had become a star at age six, and had played many notable roles on the screen. Julie London and Bob Flanigan introduced Jane to Ken Errair that night.

We went back to Fack's on Market Street in San Francisco. On February 13th Bobby Troup and Julie London were there and Roy Kral and Jackie Cain came in. The King Sisters showed up, too. We had them come up and sing while we played the backgrounds. By this time bachelor Ken Errair had become a changed man. Jane had really stopped his clock. He wasn't looking for love anymore; he had found it! Ken had always told us he was going to Hollywood one day and fall in love with a famous pin-up girl. And he was a little sheepish when we kidded him about it. "Ah ha! You found your movie star and now you can follow your plan." Love and romance had never happened to him before. It was a beautiful thing to see.

Bud Abbot and Lou Costello came into Fack's one night. They were putting together a tour to Australia and they wanted to take us with them. It started us dreaming, but it never did happen. By Saturday night the 19th, my diary says, "Too many people - 600 sat down, 400 stood and 400 looked in." That's the kind of business we were doing.

We were rehearsing an Errair solo, "Don't Take Your Love From Me." His solos went over so very well. You have heard our "Nearness Of You" and "In This Whole Wide World," but he also did "Tenderly," "Don't Blame Me" and "What A Difference A Day Makes." On March 14th we recorded some more transcriptions. The songs included "Kate," "Sophisticated Lady," "Oh You Crazy Moon," "Joanne," "Old Rocking Chair," "You've Gotta Show Me," "Don't Take Your Love From Me," "I May Be Wrong," "What A Difference A Day Makes" and "Best Man." These tunes were released in March, 1998, by the Four Freshmen Society on a CD called *Through The Years.*

At this time, we started rehearsing "Day By Day." We got the idea to do it with a Latin beat and Dick Reynolds came up with the background. It was to be released on the back of the "A" side of "How Can I Tell Her." "Day By Day" was just along for the ride until the DJs turned the record over and found it. We whipped up the introduction and ending on March 20th during a rehearsal at the Hollywood Palladium. We recorded "Day By Day" and "You've Got Me Crying Again" on March 25th.

In early May, just before finals, we did a show at the Ohio State student union. They jammed 900 people in there. We kept on proving that colleges were where we belonged. There was no dressing room at OSU so our clothes and instrument cases were behind a screen at the back of the stage. After the show we discovered that someone had stolen Errair's sportcoat and Don's shoes. We did a fraternity dance at Purdue in West Lafayette, Indiana. Usually we did our shows as concerts and another band played for dancing. But

at Purdue they wanted to dance to the Freshmen, so we were
a dance band that night. May 8th found us at the Pla-Bowl
again. We came back one more for old times sake, and for
Mac McGraw.

Five Trombones

On May 9th we returned to Columbus, Ohio, to the
Frolics. Some Pete Rugolo arrangements were to be sent to
us there. We were going to do an album with Pete using five
trombones. The Four Lads were also in town and we met
them on the street one day. I wish I had a picture of that. We
were all standing on the corner - but not necessarily watching all the girls go by! We went to Easton, Pennsylvania, next
and checked into the Easton Hotel, just to rehearse the
tunes for the *Five Trombones* album. On May 25th we went
into New York City and joined AFTRA. That night we did the
Steve Allen TV show, singing "Blue World," "Day By Day" and
"It Never Occurred To Me." In our suitcases we had Pete's
new charts for "Mam'selle," "Our Love Is Here To Stay," and
"Love." We did the Steve Allen TV show again on June 3rd,
singing "Kate," "How Can I Tell Her?" and "Street Of
Dreams."

We did a week in early June at the Rainbow Grill in
York, Pennsylvania, which was a fun job. Saturday afternoon
we did a matinee for kids in the Valencia Ballroom. It was
full, full, full! We closed on June 11th and drove toward
Ohio after work. Bob and I ran out of gas on the turnpike
but, fortunately, I only had to walk a little over a mile.

We started again at the Crest in August and were
rehearsing the *Five Trombones* charts during the day. Those
songs were very difficult for us. We were not used to doing
the arrangements as they were written, and we weren't free
to change them. Some of the chords were written so our
notes fit in among the notes played by the trombones. The
chords were, in many cases, not the ones we would have
chosen. Don let it bug him so much that he got uptight one

afternoon, tossed a glass against the wall and stomped out. We weren't sure we'd be able to talk Don into going ahead with the album. Every day we did a DJ interview or record store appearance. We closed at the Crest on July 24th.

We picked up the families in Indiana and started down to Shreveport and the Stork Club. Our rehearsals had gotten even more difficult because Don was so bothered by the new arrangements. We came back to Los Angeles, and on August 17th went in to record. We stood in a three-sided isolation booth so our microphone would not pick up the trombones across the room. The first night we started recording "Love Is Just Around The Corner." Pete Rugolo decided to warm up the musicians.

"Okay," he said, "let's take it at the trombone chorus." Then he purposely counted it off way too fast. These trombone players had all played Rugolo charts before, and they knew each other well. George Roberts, Harry Betts, Tommy Peterson, Frank Rosolino and Milt Bernhart started to play that trombone chorus, but at Pete's tempo it just became a shambles. They didn't make even two bars. Pete counted it off extra fast again, with the same disastrous result.

Finally, he said, "Okay, let's try it real slow." Then he counted it off with the tempo where it belonged and they got it. Pete told them he'd actually wanted the slower tempo all along. Everybody had a good laugh and the ice was broken. The rest of the band included Claude Williamson on piano, Barney Kessel, guitar, Shelly Manne, drums and Joe Mondragon, bass.

By August 22nd all jokes were off. We did "Angel Eyes," "Mam'selle," "I Remember You" and "Speak Low." The next night "The Last Time I Saw Paris," "You Stepped Out Of A Dream," and "Guilty." Then, on August 29th, we finished up with "Somebody Loves Me," "Love," "Our Love Is Here To Stay" and "You Made Me Love You." We probably sang better on the *Five Trombones* album than on any other because we had rehearsed and rehearsed. We knew every note. *Four*

Freshmen and Five Trombones became the most successful album we ever made, but it was also the most difficult to complete. So much of the credit goes to Pete Rugolo; he envisioned all these sounds and then he wrote them out. Don even grew to appreciate the songs. Pete Rugolo's arrangement deepened what we were doing and the Freshmen still feel his musical influence.

Wedding Bells

Ken Errair and Jane Withers were married in the fall of 1955 aboard the yacht owned by Roy Rogers and Dale Evans. We and our wives were dazzled by the hospitality and the splendor. There was room on the boat for what seemed like a hundred people, and the guest list made us catch our breath. David Rose played the wedding march and his wife, Betty, was Jane's maid of honor. Ann Blythe was glowingly pregnant. Ken's best friend, Elmo Glorio from Detroit, was best man. Ken and Jane honeymooned on the yacht, anchored in Los Angeles harbor. But it wasn't long before the Freshmen were back on the road again, primarily doing college one-nighters.

Ken's solo voice continued to grow in popularity with Freshmen fans. We featured his lush bass voice on many numbers. "The Nearness Of You" was becoming a signature song for him. And in "Gone With The Wind," there's a passionate line that goes, "Gone is the rapture that filled my heart." But every night Ken, with a straight face, sang it "rupture." Each of us would lean in toward Ken and correct him: "rapture," "rapture," "rapture."

Ken would whisper back into the mike, "But my doctor told me it's rupture" and then go right on singing. After some nervous laughter, the crowd would start wondering if he was going to replace yet another word in the song.

Everyone messed up Ken Errair's name, even the disc jockeys. It was really simple if you said, "Kenny Rare." I wonder how many times we told people that. They would say

"Ken Error," "Ken Air Air," "Ken Rrrrrr" or "Errairra." Privately we used to call him "E-rair-ee-air," and seldom used his first name. We loved him and he knew it.

I remember in Juarez, Mexico, the Cafe Charmont had a super band but they didn't play our backgrounds. We did that ourselves. The band never felt we were fluffing them off, though, because during intermission Errair would take them out the back door and across the alley, where tequila was five cents a shot. He would buy the whole band a round for less than a dollar.

The Writing on the Wall

Jane came to see Ken when she could, but she had a family of her own and a host of people depending on her for the charity work she did. Their kids wanted Ken at home, too. We all saw the writing on the wall long before Ken ever brought it up. He promised to stay until we were ready to work with a new man.

In fact, it was Ken who suggested Ken Albers to us. Albers was with that very talented Philadelphia group, the Stuarts. We agreed with Errair - we would be lucky to get Ken Albers. The Stuarts sang and played together well. They were a charming group. They had plenty of places to work in the East, but they had no record contract and hadn't traveled broadly enough to gain fame and fortune. At first, Ken Albers hesitated and we held our breath. Then in March, 1956, he said OK, and we celebrated!

There were a few more colleges to play with Errair and a week at the Town Casino in Buffalo, then two weeks at the Crest in Detroit. Our final one-nighter with Ken was at the Shrine Auditorium in Los Angeles, with the great Count Basie band.

In the next few days we recorded "For All We Know," "Lonely Night In Paris," and "Easy Street" with Ken Errair. Ken Albers was in Los Angeles during these mid-March recording sessions. Of course, we had to get new uniforms, take new group photos and re-write our publicity material so the promoters of the upcoming jobs would advertise the correct Four Freshmen. Oh, and we had to rehearse, too!

Ken Errair had been a giant player in the growing success of the Four Freshmen. We wished him well as we said good-bye.

Another change was happening to us. The families were staying at home more and more while we did one-nighters. Some of the kids were starting school, so staying in one place made sense. But there was still a lot of travel in store for them when school was out.

THE MULTI-TALENTED MAN

Even Ken Albers would admit that he had it easy
when he started with us. In 1956, the *downbeat, Billboard,
Playboy* and *Record Whirl* magazine polls all chose us number
one. With the multi-talented Albers on board we began a
month long tour on April 1st. The group included Nat King
Cole, the Ted Heath band from England, June Christy, a
pretty dancer named Patty Thomas. and a comic, Gary
Morton, who got laughs everywhere he went. The Heath
band, featuring the best jazz players in all the British Isles,
had never seen the USA, and we took great pride in showing
them around our country.

An All-Star Tour

The tour began in San Antonio, Texas, and went on
to Ft. Worth, Houston, College Station, Wichita Falls and
Dallas - all in the first week. We all rode in a bus - "coach" to
our English friends. Ted Heath presented himself as a very
proper gentleman, and he, along with his pretty wife Moira,
chose seats on the right side, near the middle of the coach.
Ted was rather aloof when the tour began but the more
experiences we shared, the closer he got to us all. A band bus
will do that to a person!

Due to the temper of the times Nat King Cole and his

trio didn't travel with us. They either flew or hired a car. The hotels where we stopped would not take them because they weren't white. Our generation grew up listening to Nat King Cole's music. He was everybody's favorite piano player, and then he became everybody's favorite singer. In a word, Nat was just gorgeous. He always dressed in the latest Hollywood styles and his valet kept him spotless. He was very dark, almost purple, and in the theater lights, he radiated. I never heard anyone say anything bad about Nat King Cole. Ever.

That's one reason we were so shocked in Birmingham, Alabama, when a man came right up over the footlights, across the front of the stage, and tackled Nat and the microphone in one fell swoop. The mike whacked Nat on the chin and almost knocked him out. A half dozen policemen came from out of nowhere and took charge. Two of them wrestled the attacker to the floor and two others helped Nat to the dressing room. The rest stood guard against - who knew what? It could have turned into a bloody riot.

At that time it was illegal for white and black entertainers to work on the same stage without a curtain separating them, so the Heath band was playing behind a see-through curtain called a "scrim." Ted had left the band in the hands of his lead alto player, Les Gilbert. Les had the band stop playing Nat's music and play "God Save the Queen" - the melody we know as "My Country 'Tis Of Thee." The audience stood at attention. By the end of that short melody the situation was well in hand. As the police helped Nat off stage, Nat said quietly to someone, "The Queen doesn't need help. God save me!"

One man in the crowd yelled out, "Please have Mr. Cole come back on stage so we can apologize to him." That's what everybody wanted. When Nat finally came back to the microphone, they applauded forever. They might still be clapping, but Nat held out his hands and quieted the crowd. Then he said, "I don't want any trouble. I just came back home to sing my songs." (He was born in nearby Montgomery.) Nat didn't work the next few nights. Racial tension was ready to explode down there.

He was back with us on April 19th when we played Don's and my hometown on Don's 29th birthday. After the show there was a party at my house and everybody was invited out for food and drinks. The band and June came, but Nat and his trio did not.

We had recorded "Graduation Day" with Ken Errair. It was being held for release until just before senior prom time. We rehearsed it on the bus and the Heath band smiled at the simplicity of the arrangement. They believed the Freshmen should always have done complicated songs like "Angel Eyes." Our tour ended May 1st at Carnegie Hall in New York. A disc jockey taping an interview asked Ted Heath, "What impressed you most about the USA?" I heard him say, "The size of Texas!"

The Albers Touch

I think it was the song writer Roger Miller who said, "Luck is some people's nickname for God." We were really lucky to get Ken Albers in our group. He was so full of musical ability. He could write new Freshmen arrangements and rehearse us to the max. Man, we needed him!

Bob, Don and I had never been whizzes at reading or writing music. We could hear a tune a few times and know it, harmonize it by ear and memorize it, but that took so much time. Capitol wanted at least two albums a year, plus some single records, and we also needed to learn new tunes for the shows. Ken could write them out. That way we didn't learn only a part of the arrangement, and then forget it before we could finish memorizing it later. Now, the notes were there right before our eyes. Dick Reynolds and Ken Albers made it possible for us to keep up with our record deadlines, even though we worked almost all night and traveled all day, sometimes for months at a time. With written notes we had the best of both worlds.

For instance, we sang "How Can I Tell Her" just the way Dick Reynolds wrote it. Except for the ending. That closing part, "Ho-ow-Ca-an I-I-Tell Her Of My Love" was done by ear. Each of us suggested a dozen ideas per chord and we tried them all until we got it to sound the way we wanted. We spent as much time on the ending as we did on the rest of the song, but that's the identifiable Freshmen sound that always grabs people.

In May we spent a month in Paradise - at Lau Yee Chai's restaurant in Honolulu. That month we did a lot of rehearsals so Ken could learn all the old songs and we could learn the new ones together. We had our families with us and they had the time of their lives. Sue and I and our boys stayed at Henry Kaiser's Hawaiian Village back when it was grass shacks in circles around swimming pools. Now it's the Hilton Hawaiian Village and instead of grass shacks they have skyscrapers.

As I mentioned, "Graduation Day" was recorded and ready to be released as planned. In Hawaii we got word that a Canadian group, the Rover Boys, had also recorded the tune and were already getting plays on American radio. We called Capitol and they put ours out at once. But suddenly there were records of "Graduation Day" by the Crew Cuts, Lawrence Welk and heaven knows who else. Our "exclusive" became the hit version, but sales were so divided that none of the renditions went very high on the charts.

Something Amiss

After Hawaii we worked in San Francisco and then at a ballroom in Denver. I tried to play badminton one afternoon but my muscles just wouldn't work. Was it the altitude? I couldn't figure it out.

Toward the end of August we worked the Lorain County Fair in Ohio and by now I was really feeling bad. My weight had dropped from 150 to 124 pounds. We sang at a ballroom on the lake in Brooklyn, Michigan, one night, and the Crystal Palace near St. Joseph the next. When I slept my mouth would stick shut. One night I tried keeping chewing gum in my mouth to keep it moist, but I woke up with my mouth glued shut by the chewing gum. It had to be that we were working too hard in the hot and humid weather. "When we work a cool place I'll be all right," I told the guys.

By the time we worked the Crystal Beach Ballroom in Vermilion, Ohio, I could hardly move. My muscles felt like taffy. I was so dizzy it wasn't safe for me to be near the edge of the stage. Between shows I laid down on a row of four folding chairs in a little room behind the stage. The other Freshmen woke me for the second show.

August 27th was a night off in Detroit, which was my first chance to see a doctor. He tested my blood and he started acting like I was going to die right there on his little padded table. He ordered me to the hospital immediately. Diagnosis: diabetes. Insulin regulation must begin at once.

I said, "Doc, if I'm going to the hospital for two weeks let's do it in Indiana. I have a home in Columbus, and a wife and family."

That afternoon Don and I flew to Indianapolis. Sue and my brother-in-law, Roy Stillabower, picked us up at the airport and rushed me to the Columbus hospital. I have never been nearer death than I was that day. Next came two weeks of blood tests, injections and dietetic food. Blah! When they finally let me up to walk the hall my muscles had almost used themselves up. I needed help just to stay standing.

Everyone needs insulin to live. It combines with calories so your cells can use the calories. My pancreas had stopped making insulin and my cells almost starved before we discovered the problem.

I had to learn to walk again. One day I got as far as the hospital parking lot but I didn't have the strength to step over the telephone pole laid at the edge, by the grass. I just stood there, being thankful to God and the doctors and nurses who knew what to do to pull me back from the edge of doom. I sensed I had been saved for something worthwhile, and making people happy with our sound was the most worthwhile thing I could think of.

Back to New York

Fred Benson, Ray Anthony's manager, was handling our career. He had postponed the one-nighters we'd missed while I was in the hospital. We agreed that on September 20th we could open at the Copacabana in New York. Sammy Davis, Jr., who worked the Copa often, sent us a wire saying, "Know you'll be a smash at your opening at the Copa." We decided we were going to knock New York on its ear.

At the Copa there was a band for dancing, then the chorus line, then Joe E. Lewis, and then the Four Freshmen. The Copa clientele knew Guy Lombardo, Sammy Davis and Joe E. Lewis. They did not know the first thing about vocal jazz, Freshmen harmony or Hoosier humor. We died that first night. The kindest thing the people did was to raise their eyebrows and shrug. We had been off for three weeks and probably didn't sound like world beaters.

One night, after the show, Don said hello to one of the chorus girls who had worked with us in Buffalo or Syracuse or somewhere. Suddenly, two big guys in dark suits came up behind him. Each took hold of one of Don's arms and held it against his side. Then they lifted him off the floor and carried the 200 pound Don down the hall to a more private place.

Don later reported that they'd said, "Listen, bud. Nobody talks to da broads, 'ja hear? Nobody talks to da broads!" We wondered what else "we wuz not supposed to do."

Lawrence Welk had become very successful with the ABC-TV show he did for Dodge. I guess he must have sold a lot of Dodges, because the Chrysler Corporation wanted to put together a show like that to sell Plymouths, only they wanted a younger, hipper audience than Welk had. So they created The Ray Anthony Show, featuring the Four Freshmen and Frank Leahy, the ex-Notre Dame football coach. Each week they planned on a guest vocal artist. Early on we met Sue Raney, when she was still a teenager. She was so beautiful and sang so well. Another guest star was Don Durant, who later played the lead in the TV series Johnny Ringo. Also to be featured was a girl trio called the Belvederes, a studio group named after Plymouth's classiest car. Lulie Jean Norman, Sue Allen, and Ginny O'Connor did a super job. Ginny had been one of the Mel-Tones and later married Henry Mancini. The Freshmen often danced across the set with the Belvederes and the girl guest star during the band numbers. I confess - I have danced more on television than I have off!

That show could have been great. Ray's band had so much more spice than the Lawrence Welk Orchestra. And, as far as sound goes, the Belvederes and the Freshmen were notches above anything else on TV. But...(why does there always have to be a "but?").

The sponsor and advertising agency didn't want us to play our instruments. They wanted us to do choreographed moves, and they must have seen we were no good at that kind of thing. It was embarrassing. We looked like four strangers acting like they were singing Freshmen parts. Unfortunately, a video exists of us doing some of the tunes and commercials, and we look so d-u-m-b! Why is there often a vacuum of creative thinking at the executive level? They watered down Ray and us so much there was no fizz left. One of the execs was so afraid we would sing an "atonal" chord. (He spoke the word like you would say "child molester.") And he didn't even know what "atonal" meant; he thought a sixth chord was "atonal." We weren't much good at dancing and they wouldn't let us do the chords that made us famous. Sigh! Before long we were taking leaves of absence from the show so we could go out and work colleges. I think the show closed down after 13 weeks.

Major Moves

In January, 1957, we replaced our manager, Fred Benson, with our very first fan and our staunchest supporter, Bill Wagner. He and Vicki had moved to California from Warsaw, Indiana, because Bill wanted to get a job in show business. Bill and Hal Kratzsch had been home town friends and many times we had stopped at their house and kept them up until the wee hours, playing records and singing. We agreed Bill would manage us until something better came along for him. We shook hands on it and never did have a contract.

Bill set up our office at 6047 Hollywood Boulevard and for ten years worked tirelessly, making sense of the bookings, the recordings, the publicity and other details. Fred Dale handled booking and Harold Plant the money. If you have a group and you want it to succeed, choose people like that; people you can trust. They are as important as the members of the group itself.

Another milestone for Sue and me was moving from our house in Columbus to a place in North Hollywood. It was tough to leave family and friends, but let's face it, there aren't very many television and recording studios in central Indiana!

Each arrangement we recorded was like adding another child. We watched them develop and grow. Some fulfilled all our expectations, others didn't. And we remember the strangest things about them. Let me tell you how "I Get Along Without You Very Well" began. It was early 1957. Our college tour had two free days in Iowa, and we chose to stay in Waterloo. We needed a piano in order to rehearse. The desk clerk at the hotel didn't believe we'd clean up after ourselves when rehearsal was over, but he grudgingly let us use the piano in the second story ballroom. We were doing

35 one-nighters in a row and trying to keep our voices smooth in the cold weather. In our free time we were supposed to put together a dozen good arrangements of the songs we had chosen for the *Five Saxophones* album.

The piano was a small upright and about the color of tobacco. It had seen better days but at least it worked. Ken sat down and played the parts of "I Get Along Without You Very Well" for us. We stood around behind him, looking at the "chart" as he played. This was the only Bill Brown arrangement we ever did and it was great. Pumped up like we were, the arrangement got our imaginations going.

It's one of music's unexplainable things: some chords sound just fine on the piano but they limp when you sing them. I've heard other groups sing chords that just "laid there" too, so I guess it wasn't just us. We used the term "speak." Each chord had to be strong enough to stand by itself and "speak" - say its own name - "I'm a major 9th," or "I'm a minor 7th." When the chords really speak, quartet singing is a joy.

This was a great arrangement. But we would change a couple of bars, only to find they would not flow correctly into the next bar. So we'd fix that bar, too. A few bars later we'd dream up another bouquet of notes, so we'd change the chords leading into and out of that spot. Some of our changed parts got replaced by even better ideas - we were changing the changes! When we finished the arrangement Ken had to write out all the changes clearly so Dick Reynolds, who did the background on this one, would know what we had been up to. Ken grabbed some clean sheets of staff paper and wrote everything out again so the parts we had changed fit right in; no arrows, scribbles, erasures, tear stains or teeth marks.

We should have saved the original chart for posterity. It was a great chart but we really shredded it. We never counted Bill Brown's chords and our own, but I think the final arrangement ended up about half his and half ours.

M'mmm! I love that bunch of notes. We did the ending by ear, too, and in my opinion it's the best ending we ever did. I never hear that record without thinking back to that cold ballroom in that Waterloo hotel with the rain pelting against the window. Here's to Bill Brown, Ken Albers, Dick Reynolds (and that desk clerk!). We couldn't have gotten along without you very well. And by the way, we left no mess.

Five Saxes

In early March we recorded the *Five Saxophones* album in Los Angeles, which included "I Get Along Without You." Then we headed back to Ft. Smith, Arkansas, to do a show and to judge a beauty contest. In Meadville, Pennsylvania, we worked a college fieldhouse that had the worst echo problem we ever encountered. Well, there was one place that rivaled it - the fieldhouse at Notre Dame. Most of the schools we worked were not equipped for concerts then. Now they have nice orchestra halls.

On Sunday, April 7, 1957, in the Penn State gymnasium at State College, we did the afternoon show with Buddy Morrow and his band that I described in Chapter One. What a memorable occasion! And on April 16th Hal Kratzsch got lonely for the music business and joined the Signatures. He had been living happily in Warsaw until Bob and Ruth Alcivar talked him into coming back on the road. They recorded some wonderful things with Hal, who now called himself Hal Curtis.

We were still trying to get that *Five Saxes* album finished. We did "Sometimes I'm Happy" on April 24th. The rest of the spring was spent on lots more college campuses. In July we recorded "Julie Is Her Name," which Bobby Troup wrote for his wife, Julie London, and one night we sang it just for her. Later she recorded a song called, "The Four Freshmen," another tune Bobby Troup wrote.

The summer was a blur of Midwest ballrooms. Kids from area high schools and colleges would pack the places when we came to town. As soon as Labor Day was over we were back on the campus circuit, plus Storyville in Boston and the Safari in New Orleans. October was more college one-nighters across Texas and the South. We worked at Porky's in Ft. Lauderdale and at the University of Florida in Gainesville, with the Kenton band.

November 22nd was a true one-nighter kind of day. With too little sleep we flew out of Columbus, Ohio, to Roanoke, Virginia. But there was too much fog to land there, so we went on to Greensboro, North Carolina. We had to rent a Ford and drive the 115 miles to Roanoke. We would have made the 4pm show on time if we hadn't been arrested for speeding in some little town.

In Mount Pleasant, Michigan, they paid us in brand new 10s and 20s, with paper bands around the money. Our bulging pockets made us look like bank robbers! I don't remember how much we got, but back at the motel we undid the packets and tossed the money up in the air, threw it on the bed and rolled in it, skipped through it barefoot.

November 28th was Thanksgiving Day and we were due to sing in Saginaw that night. Don had scraped his knuckle wrestling with luggage when we flew out the night before. He was sound asleep when the flight attendant woke him and said, "That red line that runs up your hand and arm means you have blood poisoning."

There wasn't much we could do until we landed so Don went back to sleep. We took him to the hospital in Ypsilanti, where the outpatient doctor dressed his hand and gave him some medication. "You just take it easy this evening," the doctor said, "don't do anything."

We had a hall full of people in Saginaw that night who wouldn't take kindly to our canceling the show. We had planned to grab dinner on the way to the show, but we had spent too much time with the doctor. All we could find as we headed north on Highway 23 was a combination general store and filling station. Bob pumped the gas while we bought milk, bananas and Oreo cookies. We had our Thanksgiving dinner in the car as we drove to Saginaw.

In many ways, 1958 mirrored the year before. We were locked in tight on America's campuses while school was in session, and in ballrooms and night spots when it wasn't. Baby Kathy joined the Barbour family and made us complete on January 24, 1958. What a doll she was - and is. Something about daddies and little girls made us inseparable.

A Background of Stings

It was about this time that we started planning the album *Voices In Love*. It represented something of a new direction for us. Jackie Gleason had been very successful with his mood music albums like *For Lovers Only*. The songs were smooth, mellow and smoochy and, of course, all instrumental. People would play those albums as soft background music for candlelight dinners at home on balmy summer nights.

We asked, "What if we try that same kind of flavor, except with words to the songs? Instead of blaring trumpets, let's use a background of strings. Rather than being loud, let's be soft. Let's go slow, not fast." For the first time, we mixed a slight echo chamber effect into the final cut.

Dick Reynolds wrote the backgrounds for the violas and cellos and Ken Albers outdid himself with the soft brass bridges on "Warm" and "Moonlight." His contribution on "I Heard You Cried Last Night" was in a class by itself.

The cover photo was filtered through blue light, and featured a gorgeous lady, looking intoxicated with love. It was the first album cover to show the Freshmen with serious expressions, dressed in their misty, blue striped sport coats.

While *Five Trombones* was our most popular album, many fans tell us *Voices In Love* is their favorite. It was released to great acclaim on October 6, 1958, and we incorporated many of those numbers into our in-person shows. College kids told us they stayed up late night after night playing and replaying that record. It seemed to capture the mood of romance in America then.

In November we began 18 days on the road with Maynard Ferguson and his roaring band, along with the Dave Brubeck Quartet. Jazz journalist Leonard Feather was the master of ceremonies. We rode a bus through the East and Midwest, from Toronto to St. Louis to Charlottesville, Virginia, and all points inside that triangle.

Maynard and the band were spectacular every night. Slide Hampton, Willie Maiden and Don Sebesky were in the band. Dave Brubeck had the incomparable Joe Morello on drums, mellow Gene Wright on bass and Paul Desmond playing those history making musical bubbles on his alto sax. It was a spectacular package.

10

ROAD SHOW

We had done a show in Anaconda, Montana, in early
January and spent our night off in a Butte, Montana, hotel.
It was 29 below zero and the snow was blowing into huge
drifts. How to kill time?

Our next album was to be called *Love Lost* and it still
needed a title song. I got some blank music paper and sat
down at the desk. After a few minutes, I called up the other
guys and said, "Come on over to my room and let's write a
song."

We tossed around some possible rhymes and somebody suggested that the song end with, "then there'll be no
love lost on you." The inventive Ken Albers figured out a
chord progression for the ending and Don and Bob came up
with the melody line and harmony ideas. Before the evening
ended the song was scribbled out, ready for Ken to harmonize. "Love Lost" was born that night, just because it was too
darned cold to do anything else!

We rehearsed "Little Girl Blue" and "I'm A Fool To
Want You" the next morning, before we drove to Bozeman to
sing at a college. Most of the month was spent on campuses
in the West. Ken wrote the arrangement for "I Wish I Didn't
Love You So."

We spent Monday, January 26th, recording at Capitol,
getting started on the *Love Lost* album, and by January 30th

we had all the songs recorded. Just as soon as the sound engineers made the inter-cuts and spliced it all together we gave it a careful listen. We were sure it was going to be the greatest thing we ever did. Voyle Gilmore had supervised the recording. What a patient and able man.

There are vocal interludes on the album which go from song to song, changing the key from one number to the next and tying the whole album together. Dick Reynolds had written the instrumental backgrounds and most of the vocal arrangements. But he had to wait until Capitol decided which tune followed which before he could write the interludes, which we recorded a few days later.

A professional photographer had the bright idea that Capitol wanted photos of us on top of the Capitol Tower in Hollywood. That's about 12 stories up! We climbed up there on a clear, cool, sunny day, with just a slight breeze. Bob Flanigan is afraid of heights. He has no trouble in a plane but stand him on top of a tall building and he'll have a worried look on his face. The roof of the Capitol building slants down all around, but it didn't appear to us to be very dangerous. Fearless Don decided to make matters worse. He and I, of course, had been tree trimmers so height gave Don no pause. He walked over to the edge, looked down, and acted like he was losing his balance. It just drove Bob crazy. We couldn't use any of those photos because of the expression on Bob's face!

Campus Capers

We flew to Miami on February 3 for a southern tour, but most of our luggage didn't. We had to rent horns and drum equipment before we did the Dade County Auditorium show for WINZ radio. The next day all the horns came in, but my drum dolly was still elsewhere. We drove to Auburn, Alabama, and hired a messenger service to bring the dolly in from Atlanta. Ah! We're operational again. Next came Millsaps College in Jackson, Mississippi, and then on to

Hattiesburg for a show at Southern Mississippi. We finished up in Baton Rouge and Louisiana State University, where we were given the keys to the campus.

On the 15th we were back at dear old Penn State. Capitol had moved fast because *Love Lost* was released the next day. Bob Flanigan drove to nearby Harrisburg to buy a '59 Cadillac Coupe (remember those great big fins?). The next week we did a show on the court at Kiel Auditorium in St. Louis prior to a Hawks basketball game. Marty Blake was the publicity man for the Hawks and he made a practice of bringing in entertainers to play before the games. In fact, after the Hawks moved to Atlanta we worked for Marty down there.

Later that night we went to the Embers to hear the Signatures and former Freshmen Hal Kratzsch - I mean Curtis. Even English majors couldn't get "Kratzsch" spelled right! The Signatures were a strong quintet that both played and sang. Bob and Ruth Alcivar led the group. Later, Bob wrote arrangements for the 5th Dimension.

We drove into Iowa and sang at Cornell College in Mt. Vernon the next day. The motel owner was sure we wouldn't be able to find the school so he led us there in his car. From there it was on to Iowa City and the university. This was the day we started thinking of "Candy" as a cha-cha-cha number.

Fairfield, a town nearby, was hilarious. I asked the man at the filling station "Where's the best restaurant in town?"

He said, "The Turner Hotel."

"Is that the best one?" Bob asked.

"It's the only one."

We thought, "Oh my! And more so when we climbed the three wooden steps to the plank porch that encircled this weather-beaten hotel. We could smell the pie and the green beans with onion rings on top. They had middle-aged ladies in starched white aprons serving mashed potatoes and gravy with the chicken and dumplings. We should have done another album there and called it "The Four Freshmen and Five More Pounds Each" What a place! We finished with baked apples and cake. I hope the Turner Hotel is still going strong in Fairfield because I want to go back there some day and overeat. The (very full) Freshmen worked Parsons College that evening.

Our tour closed out at a couple of great Minnesota schools - Concordia College in Moorhead, and St. Olaf in Northfield. From there Ken went home to his family in New Jersey, Bob flew east to pick up that new Cadillac and drive it to Los Angeles, and Don and I flew to California.

On March 5th we all went to Bill Wagner's house. He had a brand new *Love Lost* album and we played it all evening. On the 9th we met with Voyle Gilmore and planned our next album, *Four Freshmen and Five Guitars*. Dick Reynolds and Jack Marshall would do the backgrounds.

On the 23rd the Freshmen flew to New York to do three songs on the Hit Parade TV show, so very popular back then. It was there we got word that Mother had broken her leg so Don and I headed home to see our parents. Don and I were their moral support, the only children they had, and it was always a red letter day for them when we came home. We were in and out of there for three days, driving at night to Muncie and Bloomington to do college shows.

From home we flew to Cedar Falls, Iowa, for another college date. That night we performed "Time Was" and "You're All I See" for the first time. From Iowa we went to Kalamazoo and Western Michigan University. We probably saw 20 classes through that institution!

We were in Detroit and flying out early. I was the one responsible for wake up calls and I couldn't find Bob and Ken anywhere in the hotel. There's no point in two of us going to Charlotte - we've got to have all four. Don and I scoured the place and finally found them - they had changed rooms without telling me. We drove like fools to the airport in Ypsilanti (yup, that's how they spell it!) and took off for Charlotte, North Carolina.

There were no rental cars and time was short, so we chartered an Aero Commander to Hickory, North Carolina, and Lenoir Rhyne College. After the show we flew the Commander back to Charlotte. We kept the plane and the next day flew it to Chapel Hill for an afternoon show with Stan Kenton.

Printers' Alley

We did a show with the Stan Kenton band at Vanderbilt University in Nashville a few nights later. At intermission, Ken Albers told Stan he had always wanted to play with the band.

Stan said, "Get up there, pick yourself out a chair, have another trumpet player put the charts in order for the next set, and do it." So Ken did it, and did it well!

The evening should have ended there. But after the show some of the band and some of the Freshmen went to Printers' Alley, a whole row of nightclubs off the street, and none of them legal at that time. However, the local authorities rarely enforced the law, so the places thrived.

The Carousel was really swinging that night. The Kenton players brought their horns and a big jam session ensued. People flocked in to listen. One of the other Alley clubs got jealous of all the business over at the Carousel and called the cops. The Nashville police came in and lined up the whole pack of musicians against the wall and took them off to jail, Don and Ken included!

Before the police locked them up they had the musicians stand in a hall while they took their names and addresses. Carson Smith had his bass and the others had their horns. Carson said, "Well, we're here. We might as well play." So they had a little jam session in the hall of the Nashville Police Station.

For some unknown reason they locked up Ken and let Don go. It was Don's birthday so maybe that saved him. The next morning when we got Ken out of jail, he told us he had been in a cell with a guy who had bummed all of his cigarettes. Ken is a kind man, and he got to thinking about this guy alone in jail without any cigarettes. So he had us stop at a drugstore, bought the man a carton of Luckys and took them back to the jail as a farewell gift.

Whirlwind Stops

In New York, in late April, we were rehearsing "Whistle Me Some Blues" with Perry Como's TV show orchestra. We needed a Don Lamond kind of drum treatment. The first time through the tune the drums were okay, but timid. On the coffee break I went back to the drummer and said, "On this tune we need a big heavy foot and lots of hands. We'd like to get a Don Lamond-type sound, know what I mean?"

He looked me right in the eye and said, "I'm Don Lamond."

Ow! Was I embarrassed! It had been eleven years since I had seen him, when he was with the Woody Herman band. I am such a fan of his! What we wanted was exactly what we got! "Whistle" came to life for the show.

Perry Como is an amazing man. At the rehearsal, the production crew was on the ball, intense and happy, but you could literally feel the "calm" radiate from Perry the instant he came through the door. By the time he started doing his tunes and his lines his relaxed manner had gotten to everybody.

We came back to Los Angeles and chose songs for another Pete Rugolo album, to be called *Voices and Brass*.

The Freshmen hit the road again on May 14th for a week in Knoxville at the C'est Bon. We even squeezed in an afternoon show one day at Georgia Tech - flew down to Atlanta and back so we could work that night at C'est Bon. One of our shows was taped for Monitor, an NBC radio show that ran all weekend. On closing night Bob went back to his room and found he had been robbed - they took everything.

We flew to Boston the next day, Sunday, and Monday Bob and I bought shirts, sportcoats, belts, handkerchiefs, shoes - the works.

We were in Boston to do three shows a night at Storyville, which was downstairs in the Copley Square Hotel. George Wein ran the place as a jazz joint and we loved working there. Frank DiOrio, the ex-Kenton band boy, ran Stan's lights when he came to town and he did the same for us and June Christy. Sometimes he almost had to fight the regular light man, but he did such a great job we would back Frankie and he'd overcome the opposition. Our *In Person* album had been released and was Capitol's "Album of the Month" in May. We were doing radio and TV shows every day, promoting it.

We flew into San Francisco on June 1st to work a few weeks on the West Coast, starting with two nights at Fack's. We also played a college in Concord, California, and a ballroom on the ocean in Santa Cruz. A crowd of 2,350 people showed up. Of course, it was June, summer was here. Vacation time! We flew home to Los Angeles the next day.

On June 15th we started recording *Five Guitars*. Dick Reynolds and Jack Marshall were the background arrangers and Dick wrote the vocal arrangements. Capitol didn't list which guitar players were on which date. We didn't use the same five throughout, as we had with the horns on the *Five Trombones* album. Barney Kessel and Tommy Tedesco were on most of the songs, and Al Viola and Herb Ellis were on some. George Van Epps is featured on the introduction to "The More I See You" and the solo on "Nancy."

It was late June and time to drive back to the Midwest with the kids and Sue. I deposited the family with our parents and flew to Boston to do the Newport Jazz Festival July 2nd. Were you there? My apologies. We sounded just terrible, and we had wanted to be so good for those people. Then we did a week on Cape Cod. We rehearsed "Little Girl Blue," "When Your Lover Has Gone," and "I Could Have Told You" for the shows there. That was a great week!

In mid-July we began rehearsing songs for *Voices and Brass*. We worked Hampton Beach, New Hampshire, then left New England for the Toronto Jazz Festival on July 22nd. Also on the bill that night were Oscar Peterson, Count Basie, Gene Krupa, and Dizzy Gillespie.

Back in Los Angeles in early August we heard what the technicians had put together on the *Five Guitars* album. Then it was back to the Midwest for a whole new series of dates; everything from another jazz festival in Chicago to the house trailer convention with Homer and Jethro in Elkhart, Indiana! Those guys were so musical and entertaining. We were constant fans of theirs.

On September 1st we were back in Los Angeles and rehearsing "Lonely For My Love." Ken Albers and Bill Comstock wrote that song and it really fit with those trombones on *Voices and Brass*. What a progression! The following day we got to see the new *Five Guitars* album cover, and liked it. Then, it was rehearsal at Ken's apartment at the Lido Hotel in Hollywood (we chose the craziest places to learn new songs!). The Lido had Murphy beds that folded up into a closet, making the bedroom into a living room. Each of us had stayed there at various times so we felt right at home. The neighbors put up with us as we learned "Day In Day Out."

We began recording *Voices and Brass* on the 8th of September. Dick Reynolds and Ken Albers wrote the vocal arrangements and Pete Rugolo wrote for the horns and rhythm in the background. We were also rehearsing for the "Road Show" tour with Stan, which was coming up. We got photos taken in our fancy red sweaters the next afternoon. One of those was used on the cover of *The Best Of The Four Freshmen*, and one for the cover of this book.

The Giant Iron Lung

We flew to Cincinnati to meet the Kenton band and begin the Road Show tour. Let me take you along with us. We rehearsed in Covington, Kentucky, at the Copa Club.

June Christy came in and we all were glad to get back on stage with her. Joe Castro was June's accompanist. What a spectacular piano player!

On September 28, 1959, the show went on the road. We rode that bus over to Murray, Kentucky, where Murray State is located, and we had a great crowd. This began what would be 40 days and nights of singing our hearts out, pleasing people and getting to know that bus all too well. The next afternoon the bus drove on to Nashville where we worked an evening show. It was 3am when we all got to bed. The next day we drove to Columbia, Missouri, and played the University of Missouri. We slept in Columbia, then had an all day drive to Tulsa, arriving at 6:30pm to do two shows in a theater there. Then we drove all night to Austin.

We slept during the day and did two shows in Austin at the Municipal Auditorium, with its beautiful dome. We also watched the Texas Longhorn Band rehearse. Their conductor, Vince DeNino, made us honorary members of the band. They gave each of us a white felt cowboy hat like those they wore as part of their uniform. I will always treasure mine. While we hung out with the Longhorn Band, the Kenton band drove on. We chartered another Aero Commander, caught up with them and worked that night. Next it was on to San Antonio for an afternoon show, then an all night ride to Dallas. (Are we tired yet?)

After a while, the tour bus gets to be like a giant iron lung. You can breathe in there, but there's not much else to do. The seats were too small for some of the bigger guys and they were too close together for guys with long legs, like Stan. He always rode in the left front seat behind the driver, Eric, whom the band called "the Pres." His expert driving had earned their respect.

Stan didn't always stay in his seat. Sometimes he would stand in the well at the front door of the bus. Other times he would roam the aisle and kid with the rest of us. Or, he would have one of the band members with him on that front seat. Stan liked to play psychiatrist, father, legal advisor and parson to his guys. It was tough being away from home and people sometimes had to work out their lives by long distance phone.

Killer Pace

We pulled into the Aladdin Hotel in Kansas City about 5am on a cold October 8th, the day the Dodgers beat the White Sox and won the World Series. The hotel rooms weren't ready so we waited around in the lobby or stayed on the bus. Stan and June were both asleep on the bus and someone had left the door open. The cold wind got to them, and they both developed voice trouble, so much so that it almost kept us from recording the *Road Show* album October 10th at Purdue University in West Lafayette, Indiana. Lee Gillette and Capitol recording engineer, Johnnie Paladino, were with us in St. Louis so they could hear the show and know the songs they were to record.

As we drove through Indiana and past Greencastle, Bob Flanigan got up in the front of the bus and made up things to say about his hometown: "There's nothing to do here. People go down to the bakery to smell hot bread, or go watch the barber giving haircuts." He claimed they couldn't afford a town drunk, so people had to take turns.

The *Road Show* album captures the type of show we did virtually every night of the tour. People braved the rain and filled the place. When the show was over Stan told them they could stay while we re-did some of the things that weren't played quite right. They stayed! Then it was time to load up again, stop to eat and climb back on the bus for the all night drive to Milwaukee. This killer pace seemed hard but it was honestly quite a bit easier for the Freshmen than when we did one-nighters by ourselves. On this tour the rooms were reserved ahead of time and the transportation was provided. Our paycheck came from the tour promoter, so we didn't have to haggle or figure a percentage of ticket sales. The tour was a real vacation for Bob, who normally reserved the airline tickets, rental cars and hotel rooms as we traveled. And we also didn't have to drive all night by ourselves. All we had to do was remember to change our watches when we entered a new time zone.

So it was on to Milwaukee and Madison, Chicago, Valparaiso, Columbus, South Bend, and Saginaw - a town a day. In Youngstown we had to put on our uniforms in the bus; we didn't even check into a hotel. Toronto was next. We did a Canadian TV show there with Stan, June and Mel Torme. We worked in the gym in Columbus, Indiana, the Hill Auditorium in Ann Arbor, the Indiana Theater in Indianapolis, the fieldhouse at Urbana and the civic center in Lansing.

After Lansing, we drove east with the cold rain sliding down the windows. We were in our own little world, closed off from everything, except when we stopped to entertain or eat. It rained all through Canada and into Niagara Falls and Buffalo. We had a night off on the 26th. Wait! A night free? What is that? We felt like we had worked every night since Deuteronomy.

On Stage

One of our memorable stops was Pittsburgh. Carnegie Hall there is my favorite place to perform in all the world. I would take it with me from town to town if I could. The stage floor was soft poplar wood and it slanted down slightly toward the footlights. It reflected all the sounds we made out into the audience. The red velvet seats came right to the edge of the semi-circular stage. You felt like you could flip a coin to anyone on the main floor. The balconies curved wondrously around the stage. Hello, everyone in the balconies! They weren't very far away. Behind us were real organ pipes. Add to that a good sound system and an "arc" light man and it's heaven, just heaven, for us Freshmen and the listeners.

A theater in Rochester, New York, was next and there we ran into a problem. The musician's union man was there to collect "traveling tax" from the band. Stan was having a running disagreement with the union. If they would be willing, Stan's accountant and the union accountant could get it all straight after the tour. But this union man wasn't going to wait around and negotiate. He wanted the tax now, on the spot, or he was going to bring down the curtain. No amount of reasoning was going to change his mind.

Standing his ground, and grimacing there by the big thick rope that operated the curtain, was a big no nonsense guy named Leo Curran. Leo had traveled with the band as road manager off and on for many years, and his loyalty to Stan was not measurable in normal terms. Leo is a big guy with a glint in his eye and a firmly set jaw. His big, hairy arms were folded across his chest and his feet were planted far apart. That night Leo did with charismatic muscle what no amount of reasoning could have done to get the problem settled: he stared the union man down. And the curtain stayed up.

After Carnegie Hall in New York the tour ended at Symphony Hall in Boston on November 4, 1959. We said fond farewells to Stan and the guys in the band, "Pres," and a special good-byes to June, and Stan's wife, Ann Richards. The next day there they were, on the plane with us to Los Angeles.

The Tapes

We were at a party at Bill Wagner's house on November 10th when we first heard *Voices and Brass*. They also had tape of *Road Show*. It was uncut and un-doctored, it was brutally frank. June didn't like it at all. She moaned, "Oh, we can't let that go out."

We countered, "But June, that's what a 'live' album is about - the mistakes, the hoarseness - it's all part of the soul of the record. This is the reality of the Road Show in all it's glory!"

Finally, she promised to listen to the tape again after the electronic guys had finished doing their tricks. When the record was released most of the hoarseness Stan and June had in their voices had been electronically removed.

The album got an enthusiastic response, but I think June was still sorry we talked her into letting it come out. The emotion and soul in that album could never have been created in a studio album. I still play it often and it brings back fond memories.

On November 18th we got the inspiration for the *First Affair* album. It was to be all love songs, and we'd use harpsichord and woodwinds in the background. They used two children on the cover. We heard they were the photographer's kids, but we never met them. (We never met the pretty girls on our other album covers, either!)

On The Road Again

In late November we toured the South. We flew to Norman, Oklahoma, and Don left his glasses on the plane. In Little Rock, I started writing the lyrics to "First Affair," and they were complete by the next day. We sang in Louisville and drove to the Cincinnati airport after the show. But there were no flights out until 6am. We flew to Memphis and drove to the Mississippi College for Women in Columbus. Playing colleges was fun, but playing women's colleges was even more fun! They would squeal and squirm and scream and flirt.

In Atlanta, we worked for Mickey Morano at the Steak and Trumpet. He was the man who had hired us at Savannah, Georgia, in 1948. "Candy" was almost ready to perform. On December 10th, Ken Albers' 35th birthday, we received word that the Dorothy Stevens models had voted us their favorite vocal group. Thanks ladies! We did Vanderbilt in Nashville and the University of Colorado in Boulder, on the way home to Los Angeles.

I have a note that on Christmas Eve, our 23-month old daughter went to sleep by her stocking near the fireplace, waiting for Santa. Later, we carried her to bed for the night. We ended 1959 with a house warming party at Julie London's. She and Bobby Troup were now married. Julie had pneumonia so badly she could hardly function.

On January 7th, 1960, we appeared in Los Angeles, opening at the Crescendo with the Kenton band. Mort Sahl was to kick off the show but he got sick so Don Rickles replaced him. On the 12th, the *Road Show* album was released and we did some of the songs with Stan on Sunset Strip. That night the Damons, a five-part group, came to our dressing room downstairs and sang for us. We thought they were great, but they never really caught on. Later, three of them reorganized and became the very successful Lettermen.

In late January we recorded the *First Affair* album. Don's black Chrysler Imperial was stolen. That was the model with the bullet-shaped taillights that stood up above the tail fins. Don loved that car, and fortunately he got it back in a couple of days, but the incident caused quite a stir. On the 29th we flew to Fresno to do a show with Chico Hamilton and Anita O'Day. The DeCastro Sisters were working in the lounge at the Hacienda. They impressed us. They sang with a lot of strength. (It's pretty hard to impress the Freshmen with a trio!)

On February 1st the *Voices and Brass* album was released and "Candy" was the tune the DJs played most. In mid-month we heard the *First Affair* album for the first time at the Capitol studios. This was our era of albums.

THE SIXTIES: A SOMBER START

Franklin Hobbs did a late night radio show called Hobbs House on WCCO, Minneapolis, a 50,000 watt station which covers the Midwest down to Texas. What an able, gentle man. We did his show while we were in town at Freddies, where Frankie Avalon and Hubert Humphrey came to hear us.

Piano bars were a big thing in Minneapolis in 1960. People would sit around and sing with the piano player half the night. Our hotel had an "organ bar," and the organist told me one evening about a guy who had been going around telling people he was Ross Barbour of the Four Freshmen. He reportedly would sing a song or two and people would buy him drinks. His goal was to impress young ladies and take them home. He was giving me a bad name around town!

We decided to cruise the piano bars between our shows. We'd announce we were performing at Freddies, pass out pictures of the Freshmen and mention there was an impostor on the loose. That way they could check the picture before buying him a drink. One lady he had tricked phoned me and gave me his description. I went down to the police station to report the matter but they said there was nothing they could do. Months later we learned the impostor's name, but by then he had stopped posing as me.

We finished Minneapolis in early March, right at the time Elvis got out of the Army. It was on to a bunch of college dates in the Midwest, which ended in Philadelphia on March 13th.

The First Dilemma

While we were in Philadelphia we got word that Bob's wife was facing some difficulties and his marriage was in jeopardy. Bob's world began to disintegrate. At first, he was going to fly home to Los Angeles but some of his friends there called and said, "Stay there and let the dust settle for a few days." That night we worked at the famous Symphony Hall. I honestly don't remember much about that evening. Our thoughts were on the dilemma in Los Angeles and our hearts were breaking for Bob.

The next day we flew to New Orleans, where Bobby Troup and Julie London met our plane. The news they brought from California left no doubt that Bob's wife was through being Bob's wife. We worked the Loyola fieldhouse that night, and tried not to let our demoralized condition detract from our performance.

Over the next few days we tried to regain our emotional equilibrium as we played mostly college concerts across the south. On March 18th we played a women's college in Lynchburg, Virginia and really broke the place up! Remember, our music is a vacation from real life and we really needed one! We kept going because we loved to entertain, to do people some at least some temporal good. I believe the only way to find self respect is to do something good for other people. And again, it was also a way of forgetting our own woes.

At Syracuse University we played to the biggest crowd they ever had. Then we worked the Chanticleer Club in Baltimore. The Signatures were on that show, too. At Chapel Hill, North Carolina, we performed in the campus gym but we did just fair. We met in Bob's room after the show to decide what to do. We went back to Los Angeles on March 25th. Bob would try to put things back together, but it seemed impossible.

We had some April dates in the Midwest so Sue and the kids and I flew to Indiana to see our parents. I rigged a big rope up in the barn for the boys to swing on and land in the hay. We went fishing in the creek and built a fort out of driftwood. We even swung on some vines like Tarzan and imitated his yell.

Bob flew to Indianapolis ten days later and drove down to Columbus, picked me up and we headed to Castle Farm in Cincinnati. We sang some spots in Ohio and Michigan, celebrating Don's 33rd birthday on April 19th, the day we played the historic Albion College in central Michigan. A few days later we sang with the Glenn Miller band at Lehigh University in Allentown, Pennsylvania.

On April 23rd we appeared at the Sunnybrook Ballroom in Pottstown, Pennsylvania. Then it was on to Latrobe to sing at beautiful St. Vincent College. The crowd was a group of student priests wearing their black cassocks. They cheered us on and enjoyed the show. April 29th was the first warm spring evening in New Brunswick, New Jersey. We could see lovers walking hand in hand as we drove through town. The winter had been an especially bad one and we drew only about a half dozen people! We couldn't compete with the wonderful weather. We drove to Pittsburgh and Carnegie Hall where we had a capacity crowd.

Early May found us at the civic auditorium in Grand Rapids, Michigan. It was memorable because Ken Albers had sprained his ankle and his foot swelled up so much he couldn't get his shoe on. So he crunched down the back of the shoe and stuck his foot in the front. He couldn't lift that foot because he'd lose his shoe, so all night long he had to drag his foot when he crossed behind Don and me to get the bass from Bob. On nights like this it's fun to laugh at yourselves!

When we checked out of our hotel in Ypsilanti two nights later we were forced to carry our suitcases down many flights of stairs due to an inoperative elevator. I almost blacked out with an insulin reaction. Fruit juice saved my life. We grabbed a DC4 to Pittsburgh and worked in the gym at Carnegie Tech and chose their yearbook queen that night.

Our Happy Note - The College Campuses

Those college dates were something else. Often the kids sat on the floor of the gym and clapped along on the upbeat songs. They were into the Freshmen sound and we loved it. They brought out the best in us.

In Chicago, on May 8th, we checked into the Croydon Hotel and discovered the Kenton band was there. Yippee! We worked at the Loyola University gym with the Salty Dogs (a Dixieland group) and a new comic who wanted to start working specifically in colleges and universities. He really broke it up that night in Chicago and we were delighted to have been part of Bob Newhart's first college appearance.

The whole next week was one-nighters around the Midwest. Don's clothes bag was destroyed by the airline on the way to Des Moines but we still managed to play at Drake University, where we did an outdoor show by a reflecting pool. An entire hillside was covered with people.

In Washington, DC, we opened at the Casino Royale. That week, Ike and Khrushchev ended a summit meeting on poor terms. Castro was causing trouble in Cuba, Syngman Rhee was just ousted in Korea, and John F. Kennedy seemed to be a hot presidential candidate. We rehearsed each afternoon, trying to work through the awful strain Bob was under.

We went to San Francisco on June 9th for a Stanford University dance, held at the Mark Hopkins. Ken surprised us with new white caps on his front teeth (he'd had a very prominent gold tooth in front). But the caps were a little too long (don't they call that being "long in tooth"?). They messed up his trumpet playing until he got them shortened.

You know about the great brass sounds he's made since then. We headed down the California coast, doing shows in Santa Cruz, Oakland, and Long Beach. On June 19th Bob asked us to go to his house and help him clean out the refrigerator. His wife was gone and his kids were with their grandparents in Florida. It looked like the end.

We began two weeks at the Trade Winds in Chicago on June 27th. A lot of entertainers came to hear us - Rosemary Clooney and Buddy Cole, ZsaZsa Gabor and Fran Allison of Kukla, Fran and Ollie fame. We never got tired of seeing other musicians like this. Heading home on July 11th, we met the Hi-Los in the Chicago airport. Bob always threatened to leave us and go sing bass with the Hi-Los! The next day we saw the cover of the *First Affair* album, with the two kids on it.

On July 13th we rehearsed, and John F. Kennedy was nominated on the first ballot. We were learning the "Hong Kong Blues" for me to do. In the days that followed we recorded the beginning of the *Freshmen Year* album, including "If I Knew Then," "Sentimental Over You," "Fools Rush In," "Show Me The Way To Get Out Of This World," "Funny Valentine," "But Beautiful" and "Their Hearts Were Full Of Spring."

Two More Setbacks

A week later Don and I journeyed to our parents' farm to help mow weeds. Daddy was in the hospital with a kidney infection. During the rest of August we hopped across Indiana, Ohio and Michigan. We were still a bundle of nerves. Twenty some years later they would ask, "If love is not forever, then what's forever for?" Bob wasn't the only one in agony; Ken and his wife, Alice, were trying to make sense out of their life together.

But there was more. Don's doctor, and all of us, were beginning to see that tensions would not be resolved until he got out of the group and into a career of his own. Capitol wanted to sign Don to a contract, and things could turn out fine for him. But how would we replace him? I hated all these problems, and we seemingly couldn't solve them.

The ballroom at Monticello, Indiana, hosted us on August 19th. Bob's parents came to see the show and give him some emotional support. The Capitol man showed up that night and played the *First Affair* album for us.

The Detroit Jazz Festival opened on August 21st with Dakota Staton, the Basie band, Joe Williams, Horace Silver, and the Four Freshmen performing under the stars.

By August 25th we were back in Pittsburgh. Ken Albers called Bill Comstock to ask if he would take Don's place when we made the change. Bill gave us a preliminary yes. The next day in Erie, Pennsylvania, I asked Bill Wagner in Los Angeles to find the arrangements to ten songs Bill Comstock could start learning. We worked at Waldemeer Park Ballroom and drew their biggest crowd in three years. Things were so good and things were so bad, all at the same time.

A day later we were back in Boston to do the Boston Jazz Festival. Duke Ellington, Dinah Washington, and Oscar Peterson were there. I recall we dressed in a railroad car! Then it was on to Philadelphia and Connie Mack Stadium for the Philadelphia Jazz Festival. The stage was near home plate, and while another act was entertaining I tip-toed out in the dark to the pitcher's mound and threw a few strikes with an imaginary baseball!

Don's final night with the Freshmen was September 5, 1960, at the Lagoon in Salt Lake City, with 2,200 people on hand. What a finale! In all honesty, Don had been desperate to shed the pressures of the group, the way we worked, even the songs we sang. He was not happy, and you don't have an effective group if you don't have a happy group. We all dreaded the months ahead with a member change and the confusion it caused. We had high hopes for Don's success, but music is an unpredictable business. And we were far from sure the Freshmen could stand to lose Don. Our own future was up in the air.

Enter Bill Comstock

Bill Comstock arrived in Los Angeles on September 19th. He and Ken Albers had been friends for years. As young men they had performed together in the Alan Poe Quartet, and later with the Stuarts. In 1956, when Ken Albers left the Stuarts to become a Freshman, Ken Errair had formed a quartet and Bill Comstock was Errair's right hand man - writing arrangements, playing guitar and singing. Later Bill performed with an instrumental group backing Dick Contino, the accordionist, and traveled with him, so Bill knew what life on the road was like.

Bill could hear and sing the right notes in the right chords. He was just the man we needed. September 20th was our 12th Freshmen anniversary and the next day we went to Bill Wagner's house for our first rehearsal with Bill. Then we over-dubbed with Don that evening.

That weekend we finished the *Freshmen Year* album with Don and by September 25th Bill Comstock was ready with 21 of our arrangements. The Kennedy-Nixon debates were underway but we were too busy to notice.

The following Monday we met with Voyle Gilmore, our A and R (Artists and Repertoire) man at Capitol. We needed to make something positive happen, so we decided to do an album of happy tunes with Billy May and his band. Capitol titled it *Voices In Fun*. The national media had gotten things all wrong and were reporting that the Four Freshmen had broken up!

Our first appearance with Bill Comstock was on September 30th in Tempe, Arizona. We were tickled to pieces with the way Bill fit in. Some 3,800 people turned out the next night at Cornell University in Ithaca, New York.

After playing Eastern Illinois in Charleston, we rehearsed "Fools Rush In" and "Hearts Were Full Of Spring" in the car while we drove in the fog all night to Chicago. We began recording *Voices In Fun* with Billy May in early November. At night we worked the Santa Monica Civic Auditorium.

We were already planning the next album. It would be called *Stars In Our Eyes*, and feature Freshmen toasts to other groups.

Another big series of campus dates followed. At the Mountain Lair Ballroom in Morgantown, West Virginia. we drew more people than the Kingston Trio did - and they had all those hit records! The campuses of America were still our best friends.

On Thanksgiving Day morning we stopped for coffee at the home of Susan Comstock's parents in New Jersey. We couldn't stay for dinner because we had to get to the ballroom in Mahanoy City, Pennsylvania, the hometown of the Dorsey Brothers. (We mention Mahanoy City in our record of "Atchison, Topeka and Santa Fe."). The ballroom still had its original two pot-bellied stoves to heat the place.

On December 4th we flew to New Orleans to work at the Municipal Auditorium and ate at Brennan's before the show. If you're ever near Brennan's and in the mood for a fancy meal, they can more than fill the bill. In the days ahead it was Emory University, Florida State University and Stetson University. Then came the University of Kentucky with Joni James, followed by Wittenberg College in Springfield, Ohio. We finished at the University of Akron and had the rest of December off.

During that break, Capitol changed our recording supervisor from Voyle Gilmore to Bill Miller. We had trusted Voyle from our first days with Capitol and owe him so much credit for all the good things he did for us. Ditto Bill Miller, an ex-saxophone player with the big bands, who picked up where Voyle left off and never missed a beat.

On December 30th an X-ray showed I had three gallstones. But each subsequent X-ray showed them in different places! It drove the doctors up the wall. We all heaved a huge sigh of relief when they discovered it was the three vitamin tablets which I faithfully took every day!

We worked at the Hollywood Palladium on New Year's Eve, my 31st birthday. Don was due to start recording his own songs for Capitol in early 1961. On January 4th Dick Reynolds brought us some of the arrangements we were to do on the *Stars In Our Eyes* album. The Kingston Trio hit, "Tom Dooley," became an a cappella beauty and "Standin' On The Corner," was jazzed up quite a bit.

First Overseas Tour

In February, 1961, we were on a plane heading for New York and then England. We bumped into Bing Crosby at the Los Angeles airport. I wish I had known that man. He was my favorite talker. Singer, too. But his style of talking was unmatched.

June Christy was with us and would be part of the tour. June had been to Europe before, but not us - unless you count Bob, Ken and Bill's time with the Army in Germany. Susan Comstock came with us. In London we were met by bandleader Vic Lewis, who was often referred to as "the English Stan Kenton."

Bob Miller and the Millermen were also part of the tour. They were a most talented band that played some of our *Road Show* arrangements behind us. I can't find a list of the songs we did but I'll promise you one was "Day In, Day Out."

Let me digress for a minute. When I was in grade school, I envisioned a life where I would buy a motorcycle and just go down the road until I needed money for gas. Then I would stop and pick peaches, or shovel wheat, or trim trees until I got to know that area a little. Then I would power on to some other town and do the same thing. With the Freshmen, the motorcycle was replaced by an airplane. And music replaced shoveling wheat. For me, one reason for doing either was to get to know the neighborhood. To this day I walk the streets and cross the bridges in new places. Ask me - I know the cracks in the sidewalks from Hong Kong to

Walla Walla. A big part of my time in London was spent walking Bond Street, Piccadilly Circus, the Tower of London, the auto showrooms and the marvelous British pubs.

Our first European tour opened at Hammersmith Gaumont Theater on Saturday, February 11th. The evening went well, and after the show two other quartets came backstage. Remember the Polka Dots and the Dew Drops? Vic Lewis took us to Birmingham. We stopped at a pub on the way for a sandwich, room temperature brew and a game of darts. Ken Albers is a super dart thrower and he beat us all.

After the show in Bristol we rode a coach through the foggy night. June said, "What we ought to do is sing." She started singing "B-I-B-L-E Spells Bible, J-E-S-U-S Spells Jesus." Pretty soon the whole bus full was putting in harmony parts, singing falsetto high parts, and just having a wonderful time with June's country hymn.

We were on our way to the Odeon in Barking to do a show. Later, we would go to Ronnie Scott's jazz nightclub. Scott is a great sax man and he started putting Bob Flanigan on about being Irish. Ronnie told all the Irish jokes. Bob and Ronnie had a friendly exchange of high-pitched, disparaging remarks, which showed their mutual respect. (This was before everyone was supposed to be politically correct.)

On February 20th we flew to Frankfurt, Germany. Then it was off to Wiesbaden (White Bath), named for the natural mineral baths there. The first night we dined on venison in the hotel restaurant. That's a good way to spoil yourself! From there we worked the U.S. military bases - Rhine Main Air Base and Hahn, and then caught a train to Munich. The rest of the tour took us through Germany and France.

Domestic Disappointments

June and the Freshmen flew back to Los Angeles on March 15th. Los Angeles used to mean bliss for us: home and rest. But Bob was still dealing with the mess of his divorce, and now Ken was fast on his way to a family break-up. Don had broken out with great big painful boils, and was in the care of a doctor. So there wasn't much bliss in Los Angeles for the Freshmen on this return.

Voices In Fun was released on May Day. We were back on the road and didn't have any way to play it, but we heard some of it on WCAU in Philadelphia one night. When we could rehearse, we were trying to put new numbers into the show - songs like "Accentuate the Positive" and Bill's solo, "Do Nothing 'Til You Hear From Me." We met with Bill Wagner and Fred Dale, seeking to do shorter tours. We were killing ourselves and our families by being gone too long.

On June 14th Don began recording his solo album. It was a superb first album, and it turned out to be his last. Even at that, Don's album is far from showing all the things he had in him. If you own that collection, prize it highly because it's very rare. A week later we were back in Los Angeles to rehearse the songs for our new Swingers album. In July Bill and Susan announced they were expecting.

Summer was full of jazz festivals, like the Detroit Jazz Festival at Cobo Hall, with Dave Brubeck, Julie London, Pete Fountain and Wes Montgomery. Then it was on to the Dearborn Inn, which became our home away from home. The Dearborn was the world's first motel. Henry Ford built it across from his airport where the Ford Tri-Motor planes were based. They will still rent you a room in "Pilot's Row," where Henry's aviators stayed. We usually roomed in the Patrick Henry House, one of four replicas of quaint old American homes.

In August we flew to Hawaii to do two nights in the Waikiki Shell with the Mary Kaye Trio. The airline broke our amplifier, and Mary was unhappy with her guitar so we used her amp and she used Bill's guitar. Fair enough! We flew home for one night and then boarded a plane to Europe so we could be in Milan, Italy, on August 23rd. Our agent, Fred Dale, was there to meet us. Fred spoke Italian so he also served as our interpreter. We were there to work La Bousola, a summer resort nightclub in Viareggio.

The nightly jam sessions drew players and listeners alike. Ken Albers joined the session on the final night, and his trumpet notes surprised everyone so much that when he finished a chorus they all stopped playing to applaud. Ken had a way of knowing where the good notes were.

On our return the man at New York customs wouldn't let me bring in some miniature foil-wrapped chocolate bottles of cognac. They were so good, I just couldn't throw them in the garbage, so I passed them around to everyone waiting in the line. I made that unpleasant time a happy one for about a dozen people that morning.

Back in the States we finished recording the *Swingers* album on September 15th. At that time I was involved in writing "And So It's Over," the tune we used as the closer for the *In Person II* album and for our shows. The quartet arrangement is in the back of this book.

> And so it's over. Where did the moments go?
> Oh, it's over. We hope you liked the show.
> You've warmed our hearts and we love you because you filled each pause with applause.
> And may we mention we hope we made you smile.
> It was our intention to make it worth your while.
> May all your nights be restful.
> May all your days be bright.
> Good Night. Good Night. Good Night.

Don came to see us at a UCLA concert on September 29th. He hadn't seen or heard the group since he left. I felt we were ragged from not performing, but if Don was disappointed he didn't say so.

The next night we sang at SMU in Dallas and we heard that Roger Maris had hit his 60th home run. We flew east and did Clarion State Teachers College in Pennsylvania.

After two stops in Ohio, we drove to Harrisburg, Pennsylvania, and stopped at Howard Johnson's for some tender sweet clams.

The Ultimate Blow

Bill bought a newspaper and could not believe what he read. He called Bob aside and showed him a news item that utterly stunned him. Bob took me outside the restaurant and put his hands on my shoulders. "Ross, brace yourself," Bob said haltingly. "Don was killed last night on the Hollywood Freeway."

I went numb. I guess I stayed numb all the while Bob reserved us seats on an airplane back to Los Angeles, and all the time it took to fly west. We canceled the remainder of our tour.

Don was killed about 10pm on October 5, 1961, virtually in the shadow of the Capitol Tower. He had entered the freeway from the Cahuenga ramp and signaled his way over to the fast lane. A road repair truck had stopped at the left side of the freeway and the crew was busy putting those orange cones in the lane to warn oncoming motorists. But they didn't get them out in time. Don drove right into the rear right corner of a dump truck. His car wasn't damaged all that much, but the impact was concentrated right in the driver's area. The doctors said he died instantly.

There was a funeral in Burbank on October 8th and that evening Sue and I and little Kathy flew east with Don's body, his widow, Dolores, their daughter, Donalyn, and Bob Flanigan. We landed in St. Louis and I don't recall why, but the others flew on and I accompanied Don's body on a train to Indianapolis. I just sat on the floor of my roomette and hugged my knees, anticipating the second funeral in Columbus. Don was buried in the Barbour plot at Garland Brook Cemetery. Hal Kratzsch came down from Warsaw, Indiana for the service.

Thank you, Don, for the 32 great years I knew you. It was all too brief.

The bad news wasn't over. Bob's divorce became final on October 19th. We really needed some good news. We flew home and worked the Pasadena Civic Auditorium with Dave Brubeck on October 20th. On the 26th, Ken made it official: he and Alice would be getting a divorce.

It was a strange Christmas. Bob had an apartment and his kids, Steven and Debbie, were still with their grandparents. Ken was apart from his wife in New Jersey. He stayed with his parents. Bill and Susan Comstock and Sue and I were in Los Angeles, and Dolores was struggling through her first Christmas without Don. It was a somber time indeed as we closed out 1961.

12

IN THIS WHOLE WIDE WORLD

After losing Don and seeing Bob through his fractured marriage, we viewed 1962 as a new beginning of sorts. We would travel the world together. Bill was picking up Don's part well and by January 15th our newly constituted quartet knew a total of 38 songs - every word, every chord, every breath. I've still got the list in my notebook.

Fast Quartet:
Route 66
Accentuate the Positive
Somebody Loves Me
LuLu's Back in Town
This October
Day by Day
Candy
Easy Street

Slow, with Ken on Bass:
Fools Rush In
You're All I See
It Happened Once Before
Angel Eyes
Day Isn't Long Enough
Street of Dreams

Bob's Solos:
Show Me the Way to Get
      Out of this World

Bill's Solos:
Do Nothin' Till You Hear
      From Me
Blues in the Night
Take Your Shoes Off Baby

Ross Solos:
Paper Moon
Please Don't Talk About Me
Them There Eyes
My Heart Stood Still

"Leroy" Solos:
Sweet Lorraine

Slow, with Bob on Bass:
In This Whole Wide World
Lil' Darlin
We'll Be Together Again
How Can I Tell Her
Polka Dots and Moonbeams
Love Lost
If I Knew Then
It Could Happen to You
Poinciana
Blue World
Chasing Rainbows
Tom Dooley
Hearts Were Full of Spring
And So It's Over

Shearing We're Hearing

On February 10th we started a tour with George Shearing, Nancy Wilson and Moms Mobley. We worked in San Bernardino, then San Luis Obispo, Santa Barbara, and San Jose. Eric ("the Pres"), who drove the Kenton band bus, was driving us. He was a whiz. He and could motor into any town in the world and go right to the place we were to work. He handled that big bus as though it were a toy, backing it up a narrow, crooked driveway - right to the stage door.

In San Bernardino we set up the instruments and checked out the stage, then walked the two blocks to the hotel with George Shearing. We had to cross a street and George, being blind, needed one of us to help him. He took hold of my elbow and I said, "Gee, George. I've never done this before.

He said, "It's all right. I won't let you fall." George's sense of humor sees a lot of things. And what a spectacular musician he is!

When we crossed the border into Vancouver, British Columbia, Eric had to run into the building to sign papers. Impatient with the wait, George groped his way to the front of the coach, sat down in the driver's seat, revved up the idling diesel engine and honked that big bus horn. When Eric walked back outside and saw George sitting in the driver's seat, he collapsed with laughter.

We worked Washington State University in Pullman and some great places in and around Seattle before our tour ended.

England

On March 5th Geoffrey Charles Comstock was born in New Jersey. Sue's folks and Bill were all there. By the 14th we were back on an airplane, heading for New York and then to London. The airline lost Bob's clothes, the trumpet and my drum dolly. We borrowed instruments in London to do a TV show. Jeri Southern was there to begin the tour and were we looking forward to working with her. We'd all been fans of Jeri since we first saw her in 1950. Unfortunately, she got sick at the last minute and had to cancel.

We rehearsed the show on March 16th, and it was a dandy. The Kenny Baker band was a together bunch. Matt Monroe was part of the package, too. We opened at Gaumont State Theater and met rock star Keith Richard there.

One day, near Newcastle, I walked the quaint streets and wandered through those beautiful, historic neighbor-hoods. I bought some suspenders but the clerk insisted on calling them "braces." I told him, "No, we put braces on our teeth." In Newcastle, Ken Albers beat everyone at darts again.

Another day found us in Nottingham visiting the Nottingham Castle, but there was no sign of Robin Hood! The castle is on top of a hill and around the side of the hill is the world's oldest pub, built in 1100 AD. People were smaller back then and this place wasn't easy for Bob or Ken. They had to bend down to get through the door and stay bent to walk under the heavy ceiling beams and light fixtures.

We worked Birmingham's city hall and Manchester again. Back in London, we stopped at Matt Monroe's home for tea. The next day we did a TV show. An Austin Princess Limousine was waiting to take us to Heathrow airport. On the way, we were stopped at a red light in this spectacular automobile and people in other cars were rubber-necking, wondering what famous people were in the limo. Our driver remarked, "Hmm, there's Prince Charles beside us." Sure enough, there he was, in a military uniform, behind the wheel of a Land Rover. But nobody noticed him; they were all looking at us, or at our fancy car anyway.

We flew to Milan and I wandered the streets there as well, soaking up more history. We did a TV appearance and a show in a Milan ballroom. Later we visited an Italian rock nightclub and they asked that we sing. We didn't have our instruments with us so we did "Hearts Were Full Of Spring" a cappella in a rock club! We flew on to Frankfurt and the Wiesbaden Nassauer Hotel. Dinner was venison, of course! We spent two more weeks in Germany and France, doing two different military clubs a day before returning home.

Meeting Mary

We spent the spring of 1962 on a quiet tour of American college campuses and night spots. The *Swingers* LP was released. I stepped on a board which had a nail sticking up through it. It went right through my tennis shoe and into my foot. Ouch! I couldn't use our backyard pool all summer because of that wound!

July 14th is memorable because we were singing at the Cedar Point Ballroom in Sandusky, Ohio, and Mary Scott entered Bob Flanigan's life.

On September 20th, 1962, the eve of our 14th anniversary, we recorded the *Four Freshmen In Person, Volume II* album at Long Beach City College. That was a great hall and we had a most responsive audience that night.

Then we began another tour in the East, singing at Monmouth College and Otis Air Force Base on Cape Cod, then up the Hudson to West Point. That's a proud bunch to play to. Then it was off to Purdue and a show with Duke Ellington and Dizzy Gillespie. On October 1st we sang in Waterloo, Iowa, and Ken Albers received his divorce papers.

In Atlanta we worked at Georgia Tech and Emory University. Jacksonville, a little north of Annistorn, Alabama, was next. The map had a dot by the "J" in "Jacksonville," but we discovered too late that the town is really by the "e." There was no road from "J" to "e" so we had to go around Robin Hood's Barn to get to the right end of that long word! We were almost late for the show at Jacksonville State.

Here's one I'll bet you think I made up. We worked Pfeiffer College in Misenheimer, North Carolina, on November 8th. And when we came clumping in through the stage door carrying our stuff, all the stage crew snapped to attention. We put an end to that real quick!

On Thanksgiving Day Bob brought Mary Scott to our house for turkey. Things seemed to be moving along well on that front! Two nights later, we were back on the basketball floor at Kiel Auditorium in St. Louis, working the crowd after the Celtics beat the Hawks.

In Wichita, in December, Bob Flanigan's clothes bag got lost on the plane, so he was "Leader" at the Cotillion Ballroom. We three wore uniforms and he wore sport clothes and ordered us around. Next day, just to show how things go, we flew from Wichita to Memphis to Dallas and to Shreveport. Too bad they didn't have frequent flier miles back then; we could have arranged for the whole world to fly free!

On December 10th we opened at the La Cucaracha in Juarez, Mexico. First of all, we had trouble with the immigration people on our work permit. Then the deposit check the nightclub sent Fred Dale wouldn't cash so we didn't work the 12th or 13th. Bill Wagner came down from Los Angeles to straighten things out and we went back to work Friday. I broke a drumhead on the second show and the lights went out all over the place on the third so we sang by candlelight. Is this what happens when you name a place after a cockroach? Somehow we weren't supposed to work that job!

Until you have done a few tours like this you don't know the feeling of relief you get when you put the key in your own front door. Aahhh! At least for a while there will be no more daily deadlines, changing planes, reading maps and driving strange roads. You don't have to check your motel matchbook to remember what town you're in. All that's over for a while. Now it's time to see Kent and Gary's band concert, mail the Christmas packages, put up the tree, play miniature golf, go see Kathy in the church program and take her to see Santa (she chickened out at the last minute).

On December 21st we did a Steve Allen TV show in Hollywood. On Christmas Eve day Fred Dale, who had been booking us and a half dozen other people as the agent for V.I.P. came calling. The United Talent Management Company had made him an offer too good to pass up. He decided to go with them, which meant the end of Viscount International Productions, the agency we owned.

"O.K. We're with you, Fred," we told him. It was much better for Fred, and better for us, too. As long as we had Fred Dale we felt secure.

For Christmas someone sent us the record, *The First Family* - Vaughn Meader's spoof of the Kennedy family. Hilarious! It got a lot of play that season. Santa brought our 13 year old Kent a unicycle. He could ride it, but the rest of us just whacked ourselves up trying.

1963

We were back on the road on January 6th - off to Charleston, Illinois, and Indianapolis. I went past Arthur Jordan Conservatory at 13th and Delaware and they were tearing it down and moving it to the Butler University campus. We worked Centralia and Macomb, Illinois, before doing a week at the Alamo in Detroit.

When we flew home we were met by Vic Lewis and Alan Blackburn to make plans for another trip to Europe. A few days later we visited Bill Miller at Capitol and decided to do an album with Shorty Rogers. On February 4th Kathy, our little" Huggie Bug" went off to start kindergarten. That day we met with Shorty Rogers and chose the songs for the album.

After two months in the Midwest and West, I was at home on March 4th, playing basketball with our sons. Bam! I jammed my left first finger - smashed up all the joints. The doctor put a big clumsy splint on it that went from the palm to past the end of my finger. It felt like I had a teaspoon taped to me. The finger hurt like crazy and it became the basis for a few new Freshmen jokes. On the shows Bob would say, "Hey, Ross! Did you give up your finger for Lent?" I had to play drums with that thing on there!

On March 22nd Bob asked Mary Scott to marry him! The next night we went to the Red Hill in New Jersey and then on to Warren, Ohio, and we were just awful. We couldn't hear, couldn't sing, couldn't get in tune. I started singing "Paper Moon" and ended up on "My Heart Stood Still." Some nights are just like that. In Dayton the next evening we were awful again, so we got together in the dressing room and had a long talk. We came out with a new resolve to try harder and nail those notes.

On April 1st Ken marked his seventh anniversary as a Freshman. We did the Johnny Carson "Tonight Show" from Rockefeller Center in New York.

Even 15 year professionals take hits. On April 5th we worked Los Angeles City College and the microphone quit. We did the first 50 minutes without it. Then, we rigged the mike to the guitar amp and used that for the second half of the show. Later we went downtown and bought some seersucker tux coats so we could keep cooler in the hot ball-rooms during the summer.

Sue came along in May when we flew to Columbus, Ohio. We did a show at Ohio State in their wonderful 5,000 seat hall. It wasn't big enough, though. OSU had 50,000 students and we could have filled it ten days in a row and never played to the same audience twice.

We had a night off in Washington, DC, and we went to see the Lettermen at the Casino Royale. Conrad Figueroa was playing bass with them. After the shows, he and the Lettermen often sang four part things just for fun. We sang some with them after hours that night and Conrad sang a tune or two with the Freshmen. He had learned our parts on a bunch of songs and was quite a fan, and so were the Lettermen.

Ken Albers married Nancy Rzemien in mid-May. He had found the right lady, and the wedding bells pealed. About that time we began recording with Shorty Rogers again, this time the *Got That Feelin'* album. Lots of artists were doing things in the "Gospel" vein, using lots of hand claps and a blues sound. Shorty was into this idea, hoping we would blow away all the others with high trumpets and a heavy rhythm section. We had a lot of fun recording this album, but it surprised our fans so much they didn't see the fun and it didn't sell very well. If you have one, hold onto it.

Northern Exposure

We toured Alaska in late May. At Anchorage we were met by Colonel Sam Martone who ran the Officer's Club at nearby Elmendorf Air Force Base. This nice man arranged to get us to the right places to work while we were there. On the 27th we got word that our good friend Mac McGraw had died. We called his boys and offered our condolences.

We entertained at the Officer's Club, the NCO Club and the hospital. We were even taken into the "war room." You may have seen this simulated in the movie *Dr. Strangelove.*

The big map of the world takes up one whole wall. Underneath are the control panels and telephones necessary to reach the Distant Early Warning (DEW Line) radar sites and alert the Strategic Air Command planes. Incredible.

We also went through a fur coat sales room. (Let's see, "The Four Freshmen and Five Wolves"? Naw, wouldn't sell.) The coats are kept in a cold storage room at about zero degrees. When you try on a wolfskin coat with a parka that only shows a little of your face, you try it on in the cold room.

Colonel Sam asked if we would go entertain the guys at some of the "remote sites." He said, "The Air Force will fly you to them in the afternoons." We jumped at the chance. On May 31st we were taken in a big two rotor helicopter to Fire Island in Anchorage Harbor. The guys were in this bunch of Quonset huts for an 18 month tour of duty. Their only contact with the rest of the world was this helicopter and a couple of telephone calls they were allowed each month. Talk about a captive audience! We entertained in their mess hall, then sat around and had cookies and coffee and just talked with them.

The next day Bill Comstock and I went to Mt. Alyeska Ski Resort and rode the lift up to the top. Even though it was June it was still cool, but not frigid. That afternoon we also went to see Portage Glacier. I thought it would only be dirty snow but that glacier was as blue as the sky. The lake below it had so much powdered stone in it that it was milky white. I wasn't ready for that. I expected white glacier and blue water. What a surprise!

The trips to remote sites gave us a wonderful chance to see Alaska like no other tourist does. One afternoon after our show at a Nike site we helicoptered over some big horn sheep climbing a mountain. On the other side of that mountain we discovered a mommy bear, a daddy bear, and a baby bear. Our pilot dropped down until we were only a hundred feet above them. That's close enough! Mommy bear was reaching up, trying to catch us and take us apart.

We really felt like we had done some good for our men in Alaska. They were so starved for any change in the routine. On our last night the Officer's Club chef impressed us with a giant salmon he had broiled - the biggest and the best salmon we had ever tasted.

NAGMA'S Demise

Bob Flanigan and Mary Scott were married in Las Vegas on June 23, 1963. Mary had a daughter, Jennifer and that little cutie, who was about three years old, stood between the bride and groom while they exchanged their vows. Their reception was at the Sands Hotel. Bob's balcony was right above Sammy Davis Jr's. Sammy looked up and asked, "Who's celebrating what?" He arranged for the wedding party to be right down in front at his second show that night. Six or eight of us were at the show but Bob and Mary had other things on their minds, which gave Sammy a chance to make a few newlywed jokes.

After a stint out East we took our wives and families to the Holiday Inn in Oakland, where we worked for a week. After work on August 30th we saw the Kenton band at the Off Broadway in San Francisco. A few months earlier Bob and Stan had formed an organization called NAGMA (Never Again Get Married Association). It was supposed to work like Alcoholics Anonymous; except that if a member was considering marriage the others would get him drunk and talk him out of it. Stan was president and Bob the vice president. Now the vice president had gotten married! Stan teased Mary all evening about how she had busted up the whole organization. Then he came to the table and hugged her real good and kissed her on the forehead and welcomed her into the "family."

Back in Los Angeles we went to Bill Wagner's to hear the pre-release copy of the *Togetherness* album by Bob Flanigan and John Gray. Bill also played some Bobby Doyle Trio records for us. They sang like the Freshmen. Kenny

Rogers sang the lead part and played bass. Don Russell played drums. Bobby Doyle was later with Blood Sweat and Tears, and of course Kenny has become a mega star. When I hear him sing in octaves with that crack in his voice, I wonder if he injured it trying to sing Bob's part!

On September 20th, our 15th anniversary, we headed into San Jose to work the Safari for a week, and the Bobby Doyle Trio came in to see us. We sure admired them. After the Safari we did the Oakland Music Festival for Jimmy Lyons, teaming up with Brubeck, the Brothers Four and Carol Brent. The people at Capitol wanted us to record "Charade," Henry Mancini's movie theme.

In mid-October we opened at the Wagon Wheel on the south shore of Lake Tahoe. That area destroys every sea level singer. There's just no oxygen at 6,900 feet. If you have to hold a tone - 2-3-4 1-2-3-4, it takes a week or two before you can do it.

We started November by having our picture taken in turtleneck sweaters, trying to look disgustingly suave, and then spent the rest of the month doing campus shows. Before month's end we were in St. Louis and bumped into Bob Pettit. We had worked after Hawks games so often that Bob had become a fan of ours. We, of course, were fans of his. He was the hardest working basketball player who ever wore the St. Louis Hawks uniform. A lot of respect was exchanged as we stopped and chatted on our way to different towns. What a thrill to know people like him!

On November 21st we worked Pensacola Junior College and after a good show we drove all night to the Tallahassee airport. At daybreak we took off for Tampa and then went to bed. We awakened to the news that President Kennedy had been assassinated in Dallas. Everything stopped. The nation was in mourning and our next few shows were canceled. There was nothing until the 25th, when we opened in Indianapolis.

I knew what I needed to do: go back to Columbus and see my father who was to be operated on shortly. An aunt was in the hospital, too. With Don gone I was all the family they had. I think the assassination made people feel they should hold on to those they love while they still have them. At least, that's what my heart was telling me.

After Indianapolis there were six more college concerts before we headed home. We did a special Steve Allen TV show in Hollywood. My son had a cast on his ankle and I remember Steve signing it. Steve was good to us for so many years. We closed the year on December 27th by recording "Wake The Town And Tell The People."

13

THE YEARS THE MUSIC CHANGED

It's 1964. LBJ is President. "Funny How Time Slips Away" and "Charade" were our most recent singles. And we were getting vaccinations. An Asian tour was to begin January 7th. Tats Nagashima, his brother Hideo, and their KK Productions kept a steady stream of US entertainers coming to Asia during those years.

Tats was a gentle and clever man who was educated in England and knew not only the meaning of English words but also understood Western slang and humor. He had a respectable crew of people who worked for him, and we trusted each one of them with our lives some of the time and with our equipment all the time.

Tokyo

We moved into the New Japan Hotel in Tokyo and worked the New Latin Quarter downstairs. Lots of people throughout Japan loved our music, though few understood the meanings of some of the poetic phrases like "Try to think that love's not around." That's pretty complicated for people who don't speak English! It isn't direct like, "I will wait for you."

In the theaters we would work at 5:30 or 6pm and people would come from work or shopping to see the show before they took the train out to their flats in the suburbs. Theaters in Japan were not heated so people kept their overcoats on. That worked for them, but imagine Bill Comstock's icy fingers on a cold guitar!

There was usually a master of ceremonies who announced the first three songs (in Japanese) and then we would do them. Then he'd come back and announce the next three. This took time, but it helped the audience understand us and our music.

The people who attended knew our sound, words or no words. One night a local group called the Modern-Airs came to our dressing room after the first show and sang "Four Freshmen" to us. They had learned the words and harmony from our records. They didn't understand very much English, but they were totally into the Freshmen sound.

All over the world there are people who have the same musical soul. They speak various languages, but their musical souls match ours and those of their counterparts in all the other countries. Great harmonies please people no matter what their language. We prize the friendship of the Modern-Airs and all the other groups who sing harmony in all the other languages.

In Tokyo we were introduced to our driver, "Shorty," who was shorter than almost anyone we met over there. He could barely touch the accelerator and still see through the windshield of his car. Bob Flanigan (6'4") was always ready for fun. He'd yell," Oh! You're just my size!" and run over to stand next to Shorty, who would move away very quickly. It became a standing joke. Whenever we were out of the car, Bob would sneak around and stand by Shorty, who would immediately jump away.

One afternoon Tats took us to the factory showroom of a major pearl exporter. We were allowed to visit the area where they graded the pearls by color and size. They had buckets full of matching pearls, and the women would string them and tie knots between them so quickly it was unbelievable. Of course, we bought several strings of pearls, at factory prices, to bring home as gifts.

We met Hideo Nagashima, Tats' big brother, who was also educated in England. A more suave man you have never met. With a twinkle in his eye he would salute and say, "Hideo Nagashima, Commander, Japanese Navy, D.F.T." When we asked him what D.F.T. stood for he said, "Defeated!"

One night we performed after the Siltie Sisters, three beautiful ladies from Idaho who sang and wowed the guys in the military clubs. They were six feet tall, blonde and voluptuous. After work that night, Tats, the Siltie Sisters and we Freshmen got together for dinner.

By the time we left the restaurant, it was daylight. A little Japanese first grade student was on his way to school with his satchel of books when these three tall blonde women loomed suddenly before him. He tried not to show any emotion. It would not be good manners, after all, to gasp in surprise. He looked down at their feet and all the way up to their heads, and promptly lost his balance. Bonk! He sat right down on the sidewalk and covered his mouth with his hand as if to say, "Oh my! What have I done now?" What a great moment.

Across the Far East

From Tokyo we got down to Osaka, Iwakuni and Hiroshima which, by 1965, was rebuilt and thriving. They left the shell of the building which was at the center of the atomic bomb explosion, as an ominous reminder of the consequences of war. We flew to Okinawa on January 23rd to work in the US military clubs. Two days later it was on to Taiwan to sing at more military clubs.

Later we returned to Japan for concerts in several more theaters, including a TV show. I found that everywhere I went in Japan, people would point at me and say, "Rashawa,

Rashawa." It began to get on my nerves. I asked Tats, "What are they saying?" He explained that the ambassador from the US, Edwin Reischauer, and I looked alike. Tats commented that all the round-eyed people look alike to the Japanese and that I looked enough like Reischauer to confuse them. Reischauer was very much loved in Japan. He was married to a Japanese lady, which gave him a great affinity with the Japanese people.

On February 5th I went to the American Embassy where I was ushered into Reischauer's office and left alone with the man who held US-Japanese relations in his hands.

"Indiana," I said, when he asked where I was from. "My mother came from Indiana," he said. I told him I grew up as a Quaker in southern Indiana and he said his mother was also a Quaker.

It was not a surprise that the Japanese thought I looked like Ed. He was older, grayer and taller, and the wrinkles in his face were where the result of wrestling with important world questions. Mine were show biz wrinkles, formed by smiling. We enjoyed a half hour visit together.

We wrapped up the tour with a few more one-nighters and flew back to California. Boy, does jet lag ever get to you. We arrived in Los Angeles the morning of February 9th three and a half hours before we left Tokyo! Now it was time to be "Daddy home from Asia." We had toy Samurai swords for the boys, kimonos for the girls, and pearls for our wives.

Back At It

We were home for five days, then flew to Durham to do an afternoon show for 1,200 students at Duke. Then it was on to Valdosta, Georgia, and then up to Philadelphia.

Back in Los Angeles, Capitol could not make Beatles records fast enough to meet the demand. So, for a while at least, there would be no Nat King Cole, Peggy Lee, Stan Kenton, Pee Wee Hunt, Guy Lombardo or Freshmen records pressed. The entire capacity of Capitol was unable to deal with a success as big as the Beatles. They even had Beatles records pressed by the factories of other major labels. Personally, I love the Beatles' music, and I love success. But the Beatles and their success burst Capitol at the seams and things were never the same after that. We watched it change and wanted to scream.

A New Game Plan

February and March were mostly one-nighters. Cassius Clay beat Sonny Liston in six rounds on February 25th. On March 2, 1964, we adopted a new plan. We would cut our work schedule to 120 days a year. This would give us time at home to rehearse, record, and be available to do TV and commercials. We'd also have more time with our wives and families, which was the most important thing.

April highlights included working with the Four Preps in Athens, Georgia, and playing to 8,000 people at an outdoor concert in Chapel Hill, North Carolina. Then we flew to the Air Force Academy for a show.

On May 1st we worked in Franklin, Indiana. Bob's parents, and mine, were there to hear us, along with a bunch of aunts, uncles and cousins. We had our parents stand and be recognized one at a time. I know my folks were glad to see us working concerts and not nightclubs where people smoked and liquor was served.

Another part of our game plan was to cut expenses. We planned to close the office at 6047 Hollywood Boulevard and maybe run the Freshmen fan mail through one of our homes. Meanwhile, Bill Wagner had a good thing going at Capitol Records. When he began working there, his secretary, Mary Lou, came to our office two days a week. I would go to the office between tours and try to keep up with the mountain of details that piled up while we were away. About this time I started writing our newsletter, *The Fifth Freshman*.

On May 28th Jennifer Flanigan came to stay the night with Sue and me, and her little sister Julie was born on the 29th. Now Bob had Mary had two little girls to come home to.

When Ken Albers came back on the road with us in June he brought a flugelhorn with him. That's the first time we used the horn and we loved the way he made it sound. It is part of the Freshmen sound to this day.

Shuttle Service

In mid-June we were doing the Mike Douglas TV show in Cleveland every day at 10am; then we'd take a taxi to the Cleveland airport, fly to Pittsburgh, drive out to the Twin Coaches, and work there at night. Each morning we'd fly to Cleveland again. That week all we did was meet deadlines.

A brand new group called the Rolling Stones was on with us one day. They were the newest sensation after the Beatles. Here we were, working two jobs a day and sleeping only if there was time to sleep. We were neat, clean and pressed. The Rolling Stones were not the least bit dressy. I guess we just didn't understand the direction music was headed.

At the end of July my family and I flew to Hawaii. The Freshmen would be working there and we went early to enjoy some family time. My boys rented three surfboards and took me out in that beautiful ocean to learn to surf. It didn't take them long to get the hang of it, but I just couldn't get it. So I just laid on my board and watched them.

I was wearing a T-shirt, but the backs of my legs, from my bathing suit to my heels, got badly sunburned. Each leg was one large blister and the muscles felt stiff. I couldn't stand to wear trousers and my knee wouldn't straighten out. I walked like Groucho Marx! Finally I went to the doctor who prescribed some spray foam.

We had two shows to do four nights later. I tried putting on my wool uniform pants over those blisters but I couldn't stand it. I had some nylon pajama pants so I wore them, partly to cover the foam and partly to keep the wool off my skin. That night we did an officer's club and another club somewhere. I was on the verge of passing out by the time we finished.

The next night we worked out of doors at the Waikiki Shell. What a beautiful scene it was there in the park, under the stars and by the ocean. We did the first half and the Smothers Brothers did the second half. By then I could almost straighten my legs.

Back home a week later, the Freshmen and George Shearing opened at the Safari in San Jose. George was always such a pleasure to work with, and together we had enough drawing power to pack the Safari. In the afternoons we rehearsed the vocal parts to the *More Four Freshmen And Five Trombones* album.

George had the idea he and we should do a medley of his and our hits. He would do the playing and we'd sing. Of course George performed it flawlessly. It started with his "Roses of Picardy," then our "We'll Be Together Again." Next came his "September in the Rain" then our "Day By Day," just a chorus or less of each tune. It was really nifty.

George is very focused on his work. He is an intense learner and he makes perfection his goal. He had the medley all learned and ready to perform in a day or two. We Freshmen had to have the list of which song follows which. We put George off for a few days and he quipped, "You people with eyes are so distracted it affects your learning capabilities." When we got it done, the medley was over 13 minutes long, almost too long to use in a show. We shortened it for later use at the Coconut Grove.

The trombone players for *More Four Freshmen* were different some days but the people used most often were George Roberts, Harry Betts, Bob Fitzpatrick, Milt Bernhart, Jim Amlotte and Lew McCreary. Shelly Manne played drums, Joe Mondragon, bass, Jimmy Rowles, piano and John Gray, guitar.

"Midnight Sun," the toughest arrangement we ever did, was on that album. We didn't have time to memorize any of the songs, and "Midnight Sun" really gave us trouble. All those half steps have to be right, right, right, or they are wrong, wrong, wrong! We ended up recording four bars when we got them right, then the next four bars and so on, until we finally finished the song.

On September 15th we watched ourselves on the Frances Langford TV show. She put together her favorite people and we filmed a fun show with Edgar Bergen and Charlie McCarthy, George Sanders and Julie London. We did "Route 66" with some of Bobby Troup's special lyrics. In Boston, the Capitol record man brought us our new *"Trombones"* album.

It was about this time that Bill and Ken agreed to switch parts on certain songs. Bill still sang the second part but his voice was really hurting. Ken could do that part some of the time and thus let Bill rest his voice. We came home to Los Angeles to record the theme music for the movie "Gidget," and closed out 1964 at Julie London's Christmas party.

Europe Revisited

In the world of 1965, Charles de Gaulle was the bee in everybody's bonnet. Things weren't going well in Vietnam. Cuba still threatened the peace in our hemisphere and chaos continued in the Congo. The Berlin Wall and the Iron Curtain were still firmly in place, and Winston Churchill had died. But we Freshmen were set for a good year.

Sue and I found the house we wanted in Granada Hills, which started all the Freshmen moving up there. But before we moved in we had another European tour to do. On January 6th we flew to London, Frankfurt, and then to Paris, where we stayed at the Mon Jolie Hotel. The place had seen better days and so had the lady who ran it. She carried a little dog around with her all the time. One day a flea from the dog jumped on me and I had a new flea bite every day for a week and a half. I think part of the time he traveled in my luggage! I tried everything except a flea collar - I don't think they had them there.

The auditorium in Helsinki, Finland, was beautiful - all white inside, like an ice cave. We were told that the Russians had built it for the city in an effort to win some friends there. It didn't work, though. When the building was finished the Finns said "Thank you, now get out."

Finnish television broadcast our show that night. Earlier, we tried to rehearse the show but we had no interpreter and weren't able to communicate. Finally we just shrugged - prepared for the worst and hoped for the best. I guess they had said the same thing to themselves in Finnish. The show went so well that when we closed with "And So It's Over," the people wouldn't stop applauding. We went back out to do "Their Hearts Were Full Of Spring."

We closed out our tour in Germany at the military bases. We usually did three shows a night in three different places. Some entertainers would sign up to do tours like this but after a few days they'd say, "no more" and go home.

Snowbound

We flew back home over Greenland and reached Los Angeles on January 24, 1965, my daughter's seventh birthday. Two days later the moving van transported the Barbour family to our new house in Granada Hills, where we lived for the next 22 years. We were still getting settled on February 15th when word came that Nat King Cole had died. The world went into mourning.

Bob Flanigan signed the papers to buy a house in Granada Hills, just a block and a half from ours. On February 19th we were in knee deep snow in South Dakota, at Augustana College. There, we followed a big time collegiate wrestling match. Who else do you know who has entertained at a wrestling match? We stayed at the Dearborn Inn in Detroit on the 24th, and the next day saw the biggest snowstorm in Detroit's history. The airport closed. The schools and factories shut down. Our rental car was 500 feet away, buried in deep, deep snow. We had to call wherever we were supposed to go that next night and say, "Sorry, we're snowed in."

This was a strange time in the record business. Capitol was ready to drop us, yet *More Four Freshmen and Five Trombones* was nominated for a Grammy Award!

In early April, home after another tour of Japan, we put out our newsletter. That was hard work! People thought we had a printer do it, but I wrote it and our secretary made a gelatin stencil for the Gestetner machine. We would run off one side, put on the other stencil and run off the other side. Then it went through the folding machine. We stapled them, stamped them and put on the address labels, all by hand. When I took over from Bill Wagner we were mailing about 3,000, a number which eventually doubled.

Sue and I got all gussied up and went to the Grammy Awards presentation. The Beatles won in the group category. "When I Stop Loving You" was released, with "Nights Are Long" on the back. It didn't set the world on fire. You've heard the term, the "beginning of the end?" Well, the end for us had begun at Capitol. We had to negotiate separately for each recording released.

Crazy Days

For some reason, the spring and summer of 1965 brought with it an unusual amount of pranks, trouble making and moderately clean fun. Like the night of April 20th when we flew to Ft. Wayne, Indiana. The FBI was at Los Angeles airport, investigating a bomb threat. There might have been a bomb or a terrorist on our plane, but Bob, Bill, Ken and Ross slept all the way to Chicago. The heck with the terrorist! The amplifier is all the airline lost on our way to Ft. Wayne. We appeared at the Home Show and Betty and Hal Kratzsch and their boys came to see us. Hal was designing new products for the Zimmer Company.

Then there was the night in Muskegon, Michigan. After our show we and a group called the Twi-Niters got to singing in the Black Angus parking lot. Somebody complained about the noise and the police came and cleared us out.

In mid-May we all met at the Syracuse airport, having scattered earlier to promote our new single. We were bound for Murfreesboro, Tennessee. That plane landed in Buffalo, Cleveland, Columbus, Dayton, Cincinnati, Louisville, and finally Nashville. How can they do that to us? I'm calling the FAA! We were on that plane for eight hours and were just numb. And we sang like we were numb that evening at Middle Tennessee State. You can't win' em all!

We started an hour late in Aberdeen, South Dakota, because a late plane made us miss our connection in Chicago. The audience waited and we did fine except the sound man turned down the loud things and turned up the quiet ones. That's always been one of our pet peeves.

Then, in June, we got into it with the management at Cincinnati's Coney Island. Things went so well that we played and sang way too long. The park people fussed at us because we were keeping the people in the ballroom and off the roller coaster and the midway. On Saturday there were 2,600 people who lingered to hear more songs.

Our wives came with us to New Orleans in late June and we all went to eat at Brennan's. We were there to work with the summer "Pops" orchestra. That's such fun. But in the motel the first night Sue and I and a half dozen others got stuck in the elevator between floors. Nobody panicked and the hotel dropped everything to get us out.

John Denine ran the Casino Ballroom in Hampton Beach, New Hampshire, and he was a man who made things happen. On July 24th he had the Four Aces, the Four Lads and the Freshmen to lunch. That's the only time the three groups ever got together just to talk and relax. Somebody should have taken a picture!

Interruptions even followed us to national TV. We were on the Johnny Carson show in July and sounded great, but a news special on the Mariner spacecraft's pictures of Mars blacked us out. Then it was off to the Frolics in Salisbury Beach, Massachusetts, for a week. One night after work we went back to our motel and partied with Dave Mahoney and Sod Vaccaro of the Four Aces, along with two good friends of ours, Bill and Freda Meadowcroft. We ended up in the pool at dawn splashing around and making noise. To top off that adventure the paycheck at the Frolics bounced.

We flew to Oklahoma City to work Spring Lake Park. The '89er Motel, where we were to stay, was blown away by a twister, so we registered at Howard Johnsons. We did shows at the park at 3:30pm, in the 95 degree heat. Then, at 8:00 and 10pm we sang by the roller coaster. When it passed behind the stage something in the track went "yip yip." It happened at the strangest times - "It's A Blue - Yip Yip - World. . . "

In the fall we did the Johnny Carson show again, this time in New York. Skitch Henderson's band played our backgrounds and everything went super smooth. Joe Williams, Ethel Merman and Andy Devine were there, too. I went around to Andy and said, "I don't want to be corny, but I am such a fan of yours. It's a pleasure to meet you." Andy, with that funny cracked voice said, "That's not corny. That's music to my ears!"

We returned to the hotel that evening to watch ourselves on TV but the show didn't air because of election return coverage. We must have been bad luck for Johnny.

Fred's Idea

Fred Dale began urging us to prepare an act for Las Vegas so he could book us there. He wanted us to add a girl to our group. Voyle Gilmore and Bill Miller, two of the finest men I know, called us to Capitol in late September to explain that the company had dropped our recording contract. We were dazed, disappointed and hurt. We had helped build Capitol, but now it had new executives with different music priorities. The times, they were a-changin'. We were back on network TV a few days later on the Merv Griffin Show, where we appeared with Little Jimmy Boyd ("I Saw Mommie Kissing

Santa Claus"). There was only time for us to do "LuLu's Back
In Town," but at least it wasn't blacked out by an election or
a space-shot!

In Portsmouth, Virginia, we ran into a problem we'd
never experienced before. It was a nice hall, but when they
turned down the house lights we discovered the same switch
also turned off the guitar amp. Ooops! They had to turn on
the house lights again to figure out what they had done.
Well, that's easy - we'll plug into a different circuit and
everything will be OK. They turned down the house lights
again, but this time the P.A. faded out when they dimmed
the stage lights! We thought we would never get started.

Fred Dale was still after us to develop a Las Vegas act.
He still wanted us to add a girl but I was against changing
anything. I expressed myself to Fred at great length. After I
finished, Fred said, "The girl I have in mind is Sue Raney."
Well! That's different! Sue Raney may not actually be an
angel, but she looks like one and sings like one. She even
acts like one. Fred knew what we needed and he had the
right girl in mind.

Still, in the back of our minds, the thought of us
working in Las Vegas after all those great years on American
campuses was troublesome. Sure, staying put was easier, but
Vegas seemed like a graveyard to us. A group can live and die
in Vegas and nobody ever knows. The very thought of a few
musicians playing behind us and the five of us up there
snapping our fingers as we sang, while the folks in front of us
pulled slot machine handles and ignored what we did...we
had our doubts.

It was a tough time for the Freshmen. We no longer
had a record label and we couldn't get anybody to use us for
commercials. Was our sound becoming passé? Further, it
would mean a major outlay of money to rehearse the Vegas
act. We would have to take time off to put it together. We'd
have to buy new uniforms and new arrangements. We sighed
a few sighs and wondered.

The Mike Douglas show in Philadelphia a few days later was fun. ZsaZsa Gabor and Billy Daniels were the other guests. I remember we wore raccoon coats and sang "Graduation Day" to ZsaZsa. Then "Day By Day," "Teach Me Tonight," "We've Got a World That Swings" and "Blue World." Mike always wanted us to do "Blue World."

Afterwards they whisked us to the airport in their limousine and we flew on to Charleston, West Virginia, to sing at the Athletic Club that night. The next morning it was so foggy we couldn't see 50 feet in front of us. Charleston is in a valley and when we drove up the hill to the airport, it was clear and nice. I guess that's why they put the airport there! We worked a campus in Seguin, Texas, and came back to Columbus for homecoming at Ohio State. The place was sold out twice. We could have filled the hall nine times for an event like homecoming!

14

GETTING OUR ACT TOGETHER

We flew home November 1, 1965, and began rehearsing two songs for our Las Vegas act - "It's A Most Unusual
Day" and "Consider Yourself At Home." Gene DiNovi, an old
buddy and co-songwriter with Bill Comstock, was chosen to
write the band arrangements. A week later our first practice
with a band was held in one of Capitol's studios. That night
we began rehearsing with our all-time favorite man, Nick
Castle. We hadn't worked with Nick since "Rich, Young and
Pretty" in 1951. After that he had been the dance director
for - let's see - the Osmond Brothers, Caterina Valente,
Sergio Franci, Peggy Lee and Jerry Lewis. Nick would show
us how to move without our instruments. He was a superb
dancer, and so full of good cheer his eyes twinkled.

A few days later we flew to Milwaukee on a 727. They
were having metal fatigue problems with some of those
planes. We didn't think of ourselves as heroic, but I always
figured if there was a crash with us aboard, I would walk away
and say, "Boy, that was a close one!"

We worked Divine's Ballroom in Milwaukee and did
okay, but I think our minds were more on the things we had
been rehearsing than the songs we were performing. After
work, Matt Monroe called to say he was in town, so we went
over to see his late show. He called us up to do a song. Matt

was such a great singer. His vocal quality, intonation and phrasing were just the best.

After a one-nighter in Kansas City we sang for a week at the Penthouse in Seattle. The Penthouse was one step up from the sidewalk. Months later we worked at the Edgewater in Seattle and it was four stories up from the sidewalk.

Back in Los Angeles, our rehearsals were held in "Nick's Castle," the ideal place to put an act together. His rehearsal room had a big 20 by 30 foot hardwood floor and at least two of the walls were mirrored so we could see ourselves getting it right (or wrong!). We had never danced and we were such klutzes. Nick showed us the steps and we tried to look like we knew what we were doing.

In December I gave my son his own gold Volkswagen key. Kent was 16 and taking driver's training. Where did my little boy go?

The Act

December 31st was our opening night with "The Act" at the Royal Tahitian in Ontario, California. We were pretty rocky, but who cares on New Year's Eve?

Our show went like this: We would start off with Sue Raney in a pink formal and the Freshmen in pearl gray tuxes as the front line. We would do "Day In, Day Out," a good opener. (We would always break Sue up when we'd sing, "When I awaken I awaken with a tinkle.") Then she would go off stage and the Freshmen did the next three or four songs with the band. Then we'd sing (slow groove) "Every star above knows the one we love, Sweet Sue [stop] Sue Raney!" And she would come out and do four or five songs. Then the band played her off stage and we did four or five tunes by ourselves.

After that we brought Sue back for a fun rendition of "My Bonnie Lies Over the Ocean." It was a Las Vegas "closer" if you've ever heard one. I got to play trumpet behind Sue's pretty songs and, of course, Ken and Bob played. Bill picked up the guitar to accompany Sue. It was great to have all those horns and the new arrangements.

We were in Ontario until January 9th. On a couple of nights a new comic named Richard Pryor opened the show. In our brief time together we didn't get to know each other very well.

On January 18th, after more vigorous rehearsals, we opened with Sue Raney for a week at Shifty's Night Club in San Diego, then to Bimbo's 365 Club in San Francisco. On the 28th, Nick Castle came to see his act. He sat right in front, drew faces on hotel stationery and flashed them at us. If he liked a tune he would show us the smiling face. If we did it wrong we saw the frown. It busted us up. He was our coach, we were the team, and he had us mostly winning!

Fred Dale and Jerry Perenchio came to Bimbo's to re-sign us with the agency. They knew we would sign with whatever agency Fred was with, and they also knew we had paid for a lot of rehearsal time, new arrangements, Nick Castle's services and new clothes. They sweetened the pot by giving us a "signing bonus" of $5,000. What a kind way for them to help us through an expensive time.

On February 2nd Sue Raney went home and we Freshmen flew over lots of snow from the Rockies to Cincinnati. We had to dig the Hertz rental car out of a snowbank. We slogged our way over to Hanover College (Indiana) and back. The next day we flew to New York to do the Tonight Show with Johnny Carson. Gene DiNovi had written some outstanding band arrangements for "Candy" and "Fools Rush In" for the Doc Severinsen band.

Somehow, television was always an experiment for us. We never liked the sound we got in a TV studio. That made us uncomfortable because sound is what the Four Freshmen were selling. We could never keep our faces from showing our concern. But we kept doing TV because it was such an important part of the music world.

We drove to Vegas on February 9th and rehearsed "The Act" at Ron Feuer's house. Ron, a spectacular organ player, was to be the Vegas bandleader. Two nights later we opened at the Thunderbird for seven weeks

On February 21st Sue Raney broke her toe. Her foot got so big she couldn't put on those little pink high heeled shoes and she couldn't work barefoot because the pink gown would crumple on the floor. She ended up wearing a pink sock on the swollen foot and her pink shoe on the other. What a trooper. She was such a perfect singer, so spectacularly in tune and correct. She had never sung with a vocal group before and our harmony singing intrigued her. We were so proud of her - as if she were our kid sister.

Just so we wouldn't forget what colleges were like, after two more Nevada gigs, the four of us worked Lewis and Clark College in Lewiston, Idaho.

Grunelund and Beyond

On June 1, 1966, we recorded "Cry," and the following day took the polar route to London and through Copenhagen to Sweden. A group called the Brelids met us and sang for us at the airport. We worked Lisberry Park in Gotenborg and the next morning the Brelids took us to see the Volvo factory, the shipyards and a yacht race, then to a 3pm plane which took us to Stockholm. The Brelids were big fans.

We sang at Grunelund (Greenland) Amusement Park. Here they stopped the roller coaster and shut down the whole midway until we finished. I happened to bang my watch on the microphone stand on our second night at Grunelund. As we were closing our first set, I looked down to check the time and we still had twelve minutes to go. So I added a couple of songs and checked my watch again. We still had 12 minutes to go! My fellow Freshmen informed me that we had run over and kept the park rides shut down too long. The Grunelund people were kind enough not to fuss at us - but I did need to get a new watch!

One fun day we did a half hour live performance for a hand-picked audience in a TV studio which, happily, was videotaped. The master sat in my garage for 26 years before we got it copied. It's available to today's fans through the Four Freshmen Society.

On June 11th we were driven to a shipbuilding town called Gavle, on the Gulf of Bothnia, near Finland. We worked at Furuvik Park outdoors that evening. As they came in people broke off small leafy branches from a tree to wave as a defense against the mosquitoes. They stood up while we sang, waving these branches around themselves. Can you see it? Seven hundred Swedes waving branches to "Poinciana." At the end of each song they'd put the branches under their arms, applaud and then resume the waving until the end of the next song.

Gavle is farther north than Helsinki and it doesn't really get dark up there in the summer. When we got to "Blue World," the sky was like a glass blue dome surrounding us, with little lights playing around the outer edges. It really was a Blue World! To this day I think of Gavle every time I hear that song.

The next morning we flew to Copenhagen to appear at Tivoli Gardens. Tivoli is so pretty, with its great flower beds inlaid around winding paths and beautiful trees. There was a large bandstand, with sides and a roof, and the people sat on rows of chairs in front of us on a concrete floor bigger than a hockey rink.

We flew to London on June 13th and went right to the BBC, where we did 14 songs in a 40-minute television show. The band behind us was full of Ted Heath musicians. Kenny Baker was playing trumpet with them. What a warm feeling of friendship we felt with those men we had shared so much with in previous years. The next day we did the Dusty Springfield TV show and there we met Dorothy Warwick, our number one English fan. She had knitted four matching sweaters for us. Dorothy kept the English disc jockeys playing Freshmen records. How we appreciated her! A group can't earn devotion like hers. Devotion is not earned it is given.

Homeward Bound

We flew from London to New York on June 20th and the group scattered for a few days. I went to my parents' house in Columbus and then to New Orleans to perform with their symphony.

I wish I could adequately describe the feeling of singing with a symphony orchestra, have you sense the lump in your throat and the goosebumps when the strings play those beautiful Dick Reynolds arrangements. Maybe you can feel it a little as you read - a cushiony, velvety, feathery feeling of those strings right behind you, delivering all those Freshmen sounds. Mmmm!

Back in Los Angeles, the Barbours bought a VW bus that became part of the Freshmen family. The van wasn't a week old when all the Freshmen amps and instruments went into it and I drove it to Las Vegas to open at the Sahara on August 2, 1966. Ron Feuer was the leader of the band. Raul Romero played sax, Al Longo, trumpet, Hank Nanny, drums, and Bill McDaniel bass. Sue Raney and the Freshmen did the vocals. By now we had done the show so many times we knew it worked.

In mid-September "The Act" went into Seattle for a week at the Edgewater. For our anniversary on September 20th the band gave us a wooden plaque that said, "Four Freshmen, 18 years." It had two eighth notes and a martini glass drawn on it. Bill Comstock said that meant "of rhythm and booze."

Back in Los Angeles we went to see the Kenton Band in Shelly Manne's nightclub, "Shelly's Manne Hole." Manny Cline, a Los Angeles trumpet player, kidded that he was going to open a place across the street called "Manny's Shell Hole."

We revisited Texas A & M at College Station in late October. Some of those Aggies wore tall boots and riding pants almost like a motorcycle officer's. All we had to do was mention Baylor or the University of Texas and they would hoot, hiss and stamp their feet on those wooden bleachers. It sounded like a thousand flamenco dancers! Of course, Bob deliberately baited them into doing that every time we worked there. They were to play Arkansas in football the next day so Bob said, "It's good to be here at Arkansas." That's all it took! What spirit!

Welcome 1967

As we began the new year the four of us had been Freshmen together for six and a half years. In early January, after signing with Decca Records, we began to carry a few promotional singles of "Cry" and "No Where To Go" for the DJs as we traveled. It was the only record we ever did with Decca. On January 31st we began a week at Shifty's in San Diego. Ken Errair came in a couple of nights. What a good friend he was. We hadn't seen him for a long time.

Back on the road we visited Philadelphia and worked the Mike Douglas Show. After the show we were taken in army cars to Valley Forge Hospital just outside of Philadelphia to do a show for the patients.

At Kent State (in Ohio) with Al Hirt, they sold all 6,000 seats for the show. The next afternoon we rehearsed "It All Depends On The Mood I'm In." We had a lot of fun with that one - a jazz waltz and my solo with a mellophone chorus. For some reason we never got that song recorded. After five or six more one-nighters we flew home.

Our next tour began March 9th at Largo, Florida, then to Orange City in - not Florida - Iowa! After that concert I packed the drums and carried them down the center aisle of the gym. By now the room was just empty chairs - and so quiet, as though there had been no concert just an hour earlier. What a perishable thing music is - not even an echo remained. Suddenly, from out of nowhere, I was met by a cute coed who wanted an autograph, so I put my things down and signed her program. Then, almost like a daughter would do with her father, she hugged me and said something like, "Thank you for doing what you do." She backed up a few steps, smiled, and then turned and left. I realized then that the things we had sung and played that night had not died when the music stopped. The songs had soaked in, had affected people, and made one shy young girl come back and hug a Freshman. Wherever you are, dear shy lady, thank you for appreciating us!

In late March we flew to Japan for more concerts promoted by Tats and Hideo Nagashima. Like our earlier Japanese tours we sang at US military clubs and did TV shows, theater concerts and nightclubs for the Japanese fans. On April 1st, Ken Albers' 11th anniversary with the group, we did a show for the Red Cross Hospital. This is the way to feel worthwhile - do hospital shows where the people need entertainment so badly.

At one of the military clubs they announced the beginning of our show five minutes early. Bob didn't have his pants on! We could hear the sergeant saying, "Here they are, ladies and gentlemen - the Four Freshmen!" Bob poked his head out through the curtain and shouted "Wait a minute! Wait a minute!"

We did other shows at hospitals, NCO clubs and officer's clubs. During our stay in the Philippines we sang to and with most of the vocal groups there - Rudy Angus and the Four Notes, the Tonettes and the Jubilee Four. We did a week in Bangkok, Thailand. On April 16th we flew more than 9,000 miles - Hong Kong, Tokyo, Honolulu, Los Angeles.

We started rehearsals on "Dreamsville," a Mancini tune with a Dick Reynolds bossa nova arrangement. And we found a place nearer home for our Freshmen office - 8720 Woodley in Sepulveda. That same day, April 25th, Ken Errair came to our house for dinner. Sue made lasagna and I made the salad. That was the last time we saw him.

Off the Record

On May Day we got word that Decca was terminating our contract, which wasn't much of a surprise. The next day did bring a surprise. The Los Angeles Board of Supervisors gave us a Citation of Honor for our efforts entertaining US service personnel overseas. We had never thought of these shows as anything out of the ordinary, but that day Los Angeles made us feel very important.

The Standel Music Company supplied us with a guitar and a bass, and in early May they brought over a spectacular amplifier for us to use. We didn't own them, we couldn't sell them, but we didn't have to buy them either. We were a kind of proving ground for their products.

Going through the Chicago airport we saw Homer and Jethro. It seemed like we'd see them five out of every ten times we'd go through O'Hare. We were walking along looking at the floor in front of us we heard, "Hey! Which one of you guys is it that sings out of tune?" We knew it was them immediately.

May 31st was our first rehearsal in our new office. We were trying to polish "Dreamsville," "Atchison, Topeka and Santa Fe" and "I Want To Be Happy." The next day we got word that Jack Tracy of *downbeat* magazine was now with Liberty Records and was interested in us. We took hope. For a while we felt like old war-horses turned out to pasture. We met with him and did "Dreamsville" and "Bye Bye." Liberty liked the group but they didn't like those tunes.

In June we performed for a week at the Three Rivers Inn, near Syracuse. While there, word came that Liberty had said no to the idea of signing the Freshmen. We knew we couldn't remain a major force in the music world without a record contract. This was also a time that the Freshmen were getting pretty fed up with each other. There was a lot of tension, partly because we were unhappy with the way we sounded, partly because there was no record contract. Of course there were personality clashes - every group has them. Our dream seemed to be in real trouble.

One afternoon, Bill and I bought a watermelon and ate it sitting by the canal. (The Three Rivers Inn name refers to three canals that meet there.) We talked and wondered what in the world was going to happen to the Four Freshmen.

On stage we started doing "Spring Isn't Spring Without You," a Ken Albers-Bill Comstock original, and "What Now My Love," a good song for us, which featured Bob on a vocal solo. "Dreamsville" was now one of our featured songs as well. Because the words and melody moved half speed, I had an awful time learning to play, sing and phrase it with the group. I spent some lonely afternoons learning this double time rhythm and singing my part.

At Taylor's in Denver there was a request from a nice little lady for "Sweet Lorraine." Anyone who knew us knew that's been Leroy's song since 1949. So Leroy started in and the lady thought it was some kind of smart aleck personal attack on her. She gave us the worst cussing out we've ever received, using words Bob said he hadn't heard since his army days.

Yes!

Hey, there's some good news. The people at Liberty Records changed their minds and on August 15th we signed with them for a whole new string of albums. In most of the USA though, the summer headlines were about riots in Detroit and a dozen other towns. Paratroopers and riot police were busy everywhere in 1967.

We began a long association with the Hong Kong Bar in the Century Plaza Hotel in Los Angeles. It was a good spot to work and a good place for people to listen. Al DeChristopher, the manager, saw to it that things were right for everybody. It was nice, too, because musicians and show people came in - Robert Clary, Sue Raney, Joe Williams, and Kenny Rogers, who had his beard even then. A young man named Greg Stegeman was there to hear us, too.

In the Century Plaza Hotel our favorite restaurant was Yamato's, a Japanese place with separate little rooms divided by sliding screens. One August evening we were there with Bill and Lila Jaeger. Ken's wife, Nancy, was sitting quite close to the screen. She slid it open to see what the other room looked like. To her shock, she found herself nose to nose with Cary Grant. Speechless, she slid the screen closed again and mumbled to us, "Gulp, Cary Grant!" We didn't bother him again.

The next day we recorded "Kites," our first tune for Liberty. We were so eager we wanted to record the whole album in one day.

On our second night at the Embers in Indianapolis, my rental car was stolen while we were performing. Luckily, they found it the next day, with all my luggage still in it. September 20th was our 19th anniversary celebration at the Embers, with a big cake and a plaque. Half of my life had been spent as a Freshman!

I had a doctor's appointment at the end of September. He put his finger to my nose and said, "You stop smoking." So I threw away my Tarrytons right there in his office and haven't had a cigarette since. Everybody's doctor should do that.

We did an afternoon and evening show the next week in San Angelo, Texas. Bill Comstock's parents and brother lived there. Between shows we went to Bill's parents' house for dinner. After the show we drove to San Antonio and flew through the night to Miami.

You Deserve a Break Today

That afternoon we went to the Doral Country Club, where the McDonald's hamburger people were having a convention. The room filled up with people and became nerve wracking so we stayed out of sight in our dressing room. Ray Kroc, the founder of McDonald's, got tired of all the back slappers trying to make points with him so he came and joined us. Everybody was looking for him, but he "deserved a break" that day and found it, relaxing with us.

On December 31, 1967, I'd reached Jack Benny's age - 39. On New Year's Day we watched USC beat Indiana University in the Rose Bowl. Southern Cal used a running back who was looking great: O.J. Simpson.

GOING GLOBAL

We began 1968 with the strangest one-nighter we ever worked. We had driven down those marshmallow mountains from Lake Tahoe under a big white winter moon. The VW bus was loaded down with amplifiers and luggage we would leave in San Francisco. That's because the one-nighter was in Manila, in the Philippines, and we couldn't take everything with us.

Before I left the bus full of our stuff, I took one creative precaution: I covered the inside windows with newspapers, and drew big peace symbols and hippie sayings on them to discourage any potential thief. Who would want to swipe a hippie's things?

Party of the Century

Four first class tickets were bought for us by Eugenio Lopez, who was celebrating his 40th wedding anniversary in the grandest style he could imagine. Eugenio was the brother of the vice president of the Philippines, but he wasn't just riding his brother's coattails. Eugenio owned the Sheraton Hotel, the newspaper and a few other baubles like that. It was his plan to throw a party grander than anything the Rockefellers or the Fords would ever think of. He invited barons and kings and viscounts, maharajahs, grand dukes and muftis - the cream of the world's social elite.

For entertainment they imported the Meyer Davis Society Orchestra from New York, the Ten Strolling Strings from San Francisco, Lucien Amaro from the Metropolitan Opera in New York and the Freshmen! There was also a fine band from the Philippines. The man who ran the whole production was the prominent Hollywood movie director, Jack Brooks.

Let me see if I can paint you a picture of the Lopez compound. We entered through a big archway with an imposing gate. A high concrete wall went around a lawn area the size of a football field between the entrance and their giant home. A temporary 30 foot circle stage was built in the middle of the expansive lawn.

The tables for the guests of honor were on a riser in front of the stage. We were to work facing the Lopez family, with the band behind us. The lawn itself was beautifully landscaped, with flower beds and a hundred small trees. Circular tables were scattered all over the area, each with a huge umbrella. Each umbrella had a speaker in it so the guests could hear the band and the show.

Above the stage was an ingenious invention - a huge round metal frame that held a canvas covering. Unfurled, it would become a roof, should a rainstorm happen by.

When we arrived at the bandstand area to set up our equipment my first move was to plug Bill's guitar amplifier into the electrical outlet. Pfffft! Who could know that the double plugs over there were wired with 220 in the top plug and 110 in the bottom. Phooey! Another amp was brought in.

The Guests Arrive

The arriving guests looked absolutely stunning. Tuxedos and white dinner jackets for the men, and the ladies in traditional Philippine formal gowns with puffy sleeves that ballooned out. It was grand! The buffet dinner outdid anything I've ever seen. There was lobster, caviar - the finest of everything.

The trees and bushes, the umbrellas, and anything else they could decorate were covered with ruby red lights about the size of golf balls. There must have been 30,000 of them, and as the night grew darker they cast a hypnotic red glow over the crowd. We had seen this from the plane as we flew in the night before and thought it was a city block on fire, but it was the Lopez crew, testing the lights. In fact, they used so much electricity for this soiree the power company couldn't light the Lopez place and the whole city too. Some sections of town had their power turned off so the party could be a glowing success. Why not? Lopez also owned the power and light company!

The show began. Lucien Amaro was introduced and she sang a few operatic selections. But she was in for trouble. When she hit those beautiful long high notes the neighbors' dogs started singing with her! Soon other dogs from the outlying area joined in. The audience found the canine chorus humorous and the laughter dealt Miss Amaro's performance a near lethal blow.

To make matters worse one of the crew accidentally touched the "start" button that spread out the canvas roof above her. The machinery worked just fine, but the electric motor that pulled the canopy into place must have been near a microphone. Its droning hum was overpowering, and seemed to go on for a full minute. The poor lady struggled to finish, took a bow, and must have collapsed in her dressing room after such cruel and unusual punishment.

Our Turn

The master of ceremonies announced us and we came bounding on stage. The crew had moved our equipment on stage that afternoon, and then it had been moved a second time, because now the amp was so far back it was teetering over the back ledge of the stage. The mike was too far forward and Bill's curly guitar cord stretched across the stage to the amp like a tightrope. We heard an "ooops," and the teetering amplifier toppled over slowly and dramatically. Wham! Right on its face. The little curly puff of gray smoke emitting from its backside told us we had trashed a second amp.

I was on the microphone saying warm and positive things like "Good evening, ladies and gentlemen. We are honored to be part of this historic event" etc., etc., while Bob and Bill negotiated backstage with Meyer Davis' bass player, trying to borrow his amp. He had watched us kill one amp in the afternoon and another just then and wasn't eager to help us out. But finally he relented. You could watch him unplug it at the back of the bandstand, hand it to the trombone player, who handed it to the sax man, who handed it to Bob, who handed it to Bill. It was with great relief that we counted off "Somebody Loves Me."

They had given us a bundle of money to do this show and we were loaded for bear! By golly, we're going to thrill them! We sang with great fervor, and after each tune we would bow toward what little applause we could hear, and then jump into the next song. We finished a ballad and there was no applause at all. Suddenly, the emcee stepped in front of us and grabbed the microphone. "That's the Four Freshmen, ladies and gentlemen!"

Wait! We were still scheduled to do "Day By Day," "Blue World" and a closer. While we were changing instruments to do the next song, this clown shut us down! Off mike, the emcee was saying "Get off. Get off!" By that time we were bumping into each other. We were still pumped up to do our three strongest songs, and we were through!

We stood in the dressing room staring at each other. Our feelings ranged from anger to depression to disbelief. The master of ceremonies must have been a brave man because he came into the room, even though he must have known we were ready to lynch him. He raised his hand to ward us off. "The sound system failed," he moaned. "The only sound was on the stage. The people under the umbrellas heard nothing and thought the show was over. They were standing up and talking. So I was told to get you off stage!

All of a sudden someone ran in and got him. There was yet another crisis. The Lopez grandchildren were all inside a hollow cake, scheduled to be transported down the street, through the entrance gate, and up to the stage. There was just one problem: the cake was two feet too wide to get through the gate! It was stuck on the street, holding up traffic, with the kids still inside.

By this time we had moved from shock and anger to uncontrollable laughter. We had come all this way... ha ha! They did all this planning...spent all this money to hear the neighbors' dogs howl.. ha ha! And the roof motor roar.. ho ho! And two amps blew... ha ha! And the umbrella speakers failed.. and they kicked us off the stage.. uuumph! And now the dumb cake won't go through the gate...

The Lopez family graciously urged us to stay the rest of the week and enjoy the guided tours, the yacht trips and all the rest of the festivities planned for the dukes and earls and caliphs, but we needed to get home.

Today Kind of Thing

We stayed busy in our new office the rest of the month, sending out *Today Kind Of Thing* albums to disc jockeys across the country. We took several days to promote our album in Philadelphia, Pittsburgh, Cleveland, and Cincinnati. Then it was back to the Pier 500, near Detroit, where we made it a point to do the Morning Show on WXYZ-TV. The producer, Mike Krause, was such a Freshmen fan.

This time we lip-synched our record of "Whistle Me Some Blues." We always had the monitor speakers turned up loud so we could actually sing and still hear ourselves on the playback. But on this particular morning it was too soft. Mike realized the volume was too low and ran into the control booth to turn it up. Just inside the booth he tripped over the cord to the turntable and the sound went off completely.

We went on singing, hoping to be where the record was when the sound came back up. Of course, when Mike got the record player plugged back in it started right where it had stopped. We blushed and sang that part of the song again. We gave the viewers a real wake up call that morning! Mike Krause was so apologetic about his gaffe, he just put himself through hell. Hey, Mike, piece 'a cake! We just did the Lopez party in Manila! Mike Krause went on to marry Joan Lunden and direct her shows for years.

Behind the Curtain

On February 22nd the Freshmen began an amazing tour of Europe. Alan Blackburn was at the London airport to meet us and take us directly to the Rolf Harris television show.

The next evening, Moira Heath took Bob and me to see her husband, Ted, at their home. Sickness had reduced this forceful giant of a man to a mere shadow of himself. We returned to the hotel with a little sadness, thinking, "Time gets us all."

At this time in our career neckties were out, tie-died jeans were in. So we met the culture half way and wore turtlenecks with our uniforms.

On March 20, 1968, we began an unforgettable adventure. We flew to Vienna and crossed the Danube into Czechoslovakia. The Czechs had just declared freedom from the Soviet Union and the people were so pumped up for independence it was unreal. We were part of a cultural ministry trade. They were still a communist nation and they wanted freedom.

The Iron Curtain there was a barbed wire fence, maybe ten feet tall, with a guardpost at the gate. Then there was a 200 yard stretch of no man's land before the gate of the other barbed wire fence. The first guards took our passports and disappeared. Not very encouraging! Another matter raised our eyebrows. Some guards had a horizontal mirror on wheels with a handle like a lawn mower's. They used this device to look under cars to be sure there was no one clinging to the underside. We breathed a sigh of relief when they returned our passports and let us proceed to Bratislava a few miles away.

That's where we met Igor Ondreas, our interpreter. He looked like a Russian cosmonaut, with a ruddy complexion and short hair with a sort of messed up look. We were careful about what we said in the hotel because we figured the rooms might be fitted with listening devices.

That day we also met Waldemar Matuska. He was my size with an Abe Lincoln beard and a twinkle in his eye. We could see he was full of fun. There was a theater in Prague where Waldemar was featured in stage plays and shows the year 'round, except this week, when he and his little band were to travel from town to town with the Freshmen. Waldemar's band was called "Mefisto," meaning gypsy or vagabond. They did the first half of the show and we did the second.

We were honestly surprised at how excited the people were about the Freshmen sound. Radio Free Europe had been beaming free world music to them for years, as had Armed Forces Radio and Radio Luxembourg and others. It had been illegal for the Czechs to listen to these stations until the Dubcek government took over. But these people had secret listening rooms where they would go and tape the radio shows. Then they would cut and splice the tape and end up with a reel-to-reel package of Sinatra or Mancini or the Freshmen. After the show we signed a lot of tape boxes! Igor explained how they had risked life and limb to create those tapes. Now, in their new freedom, they could bring them out of hiding. But their owners were still cautious and would look both ways when they held out the boxes to be signed.

On March 21st we flew to Prague on a Russian plane. It was like a DC4 with two engines. I think Dr. Seuss invented it! For a thousand years every war in Europe has gone through Prague. Hitler, Napoleon, Kaiser Bill and maybe even Attila the Hun came through there, tearing things up and wrecking the town. So Prague built many of its buildings underground. The theater we worked, the Lucerne, was a good example. We entered by going downstairs from the sidewalk to the ticket booth. From there we entered the theater at the second balcony level. Two balconies circled all the way around the main floor below. The chairs there were movable so it could also be a ballroom or a sports arena. That night the stage was at the end of the main floor, with its back almost even with the front of the balcony. The place held several thousand people.

To our delight they had good microphones and sound, and good lighting. The audience was so very excited. One of Bob's comedy bits was to spray his trombone slide with water and made people think it was gin or whatever. There he called it "Slivovic," a clear Czech plum brandy that will take your head off. Bob couldn't reach most of that audience with comedy in English, but he sprayed that water in his mouth, told the people it was Slivovic, and it brought the house down.

That night we met two men who had been my penpals and readers of *The Fifth Freshman*: Ludvik Sereda and Vaclav Czicovsk. For me it was like meeting some long lost relatives.

It was back to Prague on March 23rd. We ate dinner with Waldemar in a Chinese restaurant (that's Red Chinese; the Iron Curtain kept out the others). Was that good food! We ate until we bulged! They served a drink called ShenShan. It came in a thimble-size glass and I swallowed about half a glass. Aaargh! It was like kerosene.

We did our final show that night back at the Lucerne. It was Saturday night and we had an excited audience. Waldemar had never spoken English in public, but this night he announced the second half by saying in English, "Ladies and Gentlemen, here are the Four Freshmen." The crowd went wild and we felt so complimented. My, oh my, it was a thriller of a show! I had practiced so I could say, "Good evening, people of Prague" in Czech. I also learned to say "thank you," but I got it mixed up on the show and said "good evening." The people forgave my mistakes.

We did the songs they had heard in their secret rooms. At the end of the show a young lady gave each of us a bouquet. We bowed and held the flowers close to us. During the applause Waldemar came back on stage with a big bottle of Slivovic and presented it to Bob as a surprise. The people screamed with laughter, applauding like crazy. I went up to the mike and the audience quieted long enough for me to say "May sma camaradge," ("We are friends"). Then Waldemar said, "May sma camaradge" and he and I ex-changed a big European man-to-man hug. The audience was jumping and shrieking with delight. It was a great moment for them and for me. My eyes tear-up as I write, the memories are so great.

After we got off stage and changed out of our hot, wet uniforms we came out and signed more of those illegal tape boxes. There were hugs from women and men alike. It took a long time to greet everyone but we felt like ambassadors from the free world, welcoming a newly independent nation.

It wasn't far to our hotel so we walked, right down the middle of the cobblestone street - seven or eight grown men with arms around the shoulders of the man on either side, past all the stunning old buildings. I remember Waldemar started us singing as loud as we could - "Yo Yo Ya Ya" - who knows what we were singing! It was Czech and it was wonderful.

The Longest Day

The next day was Sunday, March 24th, the longest of my life. We slept for maybe three hours. I awoke totally sick. Maybe food poisoning. I lost it all and then the "GIs" took over. The ShenShan, what little I drank, was coming out my pores and tear ducts.

I met Alan Blackburn and the Czech promoter to get the money straight. Then it was back to the room where I lost it all again. We checked out, drove to the airport and my insulin told me to eat. But nothing would stay down. Bob handled the tickets and luggage at the airport while I was in the john. I heard them call the plane to Zurich but I was just unable to move. Finally, Igor came in and got me and physically pushed me onto the plane. Going up the stairs, I dirtied my shorts. I must have looked like death warmed over. The plane full of people had waited for us, and we got some stern glances. They plunked me into a rear seat and Igor barely made it back out before we were rolling.

I was in the process of passing out and I knew I had to get calories in me or die in a diabetic coma. I said "Coca Cola" to the hostess, and it stayed down. Ken and Bill helped me into the Zurich airport, where I changed clothes and cleaned up a little.

When I emerged from the men's room Ken Albers looked like a worried mother. He got me a glass of white wine and it stayed in me. That and the Coke saved my life. By the time we got to Los Angeles I was almost back to normal.

Short Stint at Home

Four weeks and three days in Europe put us behind in our recording. We began the *Today Is Tomorrow* album on April 12th. On April 4th Dr. Martin Luther King, Jr. was killed in Memphis.

In Rapid City, South Dakota, Bill Comstock and I got up early and drove out to see Mount Rushmore. A few days later we got to Symphony Hall in Boston and discovered the Kenton band and June Christy were there. It was "Road Show" all over again, nine years later. We went on to the University of Cincinnati and then I went home to see my parents. They had amputated my father's left foot and now his other foot was swollen. I wanted to stay and help, but I had to catch up to the Freshmen in New York.

In mid-May our supply of *Today is Tomorrow* albums arrived in Los Angeles. That day we splurged and bought new bright blue tux coats, white cardigan sportcoats, and dark blue turtleneck shirts. Those shirts were all the rage then.

On May 28th Richard Nixon won the Oregon primary, the start of his race for the presidency. Liberty released a new Freshmen single with two medleys - "Come Fly With Me/Up Up And Away" was on one side and "Cherish/Windy" were on the other. And while we were doing "Walk On By" on the Steve Allen Show in Hollywood, Sirhan Sirhan killed Bobby Kennedy in Century City. The decade kept getting darker.

June 14, 1969, was one of our toughest days. Ken Errair and three other businessmen were killed in a light plane crash at Bass Lake, California. It was a chartered plane, and I've always thought if Ken had been at the controls they would have made it. He could do anything! His memorial service was at Forest Lawn on June 19th. I still miss him greatly.

Asian Tour

We headed out to Tokyo on July 24th, through Seattle, where we met bandleaders Thad Jones and Mel Lewis, who were returning from Asia. Their Asian tour promoter hadn't paid them and they had to wire home for money to get back. Even though we trusted our promoters we always had four return tickets and half the money on deposit. You get smarter as you get older!

Sue's mother died while I was overseas and Sue and our kids flew back to Indiana. The downside of the entertainment business is not being able to be there when they need you.

Our Asian trip was the first tour on which we used the Standel bass, which is worn like a guitar and amplified through its own amp. We worked US military bases in Japan and flew over Vietnam at 30,000 feet. That's as close as we wanted to get! We were on our way to hot, humid Bangkok and more US military bases.

On August 1st we flew to Manila. The first night we checked into the President Hotel and went to a press party with interviews and photos. They gave us an enthusiastic welcome and a bottle of rum. I returned to my ninth floor room at 2am and was sound asleep when the sliding shutters inside my window began shaking like someone wanted in. Then everything began to sway. Then I heard explosions all over town. It sounded like someone was bombing Manila.

Are You Ready to Rumble?

I could hear a giant rumble a mile or so away, grinding its way toward our hotel. It felt like there was a broomstick under the carpet, rolling along the floor. As it got closer the noise level rose and the shaking increased. The room was totally dark, except when an explosion lit the sky like flashes of lightning. It was an earthquake, of course - a 7.5 doozie, bigger than anything we'd had in California!

That 20-story hotel started doing a hula dance and our ninth floor was where all the action was. The plaster started falling off my walls and ceiling. Sitting on my bed was no place to be, so I groped barefoot to the bathroom door, just as the mirror over the sink smashed on the tile floor. The steel structure of the hotel groaned like a ship at sea.

Where did I leave my clothes? I put my feet in my pants legs - which turned out to be my coat sleeves. I found the rest of my clothes and tried to dress in the dark while the room swayed. Finally the earthquake rolled under us and went on its way. Had we weathered the worst?

Ken Albers' room was right across the hall. Ken can sleep through anything. "By golly, if he slept through that," I thought, "I'm going to wake him. Besides, I'd like to see a friendly face right now." I picked the bottle of rum off the floor, kicked the broken things away from the door and pulled it open.

I knocked, expecting to have to wake him, but the chained door opened a crack and an eye as big as a saucer peered out at me. I extended the bottle toward him and said, "Buddy, have a drink!" I stepped into his room and we stood in the rubble and handed that bottle of warm Philippine rum back and forth a few times, celebrating just being alive.

Suddenly, there was a man running through the hall yelling, "Please come to the lobby. There is a larger earthquake approaching." Emergency lights came on in the halls and stairs so we joined the parade of people in various states of dress going down nine flights of stairs to the lobby. We met Bob, who had arrived a few minutes before the emergency lights came on, using his butane cigarette lighter to guide the way. He had found a dozen Russian tourists pushing the elevator buttons. He'd shouted, "No elevator! Follow me!" He led them down nine floors of rubble-strewn stairs and he didn't even have his shoes on.

There were no emergency lights in the lobby, just lighted candles on tables. The hotel staff was bringing in big stainless steel coffee dispensers and cups. The French tourists gathered around their candle; the Russians were by theirs. We found the "English-speaking candle." It wasn't hard - everybody was talking at once.

I thought we would find Bill Comstock there, but Bill and the tour promoter had gone on to another party. Pretty soon Bill came in. We had been told we could not go back to our rooms, so Bill laid down with a rolled-up carpet for a pillow and was soon sound asleep in the middle of the lobby.

Daylight arrived and the lobby became relatively deserted, except for that well-dressed gentleman sleeping on the floor! We finally got clearance to return to our rooms. Bob hadn't been able to get his door closed when he left his room and he returned to discover his watch and two rings were missing from his nightstand. He reported it, but the only one up there after the quake had been the security man himself. The phones were down so we couldn't wire or call our wives to tell them we were not among the thousands who had been killed.

Back to Work

In the Philippines we sang at Clark Air Force Base and drove to the Subic Bay Navy Base. Then we were driven to the Hilton Hotel where we called our wives.

On August 5th we boarded a beautiful China Airlines jet to Taipei, Taiwan. We worked at the officer's club and then flew on to Okinawa for a bunch of shows at military bases. Later, in Tokyo, we recorded our show in the Palace Hotel. Liberty made an album of it called *The Four Freshmen in Tokyo '68*. It was released in Japan and only a few of them got to the US. If you own one, you really have a collector's item. Most of the tunes had been recorded at one time or another, except "What Now My Love" and "Shadow Of Your Smile."

We flew to Honolulu on August 18th and our wives arrived on the 19th. Geoffrey Comstock, Bill's boy, came too. It was rest and recreation time for all of us in the daytime; at night we worked at the Kauai Surf Hotel.

We flew our first Super DC8 home to Los Angeles and did a *Fifth Freshman* for all the people who had been wondering where the heck we had been. On August 29th the Democrats chose Humphrey and Muskie to run for the White House at the infamous Chicago Convention of '68. We were shocked to learn of the passing of Nick Castle. Private services were held on August 30th. The next day, Czechoslovakia was invaded by Russian tanks. Oh no! Not Prague! We felt it as strongly as if it had been Pittsburgh or Denver.

We began recording *In a Class By Themselves* with Ian Freebairn-Smith on September 4th. He wrote the quartet parts and the instrumental arrangements. What a gentle, musical, wonderful man he was. "Girl Talk," a Ken Albers arrangement, and "Beautiful Friendship" were two of the best.

The Four Freshmen at the beautiful Santa Monica Civic Auditorium in the late 1950s.

With Stan Kenton and June Christy, above, in 1959 with "Road Show." (Capitol Photo Archives)

Below, the MODERN-AIRS were true Freshmen fans in Japan and sang many of our charts. We got to meet them in our dressing room in Tokyo in early 1964.

Ross on drums and singing "Them There Eyes," February, 1962, in Los Angeles. (Bill Miller)

Left, Ross, Ken, Bill Comstock and Bob (Group #4) sometimes teamed up with Sue Raney, like here at the Thunderbird in Las Vegas, February, 1966.

Below, The Freshmen flew two of their fan club presidents to Los Angeles for a few days in the early 1960's. From the left are Babs Pleischl Frederich and Dot Matviya Lydic with Bob, Ken, Bill and Ross. (Capitol Photo Archives)

Above, the great horns of Group #5, Ray Brown, Ken, Bob and Ross in August, 1977, the final public appearance for Ray and me in Indianapolis.

Below left, clockwise from top, Bob Flanigan, Dennis Grillo, Autie Goodman, Ken Albers. Group #6. (1977)

Below right, Rod Henley, Autie, Mike Beisner and Bob made up both Groups #8 and #11.

*Above - Eleven Freshmen and alums up on stage at the Freshmen
Reunion in Oshkosh, Wisconsin in July 1996. Left to right, top, are
Autie Goodman, Mike Beisner, Bill Comstock, Ray Brown and Rod
Henley. Left to right, bottom, are Garry Lee Rosenberg, Bob Ferreira,
Ross Barbour, Kevin Stout, Greg Stegeman and Bob Flanigan.*

This is how the Freshmen looked on their 43rd Anniversary in Las Vegas. The beautiful lady is not a Freshman! The hobo on the right just came for cake.

Below, Greg, Mike, Autie and Garry Lee filled in admirably as Group #15 during Bob's recovery from his heart attack.

Above, the "New Four Freshmen" (Group #18) - Bob Ferreira, Greg, Kevin Stout and Mike surround an unknown hitchiker.

Left, a bunch of songs we did over the years were published as sheet music.

Above, Ross and Bob on stage with the "New Four Freshmen," Green Valley, AZ, February, 1994.

Below, Ross Barbour, Sue Raney and Ken Albers regroup for a fun evening October 4, 1997.

Above, opening night at the Irvine Marriott for the Freshmen (Group #19), November 6, 1994. They are joined by Bob and Ross with Bobby Troup in the middle. Alan MacIntosh is at the right.

Left, the Four Freshmen display at the Vocal Group Hall of Fame in Sharon, Pennsylvania. (William J. Boyd Photography, Pittsburgh.)

Columbus, Indiana, High School Classmates Bill Hoeltke and Ross Barbour stand under the Freshmen sign that welcomes you to town. Greencastle, Indiana, named their bandshell after Bob Flanigan and Hal Kratzsch is remembered in the Warsaw, Indiana, City Park.

*Ross and Sue Barbour -
still in love! - celebrate
their 50th Anniversary,
December 31, 1998.*

*Below, Ross Barbour with the 50th Anniversary Freshmen -
left to right, Greg Stegeman, Kevin Stout, Brian Eichenberger and
Bob Ferreira.*

≡16≡

TWENTY YEARS!

We opened our 20th anniversary week at the Embers
in Indianapolis on September 16, 1968. People came from
all over the country to make September 20th a big deal.
Among the friends, fans and relatives there were Joe
Niedermeier from Pittsburgh, the Dodsons from Ohio,
Kenny Eichelberger from Missouri, Ann Schroeder from
Louisiana, Herb Hughes from Minneapolis and the Runyons
from Illinois. Of course our cousins, the Simpsons, Bob's
mother and sister Maxine and my in-laws all took part. A big
cake said "20th Anniversary." The whole crowd ate it on
closing night.

In October we were eating breakfast at the airport in
Portland, Oregon, and Pat Paulsen walked in. Of course he
was still running for president. When people asked him for
an autograph he would pull out a rubber stamp that said
"Stamped by Pat Paulsen." Kenny Rogers and the First Edi-
tion were there, too, en route to somewhere. Louis
Armstrong was to have done the second show with us in
Laramie but he wasn't there so we did both halves ourselves.

On Halloween we worked at Pacific Lutheran University in Tacoma. We knew it would happen one day: a member
of the faculty came backstage at intermission to see what Bob
had in the spray bottle! The teacher squirted it in his mouth,
discovered it was water, and we were out of trouble.

We were back to recording the *Class By Themselves* album on November 5th. The band included John Gray, Don Randy, Johnny Guerin, Irv Feldman, Buddy Childers, Harry "Sweets" Edison and Tommy Shepherd. The next day Richard Nixon became president-elect.

We went to Boston for a week at Paul's Mall. By now we were using four microphones and a mixer, which provided much better sound. Then we were back on the Mike Douglas Show in Philadelphia. Chet Huntley and Walter Cronkite were the other guests, two very respected men. We lip-synched five tunes.

We replaced Peter Nero on the Peggy Lee Show for one night at the Riviera in Las Vegas on November 30th. The stage manager, a crusty old guy, didn't care if we were good or not. All he wanted was for us to do 35 minutes - no more no less. I figured it out and our segment ended in exactly 35 minutes. He was so impressed!

The Four Fevers

We had often said that the first one-nighter on the moon would be either Louis Armstrong or the Freshmen. We went to the "Moon" in Hamtramck, Michigan, for two weeks from December 2nd to the 14th. We stayed at that snug Dearborn Inn, of course. Harry and Pat Dodson came to see us and we did his arrangement of "This Is All I Ask." He wrote all the love he could put into that bunch of notes.

On December 10th Bob caught the flu, so we took him to the hospital for a shot. We did the show, but Bob was about a half beat behind. He was dizzy and didn't make much sense when he talked. For the second show we got him a bar stool to sit on so he wouldn't fall over. As we were going up to do the third show the boss stopped us. "I can't stand to see him go through another one of those. Just take him home and put him to bed." That's what we did.

He was sweating the next day so we knew he'd make it. That night it was business as usual, but Bob was still shaky. We finished the Moon after a couple more trips to the doctor. On December 15th we did our first 50-minute set at

Las Cruces, New Mexico, and Bob hobbled off at the intermission, saying he couldn't sing any more. The second half was strange; Bill sang solos, I did mine, Leroy did his and we squeaked by. We entertained them though! Of course the rest of us caught Bob's bug, too, and the sickest quartet in music history went home for Christmas.

Annual Reports

We worked 180 days on the road in 1968, and were at home 185 days. We were reaching our goal of having a life with our wives and kids. In the Rose Bowl on New Year's Day, Ohio State's Jim Otis and Rex Kern scored 27 points and USC with O.J. Simpson scored 16.

We flew to Miami on January 8th to work at the Cross Way Inn, and Bob forgot his shirts. We're supposed to be practiced packers, but we still forgot stuff. I had left my electric razor behind on the previous tour.

Three of us flew to Green Bay on the 20th but Ken stayed in Cleveland to get an aching tooth fixed. The next day we got together with our Granada Hills neighbor, Zeke Bratkowski, the backup quarterback for Bart Starr and the Green Bay Packers. He took us to the locker room at Lambeau Field. What a good neighbor! We were in Green Bay to do two shows with Woody Herman at the Bay Theater. John Joseph Albers was four years old January 26th.

We opened at the Club Venice in Baltimore with four new uniform sweaters - one peach, one in tan, a brown one and a green one. Mine was stolen from the dressing room the first night. On Valentine's Day we took off for Mexico City for a week with Peter Nero at the Forum.

In March we flew to Dayton for a week at Suttmiller's Restaurant, a good place for us. But the sounds of the times were changing. For us to sound "current" we needed a bass drum so we could do Beatles songs. I went out to the Rogers Drum Factory the next day and explained that I wanted some sit-down drums, but that they had to be fastened together so we could run on stage with them. They drew some pictures and together we figured out how it could be done.

I chose a red and black 18 inch bass drum and snare drum and the Rogers people made the metal parts I needed to hold it together. The sock cymbal and the snare drum stands were fastened to the left side of the bass drum, and the big cymbal stand and the trombone stand were fastened to the right side. The bass drum beater pedal was pivoted around at a 45 degree angle. I sat behind all this on a tall throne.

During the next few years lots of drummers would come backstage to ask how it worked. I let them all try it. By fastening it all together I eliminated the tripod feet for the sock cymbal, the snare stand and the big cymbal, thereby removing five or six pounds of metal. I even signed a contract that let them advertise "Ross Barbour plays Rogers Drums."

UCLA won its third NCAA Basketball Championship in a row. What a winner John Wooden was. Dwight Eisenhower, a beloved man, died on March 28th.

The Wichita Lineman

On March 31st Bob and I went out to the Omaha airport to meet Glen Campbell's plane. We were going to be working together at the Omaha Civic Center. Glen had played his 12-string guitar on some of our records and we liked him. He had begun his musical career maybe 20 years earlier, on the radio with his family in Delight, Arkansas. He had made a lot of stops along the way, including a short stint filling in for one of the Beach Boys. As we walked to Glen's limousine I asked him, "How does it feel to be an overnight sensation?"

He knew we knew his story so he grinned and said, "Yeah, overnight!" At the time he had solid hit records in "Wichita Lineman" and "By The Time I Get To Phoenix."

We started doing weekends with Glen. During the week he was filming the movie "Norwood" with Joe Namath, and he flew to the one-nighters in his chartered Lear jet. We would work with a different orchestra in each town. Glen opened the show with three or four songs, then he would say "Here they are, my favorite vocal group - the Four Freshmen!" and we would come on and do 40 minutes.

Every night when we'd run off into the wings huffing and puffing, Glen would be there and say, like a Hollywood agent, "Guys, that was really - adequate!" We were a good combination. Fred Dale gets the credit for putting us together.

After rehearsal on April Fool's Day someone stole Bob's trombone (with the Jack Teagarden mouthpiece) and Bill's Standel guitar. Bill borrowed Glen's Ovation guitar and Bob borrowed a trombone so we could do the job. We never recovered the instruments.

The next day, in Wichita, there was a big parade in Glen's honor. The mayor gave him the keys to the city. They also gave Glen a Wichita lineman hat and he got some pole-climbing spurs. We worked the Wichita State University fieldhouse, a big round building. Glen added "Impossible Dream" to his show and dedicated it to President Eisenhower. A special train was taking Ike slowly back to his burial place in Abilene, Kansas and crowds gathered all along the route to wave good-bye. Glen's song brought a lot of tears that night.

In St. Louis the show filled the big Kiel Auditorium. Glen was drawing thousands of people everywhere he appeared, and he did a whale of a show with his banjo, and his six and 12-string guitars, along with all those hit songs.

When we got home on April 4th my new Rogers drums were waiting for me in shipping cartons. Now it was time for me to sit in my garage and learn how to play sitting down, something I had never done before. I'll bet my neighbors got sick and tired of hearing, "Boom-chick Ba Boom."

The Freshmen went out to the Standel factory showroom and tried different guitars and amps and public address systems. I took my new drums along to make the tests authentic. Bill was feeling ragged and the next day his doctor put him in the hospital with pneumonia. We canceled jobs to give Bill time to get well.

We hired Shirley Barron as our secretary. She spent two days a week in our office. We would call her for things and fans would call and write her. It was a lonely job when we were on the road. And when we were home she had four "bosses" who kept her busy.

Freshman For a Night

The doctor ordered Bill not to go back to work until May 15th. We had a job in Oakland on May 9th that had been widely advertised as "Glen Campbell and the Four Freshmen and we couldn't back out gracefully.

Conrad Figueroa, in Albuquerque, could do 20 or 30 minutes of our stuff with no problem. He had sung Bill's part on our arrangements with his group locally and had traveled with the Lettermen as their bass player. We got him to Los Angeles and rehearsed with him on May 7th and 8th. On the 9th we went to Oakland.

Fred Dale was there to see that we did OK and Jim Pike of the Lettermen was there to see that Conrad did OK. Conrad did just fine, bless his heart. The band played the backgrounds so Conrad didn't have to worry about that. We worked on a six foot high stage in the middle of the arena full of 14,000 people. We each had a microphone and we faced various directions so no one in the audience felt left out. That's the only time in our history we ever had a "Freshman for a night."

On May 10th our neighbors Charlie and Ann Snowden and Tom and Rose Sullivan staged a surprise mock wedding for fellow neighbors Don and Marian Yager for their 25th anniversary. We got Don into an old army uniform and the wives dressed Marian in a bridal gown from the Goodwill store. Their original maid of honor couldn't be there so I stood in. I tell you, I'm a devil in a yellow dress, high heeled shoes, a wig and long eyelashes! My foam-filled form was something Flip Wilson's "Geraldine" would envy.

We started work again on May 15th. Bill's pneumonia was gone, but he was still weak. We had been off since April 3rd, except for that one night in Oakland. We worked in St. Joseph, Michigan - my first appearance with the new sit-down drums. We did the next afternoon at Dan Royan's Ford dealership in Columbus, Ohio, and the next at Hunter Air Force Base near Savannah, Georgia. Those three days about wore Bill out!

We were back with Glen Campbell in the Coliseum in Portland before 10,000 people on May 24th. The next night 14,500 people were at the Seattle Coliseum.

Back home we rehearsed "Summer Has Gone," a Bill Comstock original we used in the show for a long time. We also started learning a Dick Reynolds arrangement of "Come Back To Me," a song with a million words. That one took us a while.

On June 5th we flew to meet Glen Campbell at the Chicago Amphitheater. Glen had a nifty way of getting away from the crowd of autograph seekers at the end of his shows. The band would still be playing Glen's closing song and he would walk out and bow and wave, then do it again. Then he'd immediately turn and run through the stage door to his waiting limousine. The band would still be playing and already Glen would be blocks away. By the time the throng got to the dressing room for autographs, Glen was in his hotel room reading *Variety*, the showbiz paper.

Those days, trying to be more sixties-ish, we were wearing a "do your own thing" uniform. Mine was a red shirt with blousy sleeves and black pants to match my new red and black Rogers drums. Bob wore a long sleeved pastel striped velour shirt. Ken and Bill were dressy, with a sportcoat and no tie. None of us matched in style or color. Other groups worked that way, but as time went by we realized Freshmen fans wanted to see us wear matched clothes. "Let the trashy groups do what they want to," they scolded us. "The Freshmen are respectable and should dress alike."

In Cincinnati one day the Modernaires were on the Bob Braun WLW-TV show and we were kept hidden while they sang "Jukebox Saturday Night." When they started into "Blue World," we came out from four different directions and stopped them. It broke up the whole show.

The summer was filled with bookings in Atlanta, Cleveland, Chicago, and New York. On August 30th, 31st, and September 1st. Glen Campbell and the Freshmen did shows at the Indiana State Fair. Bob's mom was brought from the hotel to the stage door in a police car. We thought she would enjoy that but she said, "I hope nobody from Greencastle saw me. They might think I got arrested." It was even funnier than it might seem, because no one would ever have any reason to arrest Aunt Nellie.

Getting Serious With Leroy

On September 10th I spent an afternoon video taping "Leroy" (my little voice) for Dr. Bernd Weinberg, a voice researcher at Indiana University's Medical Center. They were exploring the possibilities of using the Leroy voice (called buccal speech) as an alternate way of speaking, which could be taught to people whose voice box had been surgically removed.

They published quite a study of the Leroy voice in the September, 1971, issue of the *Journal of Speech and Hearing Research.* They used pictures of me making the sound, or I should say Leroy's pictures are in there. When I was a kid, mother used to worry that my doing the sound would make my cheek get all baggy. Now I'm featured in medical journals, listed as "an excellent buccal speaker."

From September 19th to October 9th we worked with the Si Zentner band at the Tropicana in Vegas. Bob and Si, being proud trombone players, delighted in heckling each other during the show. "Hey, you're playing sharp" or "That's too much vibrato." We celebrated our 21st anniversary at the Flamingo, September 20, 1969.

When we got back to Los Angeles we were so eager for the world to hear "It's Not Unusual" and "Meditation" sung our way that we did them on the Della Reese and Joey Bishop TV shows. In late October we were back in Atlanta at the End Zone. One evening the Freshmen and the Modernaires went to eat together at the Abbey, an old church re-done into a fine restaurant. The waiters dressed like monks.

We started two weeks at the Moon in Detroit on December 1st. A customer stuck out his hand to shake mine and in it was a marijuana cigarette. I thanked him and assured him as I gave it back, "We're not into that." As far as I know none of the Freshmen ever got involved with drugs of any kind, thank heaven.

One afternoon I was to represent the Freshmen on a radio show aired from a small restaurant in downtown Detroit. When I got there, Rich Little, the incredibly gifted impressionist, was waiting for the DJ, too. We were early and the DJ was late so we had a chance to get to know each other.

That year we worked 189 days on the road and 176 days were spent at home. Pistol Pete Maravich was setting all kinds of basketball scoring records at Louisiana State University.

A New Decade

We bought new uniforms for 1970 - navy blue blazers and red and navy plaid pants. We kept the pants for at least two years.

Bob's father, Lee, died on January 14th. We were working in St. Louis so I was able to bring my mother and father to Uncle Lee's funeral in Greencastle. Bob and Mary stayed a few days with Aunt Nellie, and on the 21st we opened at the Washington Plaza Hotel in Seattle. There we began rehearsals on a solo for me - "The Hong Kong Blues."

In February we flew to Tokyo and sang at military clubs and Japanese theaters. One evening the Nagashima brothers, Tats and Hideo, took us home to meet their father.

He was on the board of directors of the Mitsubishi Bank. We felt honored that the brothers thought that much of us. I don't think they did that with other entertainers.

My Leroy voice delighted the Japanese audiences. They love miniature things and Leroy was our miniature thing.

Next we flew on to Manila and worked at Clark Air Force Base. Then it was on to Hong Kong where we worked in a club called the Go Down. Radio Hong Kong broadcast the show.

In Bangkok we worked the Cafe De Paris. It's a small world. Before flying out, I had a minute in the airport gift shop. A lady nudged me and asked, "George, what do you th - Oh! You're not George!"

Her pronunciation was a dead giveaway. I asked her, "What part of Indiana are you from?"

"Bloomington," she said. That's 40 miles from my hometown.

When we got to Taipei we worked a club with Bill Risley, the hypnotist. His closer was to hypnotize a cobra, then kiss it on top of the head. What a scary show! He told us he planned to go to the Himalayas, hypnotize an Abominable Snowman and bring him back alive!

On March 4th we flew to Okinawa to do three shows a night in three different military bases. Whew! UCLA won the NCAA Basketball Tournament for the fourth time in a row. Someone said, "NCAA stood for 'No chance against Alcindor!'" John Wayne finally got an Oscar and "Raindrops Keep Fallin' On My Head" was the song the Academy chose. Leroy started doing "Raindrops" that very night!

We got down to Monroe, Louisiana, to do a concert on campus. Can we knock them out in a college? Does a cat have a climbing gear? After the show the people from Bogalusa, the Knights, Kains and Mitchells, had us come to their motel room. They had a tub full of crawfish cooked in red pepper. Mmmm! That's almost heaven.

Scott Flanigan was born on May 16, 1970. Bob and Mary had Jennifer, Jill, Julie and now Scott! On May 21st we went out in the countryside east of Los Angeles to have our pictures taken. One of those shots was used on the cover of the *Return To Romance* album.

Vocal Majority

The last week in May was fun at the Losers Club in Dallas. We got with the Vocal Majority conductor Jim Clancy. I'm bragging when I say he's a friend and a Freshmen fan. Clancy said, "Hey, let's sing, 'It Never Occurred To Me.'"

We said, "It's been years. We've forgotten it."

Clancy said, "It's OK. I can give you your parts!" Jim sings a fifth below anyone else in the world, but he can shift into falsetto and do Bob's part or any of the others. He is such a respectable man!

It was on to Denver to the Radisson Hotel, where two members of the Who, Keith Moon and John Entwistle, came to see us. We sat with them and enjoyed their British accents.

On June 11th we met Bob Ashton, who changed things for the Freshmen. It was through Bob we got the *Return To Romance* album recorded. We started planning the album that very night. We flew home from Denver with autographed pictures of the Who for our kids.

Back in Los Angeles we began rehearsals on "What Are You Doing The Rest Of Your Life?" What a song! It has one of the two or three greatest bridges of all time. In early October Capitol released a three-record LP boxed album titled *Stan Kenton, June Christy, Four Freshmen*. Our week at the Pfister Hotel in Milwaukee was a busy one. We dropped down to Chicago and recorded a commercial for John Deere lawn tractors. I phoned Hal Kratzsch, who was in a hospital in Chicago. Cancer was taking him slowly, but he still had hope. On Sunday afternoon Zeke Bratkowski gave us tickets to the Packers game at Milwaukee County Stadium. We put on all the clothes we had in our suitcases - two or three of everything. We watched the Packers and the Eagles in our earmuffs, mittens and scarves, but we still almost froze to death.

On October 27th I went to Chicago to see Hal. Betty met me in the hospital lobby and took me to his room. She is still so very pretty, and she's one of the most durable people I've ever known. Hal was taking a new medicine and expecting to be the man who conquered cancer. The 22 years Hal and I had known each other gave us lots to talk and laugh about. We didn't cry much, but we did some. It's okay to cry with your friend when he's dying. And it's okay to cry like I am now as I write about it.

In Los Angeles on November 12th we met with Dick Reynolds and Lee Gillette. Lee had been our recording supervisor at Capitol in the mid-50s, and he knew how things were supposed to sound in the recording booth. He was a take charge guy and was going to supervise *Return to Romance*. Dick, our arranger since the 50s, was to write the backgrounds for the album, so we were in good hands.

Back to Britain

It was bitter cold two days later when we landed in London. On the 18th we did a show in a theater in Hull. We did the first half of the evening and Buddy Rich and the band did the second half. Buddy's band was sounding great, breathing fire and really romping. Our equipment was set up on the little apron of a stage in front of Buddy's higher stage. During his show he left his drums and sat down at mine to talk with people. My drums were like toys compared to his. He pecked on my cymbals and made a snide remark, pecked on my snare drum and made another crack.

The audience didn't take kindly to Buddy's bad-mouthing the Freshmen drums. We had just pleased them for an hour. Leave it to the British to make sense of a bad situation. A man in the audience stood up and yelled, "I say, Buddy! Why don't you shut your bloody mouth and play your drums?" Now he was angry at the audience! But he went back to his drums and played astounding things for the remainder of the show.

That night, Wednesday, November 18, 1970, both Hal Kratzsch, the founder of the Four Freshmen, and Hal Dickinson, founder of the Modernaires, passed away, victims of cancer. Two days later, I went wandering around town as I did so often. This time I went inside a grand old church, built in the time of knights in armor. It was 40 degrees outside and almost 30 degrees inside. I was thinking of the letters I had to write to Betty Kratzsch and Paula Kelly. It's never easy, is it?

Return to Romance

We did the Lesley Crowther TV show in London. Harry Robinowitz flawlessly conducted the orchestra behind us. He knew when things should slow down, when the tempo should stop. The sensitivity of that master conductor astounded us. Harry Robinowitz, wherever you are, we are fans of yours.

We flew to Madrid on the 26th of November and worked the US air base at Terhune. We were all sick. In the officer's club we asked if there was a doctor there who could stop Montezuma's Revenge. Into the dressing room came a doctor who gave us some little pills. "This is Lomotil," he said. "Each of you take one. That's usually all it takes." That's all it took. We made it a point to have those little rascals with us from then on.

The first air base we visited in Germany was Ramstein, and Bill's guitar wouldn't work so we borrowed a guitar from the house band. Lo and behold, it was the Standel guitar that had been stolen from our dressing room in Kansas City on the Glen Campbell tour! After the show we thanked the guitar player and asked how he happened to have that guitar. He said he'd bought it from a man who bought it from a man who...

In Los Angeles, on December 15th, we recorded some of the backgrounds for *Return To Romance*. Ditto the next day, and the next. This was all done at the Devonshire Studios in Hollywood. Bill Comstock owned a share of that nice place and he felt right at home. We began recording the voices for the LP on December 22nd. They came easily because we knew the arrangements so well.

The "Dinner of Champions" honoring the Rose Bowl players, their parents, and fans was held at the Hollywood Palladium. Woody Hayes and the Ohio State team were there to be entertained and honored. The star-studded show had Pete Barbuti as the master of ceremonies. When it came our turn he was in front of the curtain and we were set up behind it. Pete was still doing his bit when a stagehand opened the curtain, and Pete had to walk to the side of the stage and have him close it again. Yes, that was us with egg on our faces during the mistake.

When Pete finished he said, "Here they are, the Four Freshmen," and the curtain opened again. We had checked out the sound in the afternoon and we could hear ourselves just fine. But in the meantime someone had turned something off and we couldn't hear ourselves sing at all. We moved the whole group forward during the tunes in hopes that would help.

Our plan was to do four songs, and the curtain man knew that. But he closed it after "Blue World" and we still had "Day By Day" to do. The curtain closed during our bow and it dragged over the drums and messed up my hair as I fought to rescue the microphones. Being entangled in a motorized velvet curtain is like wrestling with a walrus. We must have looked pretty silly, but we had been through worse. No one ever admitted pulling the curtain. Oh well, as Ken Albers used to say, "That's showbiz - one big anticlimax after another." Though we weren't paid to do the show, we were given Rose Parade tickets and seats at the Rose Bowl game. That's like receiving gold!!

On December 31st, my 42nd birthday, we added trombones to *Return to Romance*. We finished the album on January 5, 1971.

17

WHO'S ON SECOND?

Music continued its sixties shift into the seventies. Most new and successful vocal and instrumental groups were rock which, at first, would seem to make what we were doing passé. But not really. We felt we were unique.

The Grammy Awards in 1971 were given to "Bridge Over Troubled Water," by Simon and Garfunkel, "I'll Never Fall In Love Again," recorded by Dionne Warwick, "Everything Is Beautiful" by Ray Stevens and the Best New Artist award went to the Carpenters, all quite mainstream stuff. George C. Scott, by the way, won an Oscar for his portrayal of "Patton" and Helen Hayes got one for "Airport."

A Good Year

We tried to be open to the changes. In April we worked for Joel Rothman for the first time, the start of a good and long relationship. He opened new hotels for Marriott and he brought us into his various locations so we would draw the local people. Then, when the boss or Aunt Tillie came to town, the local residents were more likely to guest them at the Marriott.

It was back to Hawaii for us in May and we used Don Ho's dressing room at the New Reef for three nights. We followed Ray Charles and we learned something: he does such an incredible show there's little left for anyone else to do!

We came back to the Century Plaza Hotel in June and 55 of our neighbors came in to hear their neighbors - Ross, Bob, Ken and Bill - do their stuff. Near the front door of the lounge there was a big oriental gong, a five foot brass circle that made a wonderful sound. We had it all planned with Al DeChristopher, the manager, that when we did "Byrd Avenue" and came to the place where we sang "Northwest Orient"...bong! - he would do the "bong" on the gong. The crowd liked it, and I think we and Al liked it even better.

On the Fourth of July we worked outdoors in Veteran's Stadium in Long Beach. Emmett Kelly, the "Little Hobo" and best known clown in the world, was there to entertain the kids. Jack Benny was the emcee and the star of the evening. I have a tape recording of Jack introducing the Four Freshmen to the crowd.

One afternoon, while we were back in Chicago, we went to a gymnasium on 63rd Street and had our pictures taken with Muhammad Ali, who was training to fight Jimmy Ellis. The fight was in Houston on July 26th and we flew there to perform before the main event. We lip-synched "Day By Day" and Ray Stevens synched "Everything Is Beautiful."

In August we began a tour in Pittsburgh. I laid my clothes bag on top of the car as we loaded the heavy equipment at the airport and I left it up there as we drove away. Of course it blew off and was lost. All my uniforms were in there and, if I don't have uniforms, the Freshmen don't have uniforms. We did the whole tour in mismatched clothes.

The first job was outdoors at Oglebay Park in nearby Wheeling, West Virginia. There must have been 2,000 people there and we sang like we barely knew each other. That's what happens when a group has time off. John Wooden, UCLA's basketball coach, had a saying: "Practice doesn't make perfect. Perfect practice makes perfect."

Ken Albers' dad and mom came to see him at Brandi's Wharf in Philadelphia. On Long Island we had

another surprise. We stopped at a diner and there was Stan
Kenton, with band members Willie Maiden and Dick
Shearer, Eric the bus driver and Frank DiOrio. The band and
the Freshmen worked together that night with Chris Connor
at the Long Island Arena. We slept an hour and a half that
night and got up at 4:15am to do the Today Show with Hugh
Downs and Joe Garagiola at Rockefeller Center in New York
City.

We flew back to Los Angeles all set to buy new uniforms, and found a letter in our office from Alan Hewlett.
He had found my clothes bag! I called him and promised
him and his wife a night on us when we got back to Pittsburgh.

On August 30th we took those uniforms and went to
Atlanta to work at the Hyatt Regency Hotel, the most spectacular hotel we had ever seen. It was maybe 20 stories tall.
All the rooms faced the outside and the center of the hotel
was hollow all the way up to the roof. When you walk into the
lobby there is nothing over your head for 20 stories. The
bellmen call the area inside the entrance "the profanity
corner." People walk in and look up there and utter a profanity. It was just astounding.

Business was good in their Atlantis Room. Bob had
Mary join him for a few days and they took the bridal suite.
Sigh! Sue came for the final two days, and on the 19th we
drove to Jacksonville, Florida, in two cars. David Bentley was
driving one of the cars and it ran out of gas - in a filling
station! How's that for good luck? We celebrated the 23rd
anniversary of the Freshmen in Jacksonville.

Choosing the songs for the show was a real challenge
because we wanted to include all the different ways we could
perform and feature each Freshman and each kind of arrangement. We featured each horn with a solo and Bill and
Leroy with vocal solos. During the solos the other singers
could rest their voices. We did fast, medium, slow, rock and
Latin tempos. We never did get any one arrangement, by the

way, that could show off all the facets of the Freshmen. That's what we had sought to use on TV shows where we could only do one or two tunes.

Between shows we had a chance to get involved with the fans on a personal basis. I would announce that we would be set up at a table in the rear and I'd say, "We'll sell you a record. But if you don't want a record, come by anyhow and we'll give you a picture or an autograph." Then Bob would add, "I'll give you a hug!"

We invented what we called "Tele-Fan" - billfold-sized pictures of the Freshmen, with a phone number on the back to call for information on future bookings. Those little cards did us a lot of good. People would call, hear our itinerary and plan their business trips or vacations around our jobs.

Orchestra Pit

We were in Jacksonville for ten days in the fall of 1971 and Frankie Laine came in to sing with us. Frankie could sing for an hour and never do anything but his million-seller records. One night Frankie did the neatest thing. There was a heckler mouthing off in front of the stage. So Frankie said, "Mr. Spotlight Man, hit him with your light." The spotlight man put the spot on the heckler. Frankie said, "No. Don't hit him with the spot, hit him with the light!" That was the last we heard from the heckler.

We flew home October 3rd and did what we always did. Played with the kids, fixed the door latch or the washing machine, got the cars serviced, romanced our brides a little, and generally enjoyed life off the road.

On October 23rd we did a show with Henry Mancini in a nice little theater in Kalamazoo, Michigan. Mancini and the big orchestra were on the stage. We were set up on the hydraulic orchestra pit; you'd push a button and it would come up to stage level. That way we didn't have to carry the equipment and mikes on stage to do our thing. Everything worked right at rehearsal, like it always does.

After he had done ten or 15 minutes Henry announced us. We started playing down there, and pushed the button, but the stage didn't come up! We finished the first song not having moved an inch. We were still bumbling around, trying to find the trouble. People in the front row were looking over the railing at the top of our heads. Henry was at the front edge of the stage holding his baton and smiling down at us. Finally, we started up and the show continued, Freshmen style.

We opened at the Frigate in Harrisburg, Pennsylvania, in late October. That's where we met Jorgen and Betty Bjorno. They flew in from Denmark, planning to meet and get to know us during the week. They had heard us at Tivoli Gardens in Copenhagen a couple of years before. Those days began a friendship that promises to last a lifetime.

Some weeks later we opened in Evansville at the Executive Inn. That job spoiled us. They had a good restaurant-lounge; the controls for the stage lights were on a stand right beside me. I felt drunk with power. Another plus: we lived right upstairs.

During the week I went out to the high school and spoke to Brad Chaffin's music class. He had been Sue's music director at Columbus High School. I told his students that there is a life after high school; some of it is to be found on the road in the entertainment business, and you can make a lot of people happy as you earn a living.

On December 31st I celebrated my 43 years by driving to Stockton to do New Year's Eve with the Freshmen at the Gaslight Lounge. As 1972 began the war in Vietnam was still going on and our two sons were signed up with the draft board. Thank God we never had to face that. Back in Los Angeles, we were busy rehearsing for the Kenton album, *Live at Butler* and learning "She'll Be Comin' Round The Mountain."

In the middle of the month we flew to Florida, ending up at Ft. Walton Beach. At Bacon's-By-The-Sea the boss had asked Ray Brown to name a group who would bring in some new business. Ray said, "If you want the best, get the Freshmen." We alternated with a group Ray was in and we each did three shows. We ended up in a jam session after both groups were through for the night. Bacon's was full all three nights. I wish we had taped the whole weekend.

That Sunday Dallas beat Miami in the Super Bowl and there was no jam session after work because we had to start for Columbus, Ohio, early Monday morning. Ray drove us to Pensacola to catch the plane. We especially liked him - heck, everybody liked Ray. Once in Columbus we drove to the Blue Dolphin in Mansfield, to work three nights. Boy, they had good business there.

UCLA won its sixth NCAA Basketball Championship in a row, this time with Bill Walton at center. And the Lakers won their division with the winningest team in history. In Granada Hills, all of us neighbors got together for an "End of the Draft Party." The government stopped drafting potential servicemen, which meant none of our sons would have to go!

We opened a week at the Rainbow Grill, high atop the Rockefeller Center, on April 3rd. One morning we put our uniform suits on and went to the musician's union headquarters, where the president, Hal Davis, awarded us honorary life memberships in the Ashland, Kentucky, musician's union.

We were still busy rehearsing tunes for the *Live at Butler* album with the Kenton band, including "Please Walk Softly," a Willie Maiden arrangement. What a song!

Out of Range

It is always possible that a vocal group will have voice trouble, especially when a stretch of evening shows follow rehearsals every afternoon. It seemed we were having constant voice trouble in early 1972. Bill Comstock's second part was killing him. A few months before we had fixed it so Ken Albers sang the second part on some of the slow ballads.

That way Bill could sing the fourth part once in a while and rest, but this was now hurting Ken's voice. What to do?

My mother had a stroke on May 12th and I felt so far away in California. Our schedule was set and I would have to postpone seeing her. Daddy was 79 and he was not able to get around very well. No matter what job a man has, he has to pay the price once in a while.

On May 13th we were back in Clearwater, Florida, for a week at the Fort Harrison Hotel. Somehow, the 15th was a night off and I went out to the home of my favorite cousin, Joyce Baughman, for a home cooked meal. We turned on the TV news and saw that George Wallace had been shot in Maryland. The whole world was thinking, "Can't we keep anyone from being shot?"

"Please Walk Softly" was performed for the first time at the Frog and Nightgown in Raleigh. We were really just unable to sing. We realized it was not fair to put so much strain on Bill singing the second part. It was very hard on him. No one wants to replace a voice in any quartet. It hurts the member who must leave the most, but it also means stress and worry for the other three. And replacing a Freshman means taking time off to rehearse and that meant no income and endless additional hours of work to endure. It would hurt Bill's fans to see him go and it wouldn't help our image because change suggests instability. All in all it's an agonizing decision to have to make.

Bill went to the hospital for tests. He was spitting blood. But we still kept on - Twin Falls, Idaho, then Portland.

Live at Butler

After a couple days rest in Los Angeles, we flew to Indianapolis on June 20th in time for Mayor (now U.S. Senator) Richard Lugar to present the keys to the city to us and Stan Kenton. The mayor said a lot of kind and flowery things about Stan and the Freshmen. The press was on hand, and there must have been a hundred people in this big room on top of one of the city's tallest buildings.

Stan hated pomp so he proceeded to make a great, bombastic farce of a speech. He started off by saying, "Yes, to know me is to love me." I should have taped it. We were all in stitches before he was through, and I know he just made it up on the spur of the moment. It was great publicity for our coming concert at Butler. We all made the front page of the *Indianapolis Star.*

Sue and I and our daughter Kathy, then 14, rode back to the hotel with Stan and he very graciously gave Kathy his key to the city. That afternoon we sang with the band and rehearsed the things we were to do together. Bill Comstock was holding his own.

That evening we went to pick up the instruments we had air-freighted to town, but my drums had been lost. Oh no, not that! The next day Stan and the Freshmen did radio and TV appearances all over town, for which I had to rent drums. We did the first night at Butler with those rented drums. The next day we had the final rehearsal with the Kenton band and my drums arrived! We did better that night and I imagine most of our songs that got on the *Live At Butler* album were recorded that second night.

That night, after Stan's big closing theme, he said to the audience in Clowes Hall, "This is the end of the concert. But we have to record some of these things again. You may stay and listen if you like." Some people stayed and we and the band recorded on into the night.

The bus pulled out and the Freshmen went their separate ways. Sue and I went to my 25th high school graduation reunion in Columbus. All those kids were now grown-ups, but to me they were still just kids, and I loved them all again.

When we opened at the Losers Club in Dallas in July our performance fit the name of the club. Time off was necessary but it did bad things to our sound. Bill was really straining. We knew we what we had to do. On July 12th I called Ray Brown and asked if he would be a Freshman. He was so shocked and surprised he couldn't catch his breath. But he said he would love to. I told him we had to make a lot of plans about when it would happen. Now that we knew he would do it, we could go ahead and make those plans.

Ray called me the next day and asked, "Did you really call me to join the group or did I just imagine it?" It was the fulfillment of his dream. We knew he had the love of the sound, and that's the first requirement.

That day, July 13th, Bob and I went to the rehearsal of Jim Clancy's Vocal Majority, the 100-voice barbershop chorus in Dallas. Partly it was a social call and partly we wanted to see for ourselves how Clancy made his miracles happen. They are the best. After the rehearsal, they wanted us to sing to them, but it was just Bob and me. Well, Jim knew all the parts and so did his friend Frank Bloebaum. So we made up a quartet right there and did "Blue World" for them.

Ken, Bob and I were in a quandary. We wanted to be as open as we could be about Bill's being replaced. And we wanted to be fair with Bill. What we had to do was to get a guy who could sing that part and be happy doing it. We all liked Ray Brown, but what if he realized after a week of rehearsals that he couldn't sing that second part? It might mean months of instability for all of us, during which our unity would be shot to pieces.

I sent Ray an arrangement of "Please Walk Softly." If he was going to start learning the second part he might just as well start with a hard one. On July 24th Ken told Bill we would let him off the hook. He and we knew it was just a matter of time; and, maybe this way, he could leave with some voice left. It would be February, 1973, before Ray would come with us, but setting the plans happily took some of the pressure off Bill.

The rest of the summer and fall was spent filling appearances all across the country. Ken was busy copying arrangements to send to Ray. I was making up the Four Freshmen Christmas gift list - the list of people to whom we send out promotional records. Bill was working closely with Fred Dale about future bookings, and Bob worked on our airline tickets, rental cars and hotel reservations. It was a partnership and everybody worked in his free time. We got together with Bill on a number of occasions to make plans. He would finish with us on or about February 28th.

On December 11th we received some boxes of *Live At Butler* albums at the Freshmen office in Los Angeles. Shirley, Bob Flanigan and I must have sent 200 of those out to disc jockeys and friends who had ordered them.

We were back at the Dinner of Champions show at the Palladium just before the Rose Bowl and a man from the Century Plaza Westside Room tapped me on the shoulder. "The Mills Brothers are unable to appear here tonight. We want you to fill in for them." So we saved the day.

Bob told the audience, "It's only fitting that the world's oldest quartet would be replaced by the world's second oldest quartet!"

At home, we celebrated New Year's Eve together and sang "Auld Lang Syne" again. I reminisced that Bill Comstock had been a Freshmen for over 12 years, Ken for 16 and a half years, and Bob and I for more than 24. Those four guys stayed together longer than any other group of Freshmen, and we really put on a lot of miles.

18

ANOTHER NEW ERA

Marvin Pruitt, the man who sang lead with our college barbershop quartet (Don, Ross, Hal and Marvin) before we became the Four Freshmen, came to hear us in Valparaiso, Indiana early in 1973. Marvin had developed a brain tumor, and died shortly after that. We worked Pittsburgh and Harrisburg in sub-zero cold, then flew home February 4th.

Thanks Bill, Welcome Ray!

This was Bill Comstock's final road trip with the Four Freshmen. Our first personnel change in 12 and a half years was coming up. Thanks, Bill, for that one-eighth of a century!

On February 12, 1973, Ray Brown flew to Los Angeles, to begin what turned out to be a new era for the Four Freshmen. Rehearsals came first, which we did in both the afternoons and evenings. We also had to buy new uniforms, get pictures taken, write updated publicity and send out 6,000 *Fifth Freshman* newsletters. Ray also had to learn to play that Farfisa electric piano, Freshmen style.

Our initial test came on February 2nd. We moved our instruments onto the stage at Torches West, on Ventura Boulevard in Los Angeles a day ahead of time so we could rehearse right where we would work. Those two nights at Torches West went quite well. Some of the time Bill was in the group, some of the time it was Ray.

February 25th was our last rehearsal with Ray before we hit the road, and we were about sung out. Six or eight hours of singing every day will do that to you. We shared a light-hearted feeling that lasted as long as Ray was with us. People liked Ray. We liked Ray.

Sure, we lost a little every time a Freshman left, but we gained a little, too. Now, the job for us was to find ways for the new man to stand out. We opened at the Cross Creek, halfway between Erie and Pittsburgh. We were out in the country and free to make our mistakes.

We all fumbled a little in the first show. I guess we were expecting Ray to forget what to do. He didn't. Stan Kenton was in Columbus, Ohio, and called Ray after the first show. Stan welcomed him to the Freshmen and said something like, "If you're all right with them, you're all right with me!" Ray came off that call really pumped and sang, "It's Just A Matter Of Time." He broke the place up! Freshmen fan Ted Driscol brought us a marching trombone to play that night.

The always patient Ken Albers was such a help to Ray with the keyboard chords. The Farfisa electric piano was waist high, but it wasn't high enough to be easy for Ray to play. We bought four 3/8 inch threaded rods and drilled holes in the piano feet so the rods worked like stilts. Ah! There it is!

Our Standel sound system developed an awful buzz in it one night. I asked, "Why is our amp humming?" Ray answered, "Because it doesn't know the words." Now, who can fault a man like that?

One of the most emotional nights of our career was on March 14th when we met a man in Chicago who had been a prisoner of war for over six years. He told us he had clung to his sanity by remembering Freshmen arrangements and singing the harmonies to himself. He told me, "The first thing I wanted to do when I got back to the States was to go hear those Freshmen songs in four parts!" When I told the audience that story and we dedicated "Blue World" to him, I got tears all over myself. Wherever you are, friend, you're my kind of guy!

Longhairs

For March, 1973, my diary says, "I'm letting my hair grow on the sides. It almost covers my ears." At that time everybody but Ken Albers was growing long hair, including Ray and Bob. It made me feel silly, but that's the way the world was going.

By the middle of May the news people were preoccupied with the Watergate scandal and the stock market had taken a big dive. We filled in for Fats Domino at the Flamingo in Las Vegas. On May 25th we were in Indianapolis at the Hilton. I drove down to Columbus and helped my parents celebrate their 50th anniversary a week early.

The Freshmen were the evening's entertainment at the Robert Mondavi Wine Festival in July in northern California. A sprawling lawn of rich green grass filled the area inside the bend of the L-shaped winery. From the stage we could see maybe a mile of well-tended vineyards on the side of the valley stretching toward the ridge in the distance. The sun dropped lower and lower, shining back on us across this heavenly scene. I thought we were going to lose Ray Brown - he wanted to stay right there in Napa Valley.

In Des Moines, in August, we went to see a new group called Chicago. The Pointer Sisters were on first. The young people in the audience had the air in that fieldhouse so full of marijuana smoke I thought the exhaust fans would get high and fly away!

Happy 25th!

September 20, 1973, was our 25th anniversary and the first of nine nights at the Frog and Nightgown in Raleigh. Fans from across the country came and brought gifts and partied with us. We were given the keys to the city and we did a major interview that was released through Associated Press. I had an awful cough the night ABC-TV chose to film our anniversary.

When we got to Pittsburgh in October Ray announced he had married Nancy Jo Garrett. Congratulations! We did a great big show with the local quartets at Hinds Hall, then flew to New York to catch Pan Am Flight 100 to London. First we bounced all over Germany doing US military bases, then we flew back to Manchester, England.

Arthur, a quiet little round man with round glasses, drove our short, fat, pudgy white bus. We named it the Elephant Bus. Night after night he took us to a series of working man's clubs. These audiences had no great interest in modern vocal groups. They were seldom surly, just disinterested. One night the club officer announced, "All right, quiet down. We have a Four Freshmen show for you. Hey, look! The sooner we get the show over with, the sooner we can get to bingo!" When we finished, the officer called us back on stage for a bow, but the applause had already stopped. You really feel silly bowing to no applause! Afterwards, in the dressing room, Ken Albers said, "Well, we didn't bother them, and they didn't bother us!"

The next week we drove to the Boburn Hotel near Durham (they pronounce it "Dudam") and were there a week. It was out in the country, a quaint place with maybe 25 or 30 rooms.

We kidded Arthur constantly as we traveled. He was such a good sport. We would pull out of the hotel, turn right, and Bob would say, "He's really lost this time." Later, Ray would add "He's never been this lost before." A few minutes later Ken would speak up, "Oh, we're so lost!" Arthur would just peer over his glasses and chuckle.

One night, on an especially long jaunt between jobs, we repeated that "he's lost" thing with numerous variations.

This time, Arthur didn't say anything. Finally, he rounded a turn, stopped, got out, made a grand hand and arm gesture and a great bow toward our destination and said "Ta da!" We all collapsed with laughter at this uncharacteristic display.

November 22nd was Thanksgiving Day, but that didn't mean anything in England. Bob, Ken and I ate fish together. When Arthur deposited us and our luggage at London Heathrow we proclaimed him "King Arthur." We had made a crown of cardboard covered with aluminum foil, and we had a coronation right there beside his Elephant Bus. I'll bet he hasn't forgotten the Freshmen!

On December 10th we celebrated Ken's birthday by flying to Seattle and setting up our stuff at the Trojan Horse. This time I left all my uniforms at home. We wore un-matched clothes the first night, and Sue sent the uniforms super fast. We were rehearsing "Rainy Day." What better place to do that than in Seattle? On December 20th singer Bobby Darin died unexpectedly of a heart attack after surgery.

Sue and I went out to eat on December 30th, the eve of our 25th wedding anniversary, and came home to a surprise houseful of neighbors and friends. They chose that night because the Freshmen were booked in El Paso on New Year's Eve.

Watergate to Waterloo

In 1974 the Watergate scandal was getting all over Richard Nixon. The energy crunch was upon us so we used no electric Christmas decorations. Vietnam was over, just the sorrow remained.

We flew from El Paso to Denver while USC lost the Rose Bowl game to Ohio State 42 to 41. It was eight degrees in Denver, where we worked at the Warehouse. The next day Ray and I bought some long undies. Now we were ready for eight degree weather! On January 5th the country went on daylight saving time to save energy.

Back at Capitol Studios in Los Angeles we recorded "There Will Never Be Another You," "After You" and "Girl Talk" with the US Air Force Airmen of Note. Two nights later the roads in Connecticut were glare ice on top of snow. We were a half an hour late to Woodbury, where we took the place of the New Christy Minstrels.

On January 21st we were so proud. Our Kathy was named co-captain of the 100-girl slick drill team from Kennedy High! You have never seen so many tears of joy come from a 16 year old!

We stayed in the University Club in New York from January 24 - 26 and worked the Lincoln Center with Johnny Mathis. That's a great room to sing in and a great way to be seen. Johnny had a big orchestra and did the numbers the people hoped to hear. In February it was on to the St. Regis Hotel in New York and the Maisonette Room.

Ray's first anniversary as a Freshman was on March 3rd and we celebrated by working the Old San Francisco Steak House in Houston. From there we did a two week tour through the South. When we got home Sue and I went to the Odyssey Restaurant to see our sons work. They were in the lounge there for eight months, billed as the Barbour Boys, what else! They did Beatle songs and other pop stuff real well.

We were offered a job in Bermuda for late May, but that's just when Ray and Nancy were expecting their first baby, so we told the agent no. That was the way we operated from the start. Each member had veto power. We always decided things together because we were a partnership. Each member had the right to say no, and that's as far as the discussion went. The veto prevents a lot of problems in any group. It shouldn't be used often but it should be there when it's really needed.

On April 3rd I was home in Indiana, helping my folks get some things done when a tornado struck the area. It missed the Barbour house but it utterly destroyed the old brick house where Bob's and my mom had lived when they were kids. The foot thick walls, which had stood for 100 years, were turned into a pile of bricks.

On April 8th Ray's doctor told him he had hepatitis, probably from bad seafood, and that he should rest until May 5th. The energy crunch had people buying gas on even or odd numbered days, depending on the last number on their license plate. We were really itching to get back to work and on May 5th we opened at Young Auditorium in South Bend, Indiana. We sounded better than I feared we would. We were glad to hear us again! Then it was Grand Rapids, Kalamazoo, Elkhart, Boston, Pittsburgh, and El Paso. The Celtics beat Milwaukee for the NBA Championship, and on May 23, 1974, Travis K. Brown was born.

Joe Del, a neighbor of ours in Los Angeles, owned Fortin Industries and was in New York on business. He came to see us at the Playboy Club and watched me hand out pictures and autographs. "Someday when you get through making friends for the Freshmen," he told me, "I'd like you to come make friends for me."

The afternoon of August 1st we sang at the Hershey Park Ballroom in Hershey, Pennsylvania. There was a roof over the stage, but the crowd was on semi-circular concrete seats in the open air. A sudden downpour caught everyone unprepared. The audience had no place to go for shelter except the stage. There wasn't any reason to stop the show so we kept on singing, with people jammed around us, behind us - everywhere! Al Alberts of the Four Aces was the master of ceremonies. I'll bet he and the crowd never forgot that day.

On August 9th Watergate became Waterloo. Richard Nixon resigned the presidency and Gerald Ford took office. After all that I was sure the USA could last through anything.

On September 10th we spent 19 and a half hours flying to Sydney, Australia. It was our first crossing of the equator and our first visit to Australia. That trip featured the "nose duet." Ray and Bob played "La Cumparsita" on the piano with their noses. I always announced it as though it was to be a serious duet, and those two good buddies approached it as though it were. But when they started playing the notes with their noses, the people went wild. We got laughs with that for three years.

We flew to New Zealand next. Our driver, Natalie, who was maybe 16 or 17 years old, took us to a town called Rotorua. The crust of the earth is so thin there that steam comes up through the cracks in the sidewalk. People heat their houses by driving a U-shaped pipe into the ground and pumping water through the pipe. Because of the steam the town is often used as a location for filming outer space movies.

We landed in Tahiti on our way back home and Hugh Downs got on the plane. We had met him in Hawaii years before and it was good talking to him again.

Stump the Band

In December our friends Steve and Becky Labadini were visiting Los Angeles from Boston and wanted to see the Johnny Carson show. I located tickets and we got in line at the NBC studio in Burbank. A young man who worked for the show went along our row and asked, "Does anyone have a tune that will stump the band?" Steve and I were kidding around and he grabbed my hand and held it up. The young man was on me in an instant, getting my name and the song title.

There's an unwritten rule that says, as an entertainer, you shouldn't get on television shows in this manner. The staff wants Joe Nebraska and Pauline Pennsylvania, not Ross Barbour. Right then I should have said no. But stumping the band would mean we would get good seats down front for Steve and Becky and, heck, Johnny probably won't even call on me. They might not even get to the "Stump the Band" segment anyway.

Guests Raquel Welch, Lauren Bacall and George Gobel did their stuff and, sure enough, Johnny went into "Stump the Band." He came down off the stage and put the microphone right in my face. "What's your name?" he asked.

"Ross Barbour."

"Where are you from?"

"Indiana." (There was no opportunity for me to say, "Johnny, I am one of the Four Freshmen and not Joe Nebraska." The Tonight Show band was making funny noises, trying to tip Johnny off that he knew me.)

Then he asked, "What song have you chosen?"

"I've Enjoyed As Much Of You As I Can Stand!"

Doc Severinsen performed a funny country version of a silly song and Johnny said, "No, that's not it. How does it go, Ross?" And I sang,

> You made a Peyton Place of our old neighborhood
> While I ate all the soup that Campbell canned,
> I've come to the conclusion that you ain't no good
> And I've enjoyed as much of you as I can stand.

Johnny gave us four free dinners at a fine restaurant and an album of *Great Moments From the Johnny Carson Show*. I thanked him and he went on to the next person.

Johnny, here's my public apology for all the world to see! I'm sorry I did that. That show, by the way, was rebroadcast a half dozen times. Years after I was off the road people would tell me, "I saw you on the Carson show last night." They never re-ran the ones with the Freshmen as guests, it was always "that" one!

The Coach

In late January we began a different way of traveling. The Coachman Motor Home people let us use one of their Class A motor homes. That's the kind that's almost flat in the front; there's no truck hood and cab. We used it in exchange for advertising and returned it to their dealer in Chicago when tours took us to places like Japan. The "coach" was seen on lots of college campuses.

We would park it by the stage door and change clothes in it. Our uniforms hung in the closet so they never got wrinkled from being in a suitcase. We even had a coffee maker on board, which we used during intermissions. The only time we spent the night in it was when we had to drive all night to the next job. Bob was the driver. He got it gassed up, lubed and washed. It was his baby. The Coachman was a godsend.

We loved playing in the South and a three-day stint in Wilmington, North Carolina. was so very memorable. We opened there with Steve Allen's tune, "This Could Be The Start Of Something Big," then "Laughter In The Rain," with a rock beat background. At the end of that we dived right into, "In This Whole Wide World," all as sweet as butter-scotch. Wow! We had them!

We paused to introduce the Freshmen. I said, "Ken never says anything. Ken, do you want to say something?" He blushed and shook his head. I'd say, "Come on. Say some-thing." And he would approach the mike like it was going to bite him, and say, "My girdle is killing me." Everybody in the crowd loved Ken.

I continued, "From Fort Walton Beach down in Florida, the only rebel in the bunch, Ray Brown!" He had a confederate flag about a foot long sewn inside the left side of his coat. He stuck out his chest and opened the side of his coat! The rebel yells, whistles and cheers just got all over us. The people choked with laughter to see such a show of loyalty. And, of course, Bob on trombone and Ken on the bass, broke into a few bars of "Dixie" to increase the reac-tion! It was flat out wonderful!

Then I would say, "He plays trombone and bass - not just another pretty Hollywood face, the very beautiful Bob Flanigan!" And Bob would strut around, bow and increase the applause by raising the palms of his outstretched hands. He was our un-humble sex symbol. We never knew what Bob was going to do next. He kept our Freshmen humor bubbling and ready to explode. Bob and I had a few set lines.

I would say, "How do I look?" And he'd say, "Compared to what?"

Or I'd announce, "You'll have to excuse Bob this evening. He's working under a handicap."

And Bob would say, "Yeah, I'm sober."

Then I'd say, "No, I mean, Bob has been very sick."

Bob: "Yeah. I just got out of the Naval Hospital. I had a lot of trouble with my navel. It was caused by carrying the flag in the American Legion parade!" We got them howling with those lines. And the way Bob went marching around the stage with that imaginary flagstaff in his navel.

In Boston, Herb Hughes came to see us. We did a fun thing with him whenever we got the chance. I would say, "It may seem difficult to sing what we sing, but anyone can do it. Like, for instance, you there with the gray tie - why don't you come up here and sing a part with us?"

Herb would hesitate and we would coax him. Pretty soon he would be on stage with us and we would sing a Freshmen tune with him. He would do just fine and the audience would applaud him wildly. Then I would explain that first contact we had with Herb was years ago. He sent us a record of himself playing and singing all the parts on five or six Freshmen arrangements. The audience realized we had conned them, and they loved the trick.

Before we flew out of Boston's Logan Field we had breakfast in their little coffee shop and Coach John Wooden was seated on the other side of the horseshoe-shaped counter. When we were through, I introduced myself to him and shook his hand. I stammered something like, "I am a fan of no man more than you." He was so together and gracious, as he was all those years at UCLA.

Jane Powell was on our plane. We hadn't seen to her since 1951 when we filmed "Rich, Young and Pretty." It was so good to catch up with her.

We loved what we did, but we were never satisfied with our work. The only way to have a good group is to be picky-picky. We rehearsed almost every afternoon, trying to iron out rough places on the songs we performed. People told us we were way ahead of any other group, but we weren't pleased with the way we sang or the way we played. We weren't satisfied with the way we did comedy or paced the show. The goal for us was always out of reach. If we had done easier arrangements, or didn't care how we sounded, we would have all lost interest.

Saturday, September 20th, was our 27th anniversary. Greg Stegeman was in Memphis with another group and we came to town to work Dad's Place. Greg came around to renew old acquaintances. He was ready then to be a Freshmen, and had been for years.

December 10th was Ken Albers' birthday. Ken is a man who loves to sleep. So we made up a sweatshirt for him. You music students will appreciate it. On the front it had a musical staff with a G clef and one whole rest on it. Above the rest was a bird's eye, meaning to hold it. It was marked triple pianissimo (very quiet) and under the staff was "Rit" (slow it down). At the front and back of the measure were double bars and double dots (repeat it). That became Ken's "sleep shirt."

The Spirit of '76

We began New Year's Day, 1976, flying to Harrisburg to begin recording the *Mt. Freshmore* album at Don Baldwin's studios. We played and recorded the backgrounds, then added voices. We recorded Ken's instrumental solo on "Let Me Be the One," then we did all the vocal parts and the rest of the songs. Days later we recorded Ken's horn solo on "Let Me Be the One" again. Just for fun the recording engineer played back both solos at once. To our amazement, they were the same. Not just similar - exactly the same! The solo on that song in your stack of Freshmen albums is really Ken's duet with himself.

We wouldn't have left Los Angeles for our February 4th trip if we had known what was coming. We flew to Indianapolis and drove to Hanover College in southern Indiana. Just as we were getting dressed to go on stage Bob got a call. His daughter, Jennifer, had been in an accident in her Mustang and they wanted Bob to come back to Los Angeles. But a blizzard prevented Bob from leaving for two days.

Ken, Ray, and I flew to Harrisburg to supervise the putting together of *Mt. Freshmore* and at nine the following morning we finished and collapsed on a plane to Los Angeles. Jennifer was on the mend and was thankful to have Bob there.

As April approached, the Freshmen flew west. Boy, did we fly west! Los Angeles to Hawaii to Tokyo to Hong Kong and all the way to Bangkok, Thailand. The Grand Hyatt Erawan was our home there for a few days.

Trucks in Thailand are works of art. They import the hood, engine and chassis, and the Thai craftsmen fashion a cab and truck bed out of hand-polished teakwood and mahogany. They add clearance lights, mud flaps, hand-painted designs and lots of chrome. It's worth a trip to Thailand just to see one.

Claude Akins, a Hoosier friend of ours, was doing a TV series called Movin' On and in it he drove an 18-wheel tractor-trailer rig. It was fancy, but not as fancy as a Thai truck, so I walked out of our hotel in Bangkok to get a picture of one of these trucks for Claude. It was a nice afternoon and it seemed like an easy thing to do. Wrong!

Before I had gone ten steps I had to deal with a persistent beggar and politely decline his repeated requests for a handout. Finally he went on to another tourist and I went back to truck hunting.

Suddenly there was a beautiful young woman by my side. "Hello, Joe. You want fun? I show you joy!" She pointed to a door, "Follow me. I give you thrills! I give you joy." She began hugging me. I had the camera in one hand and my other hand on my billfold.

"No," I said. "All I want is a picture of a truck."

"Oh, you want a picture? I take your picture," she said as she tried to get my camera away from me.

We both repeated what we wanted a couple of times as I continued walking. She stopped when I made a right turn at a corner jewelry store with big display windows. I stopped and looked through the windows to make sure she had stopped following me. What I saw was the reflection of a man standing behind me at the curb, looking at me. Fed up, I turned to face him.

He raised both hands to shoulder level and said, "Please. I am a government investigator. The woman around the corner is a man. If you had gone with her, she would have hit you on the head and robbed you. I would have arrested you both."

I heard myself shouting, "All I want is a picture of a truck!" He waited with me until a truck went by and I snapped it, then I showed him some fancy foot work that brought me back to the hotel. Whew! I got a lifetime of experience in those 20 minutes.

Next, we flew on to Malaysia, which used to be the "Malaya" Don sang about. We thought we were in a totally remote world when we landed in Kuala Lumpur. What a surprise when the skycap spoke to us in beautiful English. He explained that England had ruled that territory for generations.

We got to Tokyo and the New Otani Hotel on April 9th. Sue flew in on the 10th; she had always wanted to see Japan. The Freshmen worked two different places every night and went sightseeing in the daytime.

One night backstage we met a trumpet player who had quit his job so he could come and hear the Freshmen! I hope he got another one! While we did a TV show, one of the local journalists cornered Sue, interviewing her about what it was like being a Freshman wife. A few days later, on April 24th in Yokosuka, we got a call that Ken's wife's mother had died. We phoned and sent flowers but we were too far away to help.

After a week at home we were off to Bermuda on May 10th. Ray and Nancy brought Travis, and Sue came in on the 14th. It was time to enjoy life and Bermuda is the place! We lived and worked in the impressive Southampton Princess Hotel, with free rooms in this paradise and 50% off our meals. They even let us leave the equipment set up for the whole three weeks. We did just one show each evening. It was heavenly. Dave Bentley from New York, and our good friends from the San Fernando Valley, Neal and Elsie Sinkeldam came to enjoy the islands with us.

One afternoon Dave, Bob, Ken, Sue and I got aboard a glass-bottomed boat to go look at some of the wrecked ships under the clear water. Bentley and I put on swim fins, masks and snorkels and went swimming among clouds of little fish by the sea garden reef. It was a day I will remember forever.

June 3rd was my parents' 53rd wedding anniversary and Sue and I were there to celebrate with them. Bob had picked up our motor home in Chicago and we met him there. We made it almost to Flint, Michigan, when we ran out of gas. I walked the mile or so to a filling station and brought back a gallon. We barely made the Sheraton Hotel show on time.

That night we stayed at the Dearborn Inn and had a big meeting, our periodic "honesty session." What are we doing wrong on the show? Everybody let it all hang out. "I don't think we should do this" or, "I don't like it when you do that." If you are going to have a quartet, you have to do that once in a while.

19

TOUGH FAREWELLS

On Friday, June 25, 1976, my father died. He was 82.
Sue flew to Indiana to be with Mother. Of course I canceled
work at the Contessa del Mar in Chicago to attend the funeral.

I didn't want to leave Indiana that next Tuesday but I
had promised to be back at work in Chicago. I left Sue there
with Mother. There were tornado warnings all over Indiana
and my plane was delayed for two hours. When we got up in
the air we were banged around all the way to Chicago. Bob
was waiting at the airport and he whisked me to our job but
we started the show late.

Sunday, July 4th, was the big bi-centennial celebration, complete with fireworks by the lakefront in downtown
Chicago. People parked their cars on the outer drive hours
ahead of time. We made it a point to stay out of that traffic
jam so we wouldn't be late to work again. After we finished in
Chicago I went back to Columbus to help Mother.

We worked inside the Eastland Shopping Mall in
Detroit, then Traverse City and on to Minneapolis for a night
at the Hippogriff. Herb Hughes was there, so we pulled the
"Anyone can sing this stuff" routine again.

In early August I flew back to Indiana to help Mother
again. Ken and Ray flew to Philadelphia and Bob went to
Goshen, Indiana, where the factory guy taught him all about

the motor home - how to fill this, how to empty that. Bob was becoming a master motor home driver. We did a show in Philadelphia, right in the street by the art museum. Then we went to Miami to do a string of shows at retirement homes.

We went into Lorain, Ohio, on September 10th to do a different kind of thing. Hobart McCoy had retired, and he and his wife Ceil wanted to do something to celebrate. It came down to taking a cruise on the Love Boat or having the Four Freshmen entertain in their basement rec room. Guess what? They filled the basement with their friends and neighbors and we did two shows for this great bunch of people. There was food and drink all evening long and lots of friendship and happiness. Ted Driscol and his brothers were there, and Harry and Pat Dodson got up and sang with us. The McCoys' dog fell down the basement stairs in the middle of a song and broke all of us up. It was a wonderful night to remember.

Three of us would wear big western cowboy hats when we traveled, but Ken wore an "eastern hat." It was a just a cap and we kidded him about it. We worked Astoria and Longview, Oregon and Olympia and Bremerton, Washington, where we sang at Holy Trinity Church. We worked a high school in Polson, Montana, and drove on to Missoula, and then Lewiston, Idaho. There is some big country up there. Sue met us and rode along for a week. Snow started falling in Jackson Hole, Wyoming. People were slipping off the road, but ol' Bob kept a steady foot on the pedal.

It was snowing nickels while we sang in Lander, Wyoming. When we left there, all the accessories in the motor home stopped working - the turn signals, the backup lights, everything. Mostly we missed the heater! There was a fuse blown somewhere, but we couldn't take the time to hunt down a repairman. We bundled up in our winter clothes and went on to Sheridan, Wyoming, to work a theater.

We did Gillette and Cheyenne, where it was 18 degrees. What's a vocal group doing out in this kind of weather? In Denver we put Sue on a plane home and then worked in Lamar, Colorado, that night. The Ramada Inn in Steamboat Springs is just what a ski resort hotel should be.

Winding Down

The entry in my diary for October 24th began to tell a tale. It says, "The time for me to leave the group is near. I'm not content with our sound. Sue is lonesome. Mother is in the hospital and needs me. It seems like all the ducks are lining up in a row. Things are going to have to change pretty soon."

A few days later we got to Durango, Colorado, at three in the morning. The motel manager had just left the keys in the room doors for us. He didn't want to be awakened just to sign us in. I played a trick there. The desk chair in the room had come unglued and some pieces were out of their peg holes. I put Elmer's Glue in all the loose places and made a tourniquet out of some string to pull it all together. By morning the chair was as good as new and the maid puzzled about the "magic chair." "How did it do that?"

We worked the high school the next evening, loaded up the stuff for the last time on that tour, and Bob drove home to Los Angeles. He was just tireless. Ray was busily talking on the CB (his "handle" was "Corn Bread"). Ken was in the back asleep. I was in my bedroll above the cab with the atlas and a flashlight, ready to provide an answer should Bob ask, "Ross, what's the highway we need out of Ash Fork?"

Bob drove from 11pm that night until five the next evening. Ray stayed at my house that night. That's when I told him I hoped to be replaced by January, which led to some deep thoughts and a long conversation.

In November we did ten days around Detroit and on the 15th opened at Maggie's Opera House in Cincinnati. It was there that I called the Freshmen together and explained that the time had come for me to be replaced. I needed to be off the road for my health's sake and for my family's. Ray had decided that when I left, he would go too. He wanted to return to Florida and not be cold again.

So the Freshmen had a new topic to discuss. Who would we get to replace Ray and me? How would it happen? Ray and I told Bob and Ken we would stay until the new people were ready, but we wanted that to happen as soon as possible.

The Kenton band and the Freshmen alternated at Maggie's Opera House on November 23rd. Stan was concerned that we treat each other fairly during this time of personnel change. We were off for Thanksgiving, which I spent with Mother in Columbus. I packed her a suitcase and she flew to Los Angeles for Christmas.

The Freshmen went on with one-nighters in Louisville, Lancaster, Pennsylvania, and Detroit in the snow, doing a show for Dodge executives.

The *Mt. Freshmore* album reached us on this trip. We had almost killed ourselves recording it the previous January. Now, eleven months later, we had almost forgotten what tunes were on the album. It was very welcome.

We worked at Howe Institute, a military school for boys, and Leroy was the star. We set our instruments up at the Detroit Athletic Club on December 11th for a job later that day. Then a limousine took us to the Silver Dome where we sang the National Anthem to kick off a game between the Lions and Rams. We sang it quite simply, except at the end. On "home of the brave," we dropped in some Freshmen chords. But the crowd started cheering at that point so nobody heard us. Well, we tried!

In order for the group's finances to work out for the best, Ray and I were talking about next April as the time we would leave. On December 16th we told Harold Plant, our accountant, that the change was coming. My diary entry for December 23rd says, "Oh, it's so good to be at home. I think I'll never leave for anything." On New Year's Eve we played at John Walton's spectacular home on the Pebble Beach Golf Course near Monterey. Happy New Year!

On January 4, 1977, Greg Stegeman came to the Freshmen office. Shirley, our secretary, and I entertained him with our shelves full of Freshmen records, publicity material, arrangements and memorabilia. Then Greg and I got down to business. I told him I'd like to see him in the group. Greg was almost over qualified as a singer and brass player. He was also a patient, cooperative young man, but at the moment, Bob and Ken needed a drummer and a keyboard player.

Mother and I flew back to Indiana in mid-January and I got her back into her house. It was a good house, and it was home, but it was 200 yards from the road and seven miles out of Columbus. When snow came she might be marooned for days. Together we planned for her to sell the Indiana farm and we would buy a place with a guest house in California. She and we could live separately, but Sue and I would be close enough to help her.

The rest of January was filled with one-nighters: Loveland, Colorado, Indianapolis and Chicago, where we entertained the people who loaned us the motor homes. On January 26th President Carter pardoned all the draft evaders.

Mid-America Marathons

Bob drove us from Los Angeles to Midland, Texas. This was the beginning of a nine and a half week tour for Columbia Concert Tours, the first time we worked for them. They sold season tickets in small towns all over the U.S. and supplied a series of concerts. The jumps were short and comfortable. We had not done tours that kept us away that long, but we could bring our wives on the road with us during the tour.

Dave Bentley flew out to ride with us when we were in Duncan, Oklahoma. He introduced the group to begin each concert and also ran the spotlights during the shows. Dave had only New York type clothes, but we got him to buy some cowboy boots in Ada. We and Dave sang barbershop openings with Jim Clancy in Dallas in the Country Squire motor home.

We found Marshall, Texas, to be a fine town. We worked in New Iberia, Louisiana, where all the tabasco sauce comes from. Down the road, we had spaghetti with our friends the Kains, Knights and Mitchells, and worked in Biloxi where I met a lady named Lorrain Barbour. She had to be a relative. The Barbours came to Louisiana from Ireland and later moved north.

The prettiest hall in the world is in Ft. Smith, Arkansas, and I don't even know its name! In Dodge City we took pictures of the motor home at Boot Hill, and that day, March 1st, we got word that Autie Goodman would join the Freshmen. He had been a mainstay of the Modernaires for years.

"I can actually sing higher than Bob Flanigan," Autie told me. Bob overheard him and shot back, "You can sing higher than I do all you want - at home!"

There was a reception at someone's house almost every night of this tour. The committee was disappointed if we didn't stay and have a piece of cake or something. We shook hands with so many people. Sometimes we would have to drive on and skip the festivities, but we usually made friends by staying to eat.

April 1st was Ken Albers' 21st anniversary as a Freshmen and we were in the mood to do something foolish for April Fool's day. We were in Iron Mountain, Michigan, and we arranged with the stage crew that I would use the off-stage microphone and say, "Ladies and Gentlemen! The Four Freshmen!" Ray would pull open the curtain and Bob would run the lights. The four stage crew guys ran on as though they were going to entertain. Iron Mountain is a small town and most of the people in the audience knew one or two of them. The crowd yelled, "Boo!" and things like that. One of the crew yelled, "April Fool!" Then we came on. It worked!

Bob drove all night and we arrived at Brainerd, Minnesota, at 6:30 in the morning. It's handy when you can arrange that kind of timing. The guys in the Kenton band used to say, "We'll hit and split and go for a too-fer." That meant drive all night after work and get to the next town after 6:30am. Then you can check in, sleep all day, go to work, and spend the night at the motel as well. You get two nights' sleep for the price of one. That's only one of the tricks the guys on a band bus know. We drove into Chicago, left the motor home, flew to Buffalo and drove rental cars to Wellsville, New York. April 6th was the end of the tour; 54 jobs in 63 days. Whew!

Two Good Men

By April 18th Bob and Ken had the two new Freshmen all set. Autie Goodman had said yes earlier. Now Dennis Grillo also said yes. Their rehearsals would take a while, so we re-set the transition time for the middle of August. In Greencastle we worked in a theater on April 23rd. The Speed Capitol Chorus from Indianapolis was there to sing, as was a quartet called the Four Flushers. Wayne Jenkins was in that group. He'd been in our freshman class at college. We lived in the same dorm and he sang occasionally with Hal, Don and me.

I love things like what happened on May 6th, when we watched a young lady fall in love with music. Sam Presley had us entertain at his big party in New Orleans. This young lady was listening when we did "Polka Dots and Moonbeams." I guess she had only been listening to slow rock and roll tunes before and had thought they were the real love songs - until she heard this. She got all puddled up in the eyes and snuggled up to the guy she was with. She was so visibly affected, it affected us as well, and we had to blink a little. These are the tunes we lived by. We love them and it's such a treat to see someone discover them suddenly like that.

In Houston we worked with the Symphony Pops Orchestra. One of the people in the audience was Igor Ondreas. He had been our guide and interpreter on our Czechoslovakian tour and had come to the free world after the Russian tanks came to Prague.

In Pittsburgh we shared the stage with Harry James and the band. I had been a fan of his since my high school days. As a kid in 1945 I wrote to his radio show, The Chesterfield Music Makers and got a picture of the band. The photograph showed the band sitting rigidly straight, and the trumpet section had their horns across their knees, all pointed in the same direction. I set a goal back then that one day I'd play trumpet with the Harry James Band. It came true in Pittsburgh. They were on stage and I was backstage. But I played a few bars with them anyway, just so I could say I did it!

We flew to Tokyo on June 2nd, lost June 3rd at the dateline, and flew to Manila June 4th. We worked four days in the big ballroom at the Philippine Plaza Hotel. Imelda Marcos built the place and was having the land next to it cleared to build something else.

We did a show in Singapore and one in Hong Kong. The two promoters of this tour had a falling out, almost a fistfight. Neither one wanted to honor the contract and we certainly didn't want to work if they weren't going to pay us. We were supposed to work again on the 14th but we didn't because of the money situation. I spent the evening with a representative of the American Consulate, hoping they could help.

On June 15th we went back to Tokyo to do the Tokyo Music Festival. That was a big deal - highly advertised and the entire show was televised. Each of the contestants did a tune or two. The "after party" was in a big room, but hardly big enough for the entertainers, the crew, and all the people connected with the show. The Time Five sang the vocal background for solo singers on the actual show. The group playing behind the singers was the Crest Four, Plus One. We had met them on previous trips to Japan. These two groups knew a dozen Freshmen arrangements so we got them all on stage with us and performed three or four songs, with all 14 of us singing the parts on "Graduation Day," "Blue World," "The Day Isn't Long Enough" and "Poinciana." It was grand!

Final Tour

We rested from the overseas trip for two whole days and on July 14th Ray and I began our final tour with the Four Freshmen. Happily, we worked again with the Kenton band on the 15th at the Meadowbrook Ballroom in Rochester, Minnesota.

Saturday, July 16th, was the first of a long list of dates when we appeared in different combinations with two other groups, chosen from among the Four Aces, Ink Spots, Pied Pipers, or the Mills Brothers. We were promoted as "groups from the Golden Age." Each group did maybe 30 minutes. Then, at the end of the show, the three groups would come on stage at the same time. Each group would do a couple of their tunes and the others would listen and lead the applause.

The first show we did was in Toledo, and it was a great success. That night it was the Four Aces, the Ink Spots, and the Four Freshmen. It made me smile when a lady asked one of the Ink Spots if they were the "originals." The answer was, "Kind Lady, when you go see Ringling Brothers Circus, do you ask if those are the original elephants?"

In Dallas, on July 17th, a tent was set up on the northeast side of the city. They called it the "Summer Top." The Dallas Symphony played on summer evenings and we worked in front of the orchestra. The symphony played some of our backgrounds and they sounded so good back there. Dick Reynolds wrote the arrangements that outstanding orchestras such as this one liked to play.

On our flight to Kansas City I showed Ken Albers how I put the numbers together for our accountant, Harold Plant. Ken would now be the one who collected the money and paid the group's way on the road.

We went back to Alma, Kansas again. Chef Gordon, who ran the place, was the first of our hosts to announce publicly that Ray and I would be leaving the Freshmen in August. On our last night there we said a hundred good-byes and packed up the instruments. Chef Gordon and his purple-clad waiters served us shrimp cocktails, turtle soup, lobster thermidor, wine and a fancy dessert. Ah!

On Friday, July 22nd, I loaded our equipment in a rental truck to head east. I drove to Columbus and got to Mother's at five in the morning. For two days I ran errands for her and fixed everything that didn't work. Then I got that big truck rolling to Lancaster, Ohio, to spend an evening with Jack Furniss and his friends. On the 26th Jack and I drove the truck to Hobart and Ceil McCoy's and played in their basement again. It was an ideal night except that Bob had the same problem he had before - when he stood up straight his head hit the ceiling.

For Ray and me, our final public appearance with the Freshmen was in Indianapolis at the Hilton Hotel. Sue and our daughter Kathy drove from Los Angeles to Indianapolis to be there for the final "bon voyage" show. We worked in the Hilton ballroom for Big George Spiros and the place was full, full, full. Mother's doctor brought her to Indianapolis from Columbus. He wanted to see that she was in good hands.

Ray and I were given plaques from the mayor. The emotional momentum carried the evening through with much excitement. Ray was honored with lots of applause, and when Bob asked for one last round of applause for Ross, I thought the people would hurt themselves clapping. They didn't stop.

What a kind way of thanking me for my part in bringing pleasure to them through - can you believe it? - 28 years,

10 months and 10 days. I'm sure some of the response was spurred by the feeling they might never again see the Freshmen. They wanted to applaud well while they had their chance.

There was one more private appearance in Union, Michigan, at the Country Squire motor home factory, one of the companies which had loaned us those great vehicles. Bill Sames, their dealer from Chicago, was there. He had arranged the deal and made sure things went well for us and for the motor home people. Those two shows right there in the factory on August 11, 1977, closed out the career of Ray Brown and Ross Barbour as members of the Four Freshmen.

Ray went back to Ft. Walton Beach and took up his life with Nancy Jo and Travis. He would come to see the Freshmen when they worked near him, and he would dial my number or Ken's once in a while, just to talk. We saw each other only once until Ray came to a Freshmen reunion in July, 1994. He actually boarded a plane to do it, too (he hates to fly). I felt as close to him as I did when we were on the road. Nothing ever came between us to change that.

August 12, 1977, was the first day of the rest of my life. Sue, Kathy and I drove leisurely to Los Angeles. Though I loved my Freshmen years, I felt like a great weight had been lifted from my shoulders. It was simply time to retire. People had seen me play drums and some trumpet, and sing the third part. I was "Leroy" on some songs, and the master of ceremonies each night. I was Bob's straight man. All that showed when we worked, and it kept me lighthearted.

Each of the Freshmen had jobs behind the scenes. The ones I performed weighed heavily on me. I was responsible for maintaining healthy finances. We had to earn more than we spent or spend less then we earned. It was my duty to wake everybody each morning and make sure we had all Four Freshmen in the car on the way to the airport. When I called them after two hours of sleep, mine was the voice they didn't want to hear. It fell to me to ensure cooperation among the members. More than talent or anything else, cooperation is the most important thing a member can contribute. If a Freshman wasn't being mellow, I did what I could to improve cooperation. Sometimes it was like walking on eggshells. This was the job I especially liked leaving behind!

Another job was to make new things happen. We always needed new arrangements. I constantly maintained a rehearsal mentality and when someone suggested that we needed new pictures, or new uniforms, or new publicity, it was me doing the talking. I would get all four of us together for those things.

The Freshmen office was my baby. It wasn't a big, impressive place, but out of that office flowed friendly contact with our people around the world. We mailed out our newsletter. I kept Tele-Fan, our phone answering machine, as up-to-date as I could. We also sold records and arrangements through the mail.

Now I had a whole new set of challenges. We moved Mother west with us. I started living regular hours and taking care of my health. Diabetes does not belong on one-nighters. I had proved I could stay alive on the road with diabetes for 21 years, but every year it became more difficult. But I made it.

I retired undefeated!

20

FROM THEN TILL NOW

1977

On August 30th the Four Freshmen - Bob, Ken Albers, Autie Goodman and Dennis Grillo - began again at the Michigan State Fair. Autie told me, "We had rehearsed in Las Vegas, and Dennis - what a talent he was. He had done a lot of writing, was great on keyboard and spectacular on trumpet."

This group, number six, had four stellar horn players. I saw them in Newport, California, on September 4th. They were still learning some of the words, but they sure could play those horns. Dennis actually wrote symphony orchestra background arrangements for these Freshmen, in ink, aboard the motor home, with all the horn parts transposed. The copyist said there were no mistakes. Dennis went on to teach at Berklee College of Music in Boston.

1978

The Freshmen came to play at Mike Beisner's jazz club in Lawrence, Kansas.

"Our club was on the second story over a music store downtown," Mike recalled, "and there was this big set of stairs out back, almost like a fire escape. I was getting ready to open for the evening and Bob Flanigan walked in the door smoking one of those brown cigarettes. Before he said,

'Hello' or anything he said, 'I hope you have some people to help us get the equipment up those damn stairs!'

I said, 'You must be Bob Flanigan. Bob, why don't you come over here and sit down. I'll fix you a drink. I've got plenty of guys to carry the stuff. Get all the Freshmen to come up here and relax.' We've been friends from that moment on."

Mike discovered the Freshmen when he was 13 and taking trumpet lessons. "I loved Al Hirt, Doc Severinsen, Basie and Glenn Miller," Mike remembers. "My trumpet teacher and I were talking about music one day and he said, 'For today's lesson, we're just going to listen.' He put on a Kenton record and my jaw dropped.

"I said, 'Wow, if I had a band, that's the way I'd have them play.' One of the albums was *Road Show*. Stan introduced the Freshmen, and I said, 'Man! If I ever sang in a group, that's the way I would want them to sound.' He played some Maynard Ferguson and I knew that's the way I wanted to play. That afternoon changed my whole musical perspective."

On September 3rd the Freshmen came back to the Marriott in Newport and Sue and I drove down. They sounded great and Paula Kelly, Jr. was among the Freshmen faithful that night. There was also a series of one-nighters with the Four Lads, the Pied Pipers and the Ink Spots. That tour was called "The Fabulous Fours."

1979

The gasoline shortage and long lines at the filling stations complicated life on the road. At home in Los Angeles I had earned my real estate license and was able to sell some homes. But the interest rates rocketed to 21% and no one was buying so I got out of that business.

On August 26th Stan Kenton died. He'd had a mysterious fall in the spring of 1977. The wait for complete recovery was unbearable for him and he went back out with the band in January, 1978, well before he should have. He disbanded again in August, 1978, intending to follow doctors' orders this time. But he was never able to regain his health.

The Freshmen owe more to Stan Kenton than to anyone else in the world. He guided us, inspired us, and in many ways adopted us. Just his stamp of approval brought us good things. We love you, Stan.

1980

The Freshmen didn't get to Los Angeles very often and I was busy in a new job at Fortin Laminating Co. in Sylmar. Our neighbor, Joe Del, ran Fortin. He's the man who had invited me to come make friends for his company if I ever got tired of making them for the Freshmen. I became Director of Industrial Relations, but while I was a trainee the letters for my title spelled "D.I.R.T." (Director of Industrial Relations Trainee). Their 13 plants made circuit boards. I became a high profile goodwill representative to the employees and loved my job.

On August 31st the Freshmen were back at the Newport Marriott. Sue and I were there to cheer them. I got on stage for a tune or two.

1981

The Freshmen worked in Hackensack, New Jersey, for Roger Rudnick on June 7th. He promoted the show as "The 40s in the 80s," and he had 1940 automobiles all around the theater lobby. He wanted me there so badly that he sent Sue and me airline tickets. Leroy did "Sweet Lorraine" and I sang "After You." It was a super night.

1982

January 30th at the Palomino in North Hollywood was Ken Albers' final night as a Freshman. They got me up to do a tune or two and we had fun. There was always sadness, though, when a Freshman left. Dennis Grillo would be leaving shortly, too. Dennis had been a Freshmen for only four and a half years, which is about the entire life span of most groups.

Kenny had been a part of the Freshmen for more than 25 years. Most people who knew us had discovered us with Ken singing, playing and arranging. His smile was such an important part of the Freshmen picture.

Mike Beisner replaced Ken in January (Group #7). Dennis was replaced by Rod Henley in April (Group #8). The Freshmen were at full speed again with Flanigan, Goodman, Beisner and Henley. Ken Albers went to work in the music library at Universal Studios and later chauffeured a long black Lincoln limousine.

Everyone who knew Mike Beisner said he was a whale of a musician. But no one had ever heard him sing. He had told Bob he could sing the parts so Bob called him and asked if he could join the group. "Bob figured he wouldn't take the job if he couldn't do it," Autie Goodman told me. "Mike memorized that third part so quickly!"

Mike remembers: "Rod Henley and I hadn't been with the Freshmen long when we worked in Atlanta in front of a symphony orchestra for our first time. You say, 'Oh, Yes! That's the way it's supposed to sound.' I was terrified. I don't often get nervous, but that night did it."

Rod Henley was equally good for the Freshmen. Autie commented, "He could take that keyboard and make it sound like an orchestra. Rod wrote a lot of nice things, and he and Mike wrote things together." This group is heard on the *Fresh* album.

1984

Look, Ma, I'm an emcee! A Freshmen fan was in charge of a big convention in Houston in January and he flew Sue and me there. I served as their master of ceremonies. In May I did a similar thing for a model railroad group in Phoenix.

August 18th was Sue's birthday and we were celebrating in Vegas. The Freshmen were at the Dunes with the Russ Gary Orchestra. (I hadn't seen them at all in 1983.) By now they were using "Route 66" as their opening song. The routine that night called for them to run up on stage from the back of the hall - right up the middle aisle. I don't know who put me up to it - probably Bob - but I ran on with them and did the opener. Then Mike ran on and I ran off. Later that night they worked by themselves in the Top of the Dunes, and I did "Blue World" with them. We were together again October 9th at the Newport Marriott. Dave Bentley was there from New York and Bobby Troup came to hear his songs.

The Freshmen worked in Monaco, October 24th to November 13th. That's the kind of a job to have!

1985

After five years at Fortin, the company was sold to Westinghouse. Joe Del took me with him to Mortensen Educational Products, Inc.

The Freshmen were at the Main Office in Simi Valley, California in early June. It was another fine chance for me to get together with them for an evening and kid around.

In Los Angeles the Society of Singers celebrated the Modernaires' 50th anniversary on October 3 with a banquet, and then filled the stage with representatives from as many groups as they could find to congratulate Paula and the "Mods." One of the Mills Brothers, one of the Lettermen, and Randy Van Horne and I were there to speak. The Clark Sisters, the King Sisters and the Andrews Sisters were all represented.

1986

Sue and I went to Las Vegas for Bob's daughter Jennifer's wedding on April 26th. The Four Freshmen sang

"Their Hearts Were Full of Spring" at the reception and I did "Blue World" with the group in a tight circle around the bride and groom.

On May 27th my friend Joe Del, had a stroke. The Mortensen company closed and I was let go in mid-June. I became a counselor at Eternal Valley Memorial Park in August. I was leading a funeral procession one day in late October and - what's this? Driving the black limousine at the head of the procession was Ken Albers! Away from the mourners, he and I got out of our cars and gave each other a hug.

Rod Henley left the Freshmen in September to get his master's degree at UNLV, but returned for July and August of 1987. His replacement was a trumpet and piano player named Dave Jennings who sang the bottom part very effectively (Group #9). This group (Jennings, Beisner, Goodman and Flanigan) began an album in Nashville. Autie remembers: "We did a bunch of good country tunes with some great players, including Grady Martin and Chet Atkins. There was a money glitch and we never finished it."

1987

I took a job at the Tailored Baby Company, which manufactured crib blankets, quilts, diaper bags - a thousand different items. The salesmen called me when they wanted samples.

On January 17th the Anaheim Marriott hosted the Convention of Music Manufacturers. The show that night was a hot big band led by Pete Barbuti, and featured the Four Freshmen (Jennings, Goodman, Beisner and Flanigan). That was the only time I saw this group. The album *Fresh* was nominated for a Grammy but the award went to somebody else.

Rapid changes were descending on the Freshmen. Dave Jennings returned to Detroit in April. Mike knew Newton Graber who had a big band in Kansas. He came with the group for just four months.

"He just didn't want to be on the road so he went back to Kansas," Autie remembers. In July and August, Rod Henley came back until a new man, Kirk Marcy, was ready.

"Kirk came with us and it was joyful because he's such a lovely person," Autie told me. Other people thought so, too. After a short time as a Freshman, Kirk received a wonderful offer to be head of vocal jazz classes at Edmonds Community College near Seattle. That made three ex-Freshmen who are educators: Kirk, Dennis Grillo in Boston and Rod Henley at Georgia State.

My job at Tailored Baby ended in May. Our kids were all grown and gone so we put our big house in Granada Hills up for sale. The house sold in July and we moved into a smaller home in Simi Valley, close to our daughter, Kathy. In August I went to work selling Chevrolets at the William L. Morris dealership in Simi and Sue started work at Rocketdyne.

In September we paid a visit to Dick Reynolds. He had won his bout with cancer for a while, and we tried to encourage him. On September 15th I became the rental manager for Morris Chevrolet. Rod Henley sent me a tape of *Freshmas.*

A major event of 1987 came through Edd Townsend, a super Freshmen fan, who began to network other fans across the world into what today is the Four Freshmen Society (FFS). FFS is like all the fan clubs of the 1950s grouped together. These grown-ups are united to encourage and support the Freshmen and help them to succeed.

The FFS would grow to over 2100 people by 1998, with an outstanding bi-monthly newsletter, *Fresh News.* Fans who want information on how to join FFS may write or call the FFS, Membership Department, P.O. Box 9804, McLean, VA 22102-0804. Phone (703) 471-4672.

1988

We started the year by burying Dick Reynolds. I did the eulogy. It was one of the hardest things I have ever done, but I made it. I guess I've always known I'd go through hell for Dick Reynolds, or do anything else he needed.

I sold Ken Albers' son Richie a red Chevy S1O pickup truck in April. He treasured that little number. On July 1st Sue and I went up to Ventura to see the Freshmen alternate with the Count Basie band at the Hotel Harbortown. Kirk Marcy was still with the group and that's the only time I heard him. Kirk left soon after that and the Freshmen added Garry Lee Rosenberg from a group that did four horn things. He also played keyboards when Mike played brass, like they did on the Ellington Medley, "Sophisticated Suite."

On Friday, September 16th Sue and I flew to Las Vegas. No way were the Four Freshmen going to have a 40th anniversary party without us! There must have been 150 fans from all over the country who had come to the Barbary Coast Lounge to celebrate with the Freshmen. Jorgen and Betty Bjorno were there. They had taken a year to go around the world, starting from their home in Denmark on a motorcycle! When they got to the Middle East there were too many wars going on so they sold the cycle and flew the rest of the way. Dody and Lucille Kain arrived from Bogalusa, Louisiana. Bill and Susan Comstock were there and looking good. We saw Palle Christensen and Eric and Kissa from Denmark, and Keith and Hazel Murray from England.

On Saturday they got Bill Comstock and me up to sing with Garry Lee and Bob. I don't remember whose idea it was, but we got Sue up to sing lead with us, like she had done at our rehearsals 40 years earlier. They gave her a standing ovation! The next Monday she told all her friends in accounting at Rocketdyne what a hit she had been in Vegas over the weekend.

1989

It was April 14th before we got together again, and the Freshmen didn't need Sue and me to have a crowd. They were in Buena Park, California, in a room that should have held 800 people at the most, but there must have been 1,200 there.

On May 13th, in Port Hueneme (Wy-nee-mee), Sue and I and the Snowdens spent the afternoon hanging out with the Freshmen before they did their show in a nice old theater. The guys wore their red coats and black shirts and trousers. The audience likes it when Mike calls an ex-Freshmen on stage, so he got me up there for "Blue World."

Greg Stegeman called me on August 17th. "I'm going to be a Freshman!" All his life he had prepared for this day. Greg replaced Mike Beisner, who became musical director for Every Day with Joan Lunden. Greg told me, "I was terrified the first month. I had to stay focused or I'd forget the chord changes on the keyboard."

With a sparkle in his eye, Greg remembers well how he discovered the Freshmen. "When I was about 15 I went through my parents' record collection and the *Four Freshmen and Five Trombones* album was in there. I just happened to put it on the record player and - boom! There it was! My ears were changed forever. I just played it to death, and became a huge fan. I ended up getting almost all the albums. Dad drove me to Los Angeles - seven and a half hours from home in Carmel, California - just to see these guys!" Greg met Bob, Bill, Kenny and me in 1967, at age 17.

"I was really thrilled," Greg recalls. "The thing that knocked me out was you dedicated 'Their Hearts Were Full of Spring' to us. Back in your dressing room, all four of you listened to the tapes I made of me singing all four parts from Freshmen arrangements. No one even talked during the tapes. I learned that night that entertainers really must be polite to the people who show interest."

1990

The reins of the Four Freshmen Society were passed to John Bangs of Oshkosh, Wisconsin. John has organized state representatives and, with Chick Trafford's newsletter to keep the fans informed, good things continued happening.

Changes in the automobile business caused my rental department to be closed and I made a job switch. In April I began doing "extra" parts in movies and TV. During the next three years I was in some 60 films. I was the man who walked by the star, or one of the people getting off the elevator. In "The Haunted" I'm a bothersome newsman in the front yard of the haunted house. "Nutty Nutt" shows me as one of the crazies - and I'm also the trumpet player in the band during the world's largest pie fight. Dean Jones played a bad veterinarian in "Beethoven." In one scene he whacks Beethoven to get the dog to "attack" him. It wasn't Dean at all in the distance shots of that dog-whacking, It was me, made to look like Dean. (I didn't really whack the dog!)

On August 3rd we saw the Freshmen again in San Pedro, California. Toward the end of the evening, Flanigan got me up to do "Blue World." Former Lettermen Jim Pike was there and sang a fifth part at the bottom. It was a good night!

But shortly thereafter came a very bad night. On August 23rd Bob Flanigan had a heart attack in Chautauqua, New York. Autie remembers: "I called Mary from the hospital. The nurse told me if Bob had waited another hour to come in, he would have been dead of a massive heart attack. We canceled bookings and stayed around Jamestown with Bob. Mike Beisner had finished with the TV show, so Mary called Mike to ask if he could rejoin the group."

The next day Greg Stegeman knocked on Autie's door. "Tell Flanigan I can sing the lead part." And he could! Autie told me, "I worked next to Bob for 13 years, and I couldn't sing Bob's part. If Greg hadn't been there, I have no idea who we would have gotten to do it. Nobody sings lead like Bob - except Greg."

Later that morning, Autie went to the hospital. "I looked in his room and there's Flan with all those tubes sticking out of him. He said, 'Dammit, Austin, I don't like this.' A week before, he had driven the van from Las Vegas to

Jamestown, New York. Good Lord! What if he'd had the heart attack out on the road?

"When God taps you on the shoulder, you'd better heed the warning. Bob did. He did all the things the doctors asked him to do, and it was one of the best hospitals in New York State."

Meanwhile, Mike Beisner planned to join the other Freshmen in Philadelphia, where they were booked at a convention. Garry Lee sang bass, Mike the third part, Autie was the second part with Greg on the lead.

Publicity pictures were taken of this fill-in group, and Bob never let them forget it. "Here I've had a heart attack, and could be dying, and in this picture you guys are smiling and looking like you're the happiest you've ever been."

When the Freshmen came to the Lido in Newport on October 14th Sue and I were there. Bob was taking it easy and letting Greg sing lead. But Bob and I did do "Poinciana" and "Day By Day."

1991

March 17th brought the Freshmen to the Irvine Marriott, with a Kenton alumni band, fronted by Alan Yankee. Garry Lee was leaving soon after that. Beisner would stay on and move to the low part.

Sue began radiation and chemotherapy in June (she's fine now), so on July 11th I flew alone to the FFS-sponsored Freshmen Reunion in Oshkosh, Wisconsin. Kirk Marcy came from Seattle and Bill and Sue Comstock from San Antonio. The mellow weekend charged everyone's batteries. The Grand Opera House was perfect for the concert, and the American Legion Post on nearby Lake Winnebago was ideal for the dinner. Oh, how we fans love these reunions!

On October 4th the staff at the Marriott in San Diego had a big surprise party for Joel Rothman's 30th anniversary with them. They knew what a Freshmen fan he was so they brought the guys in secretly. About 10pm the Latin band did a chorus of "Day By Day." Suddenly, the curtain opened and the Freshmen did the second chorus. The surprise was complete. Even Sue and I didn't know the Freshmen would be there!

1992

Ken Albers brought his Lincoln limousine to the house one evening in the spring and took us for a ride. He was so proud of that pretty thing. His company was called "Traditional Limousine Co." and his license plate read "TLC" and then a number.

July 17th was the FFS Freshmen Reunion in Columbus, Ohio, and the big announcement was that Autie and Bob were stepping down. Gasp! The new group would be Mike Beisner, Greg Stegeman, Kevin Stout and Bob Ferreira. Flanigan would travel with them some, announce them at the beginning of the show, and maybe do a tune or two.

Kevin had been part of the plan for a year. He waited patiently and kept his day job until Bob and Autie retired. Kevin is an amazing musician and was made to order for the Freshmen. Bob Ferreira, a 22 year old drummer who had operatic training in college, would sing the low part so crucial to the Freshmen sound. The album *Voices in Standards* shows how well Bob sings that fourth part.

When these "New Four Freshmen" were rehearsed and ready to hit the road, word got out to the fans that the money to cover new uniforms, instruments, arrangements, publicity photos and other start-up costs just wasn't there. Guess what? Over $50,000 was donated by Freshmen fans! As far as I know, this is unprecedented in the history of jazz or popular music. That's the kind of devotion Freshmen fans have!

It was August 30th when the Freshmen revisited the Marriott in Irvine and we brought two of our grandchildren, Natalie and Doug Bruso, to hear them. The New Four Freshmen did the show, but Flanigan and I got up to sing a couple numbers. Natalie and Doug knew me only as Grandpa, so it was a surprise for them to hear me sing with the Freshmen and get all that nice applause.

1993

On June 18th history repeated itself: Bob and I appeared as Freshmen again. The promoter of the show at the Beverly Hilton wanted "the original group," but Bob and I were the only originals still around. So we, Bob Ferreira and Mike Beisner did the show. The band played our backgrounds. It was a gala charity event. I bought one raffle ticket and they called my number! The prize was two first class tickets to Hawaii. Aloha!

The Freshmen Reunion was in my hometown on July 30th and 31st, but some of us just couldn't wait. Sue and I checked in at the Holiday Inn in Columbus on the 29th and found John Bangs, Ted Driscol, Yasushi Ichiura from Japan, Palle Christensen from Denmark, Bill Truitt and Chick Trafford in the restaurant.

At noon the next day, Betty Kratzsch arrived. Five ex-Freshmen were there: Flanigan, Comstock, Autie and Garry Lee and me. After dinner was "request night," and the wonderful sound of the new group welded us all together.

I wasn't sure the "Fresh Roots" tour that Sue and I conducted Saturday afternoon would attract anyone. But we filled the bus twice and disappointed a dozen who couldn't go see the sights Don and I knew as kids.

That evening the New Four Freshmen did a fierce show. During the break Mike Beisner and I did an epoch composition I wrote called "Durability." Ted Driscol awarded Bob Flanigan and me each an Energizer Bunny 'cause we "just keep going." The Mayor of Columbus, Robert Stuart, declared July 31st "Ross Barbour Day." He and I started first grade together in 1934.

In the fall of 1993 Dave Bentley became manager of the Freshmen. Dave has been our good friend since the

1960s and his dedication was a major factor in getting the New Four Freshmen together. The album *Voices in Standards* owes credit to Dave's efforts.

1994

Before dawn January 17th an earthquake hit Los Angeles. I fixed coffee for the neighbors on my backyard barbecue! We were spared extensive damage, but we had no electricity or gas, and we had to boil our water for a week or so.

On February 7th Bob and Mary Flanigan came with us to Randy Van Horne's "Vine Street Irregulars" party honoring Frankie Laine. The next week, the New Four Freshmen presided over another gathering of good people in Irvine: Bob and Mary Flanigan, Jane (Errair) Withers, Mrs. David Rose, Pete and Edie Rugolo, Bobby Troup, Vic Lewis from England and a thousand other Freshmen fans. A Kenton alumni band played Stan's sounds to complete a fine night!

The New Four Freshmen, as well as Bob and Mary Flanigan, Bill and June Hoeltke and Sue and I, all got to Green Valley, Arizona, on February 19th. CBS Sunday Morning filmed the pre-show reception at Bob Solheim's house and the show itself, which was a benefit for Habitat for Humanity. On March 16th Ken Albers and I went to lunch and brought each other up to date on our grandchildren.

On April 20th the doctors operated on Bob Flanigan to remove an aneurysm. When I talked to him May 3rd he said he was "one sore Irishman." Sue and I used those tickets we'd won and flew to Hawaii. The Freshmen and the Kenton alumni band were at it again at the Irvine Marriot on June 19th. Jane Withers was there with her son Ken Errair, Jr., who looks so much like his dad.

On July 15th, when Sue and I flew to Oshkosh for the FFS Reunion, we found ourselves on the plane from Chicago with Rod Henley, Garry Lee Rosenberg, and a dozen fans.

The people came from everywhere; about 250 good folks. Ray Brown was there. I hadn't seen him in 13 years! There were seven ex-Freshmen there: Rod, Garry Lee, Ray, Bill, Autie, Flanigan and me. We all got into the act at the Grand Opera House with the new guys. Eleven Freshmen posed for pictures.

On Friday, the informal night, Ray did "Just a Bowl of Butter Beans" and recited "Cinderella and her Sisty Ugglers," with the words all twisted around. People laughed themselves sick! I did a parody on "I'll Be Around." It became "We'll Be Around" and the gist was that the Freshmen will be here from now on!

On August 7th CBS showed the Freshmen segment on their Sunday Morning show. What nice coverage. Thanks, CBS. At the Ventura, California County Fair August 23rd the Freshmen knocked the people out. Backstage they told me Mike Beisner would be going home and drop the unhealthy life of a road musician. No one can do it forever. On the way out I told Mike, "I love you no matter what happens."

Sue and I showed up in Irvine to meet Alan MacIntosh, the newest Freshmen, on November 6th. They already sounded good. Greg, Kevin and Bob Ferreira were very impressed with Alan's capabilities, his attitude and his desire to make that Freshmen sound. Between shows, Bobby Troup, after a few kind words, gave me a beautiful plaque that reads:

ROSS BARBOUR 1948-1977
Co-Founder and Co-Chairman of the Board
The Four Freshmen
Presented by Bobby Troup November 6, 1994
at the Irvine Marriott in conjunction with
Ken Allan Productions
The Greatness of your music is secondary
only to the Greatness of your character

It really was a special evening for me because some of

our friends from the Knollwood Methodist Church came. Our daughter, Kathy, was there with her husband, Gilbert Bruso. He took pictures of the occasion. Our sons, Kent and Gary, and Gary's girlfriend Karen King were there. Kent's wife, Phyllis, stayed home with the grandkids, her two-week old baby, Julia, and four year old Tim, and also Kathy's kids, Doug, 8 and Natalie, 12.

1995

Early in the year the very devoted, very busy, Dave Bentley asked Bob Flanigan if he would become the Freshmen manager. The incurable road rat, most influential lead singer, incomparable trombonist and ever-durable sexagenarian (whatever that means!) took the job. Bob's contacts stood him in good stead in filling Freshmen itineraries.

In the early spring the Freshmen got to Germany with Jiggs Whigham's All-Star big band. He had some sidemen you may know - Conti Candoli, Bud Shank and George Roberts.

Then there was the Honolulu Jazz Festival, "The Star Spangled Banner" at football and hockey games in the U.S. and a tour of Japan where Alan MacIntosh astounded the Freshmen and the Japanese fans with his mastery of their language.

On June 4th, the Freshmen, with the Beach Front Property, entertained out-of-doors in Warner Center Park, Woodland Hills, California. All the listeners sat on the grass, and I did too until Greg called me to the stage to do "Day by Day" with them. I'm such a lucky man!

The annual Freshmen reunion began in Huron, Ohio, July 6th, at Sawmill Creek. On Friday noon we opened the first box of the first edition of *Now You Know*. None of us had seen the book until that moment. I signed books for four hours. That evening Fausto Yturria was our auctioneer, and people bought treasured memorabilia from the early Freshmen years.

Ted Driscol's pretty daughter and her girls' quartet did "Route 66" and other dandies. The "Geezers" (Flan, Ross, Bill Comstock and Autie Goodman with Rod Henley playing bass) did a half hour, and we wore ourselves out. If we wanted to go back on the road we couldn't pass the physical!

The next night, Saturday, the current Freshmen entertained us all in nearby Lakeside, Ohio. The limousine ride to the concert was fun. The limo had a sunroof so Bill Comstock and I stood up and waved out of the top of the car as though we were candidates for political office.

Right after the reunion I did a week of book-signing appearances in Cleveland, Detroit, Dayton, Cincinnati and my home town Columbus, Indiana. There I did an evening talk to the theater full of people who knew me when I was a kid. Later in 1995 I did dozens of book store appearances in and around Los Angeles.

November 11th, Newton Graber died suddenly. He was a Freshman from April 1987 to July 1987.

By year's end the Freshmen were doing a whole handful of new arrangements: "My Shining Hour," "Unfor-gettable," Bobby Troup's tune "The Meaning of the Blues," "Moonlight in Vermont," "Where Do You Start," and "Love Dance."

1996

It was announced January 11th, that James Winner, inventor of the auto security device "The Club," would fund the establishment of the Vocal Group Hall of Fame in Sharon, Pennsylvania. In February the Freshmen Page was born on the world's computers at http://www.opms.com/4fresh. About the same time I phoned in a radio interview with talk show host, Ray Brown. He was doing a Ft. Walton Beach, Florida, early morning show. The same week Ken Albers and I were interviewed by the Simi Valley Star. Oh, what fame!

There was a Freshmen show at our alma mater, Butler University in Indianapolis on February 26th with the Jordan Jazz Sextet, the Indianapolis Youth Chorale and the Butler Jazz Ensemble. Next day the Freshmen held workshops with the students. That's the kind of thing the school did not do when we Freshmen were there.

On March 11th, at the Warner Center Marriott, the Los Angeles area convened for a benefit for noted jazz guitarist, Barney Kessel. A stroke had left him unable to talk or play guitar. Therapy costs money, so the Freshmen, Sue Raney, Buddy Childers and his big band, Jack Sheldon and the Page Cavanaugh Trio performed so Barney could get the help he needed. Among other notable guests were Bobby Troup and some of the King Sisters.

On April 22nd we found out that Susan Comstock was in the fight of her life against cancer. The operation, treatments and people's prayers renewed her. Thank God for the giant steps made in cancer treatment.

Baby Abigail Stout arrived on June 11th and changed Kevin and Linda's lives forever.

The 1996 Freshmen Reunion started for Sue and me when we were picked up at the O'Hare Airport by Peter and Marilyn Gillquist and were taken to the Lincolnshire Marriott Resort north of Chicago. Peter's unquenchable enthusiasm is the main reason my shambles of information became this book.

The evening of July 28th the out-of-doors barbecue was followed by the very clever Chicago Gas Co. Quartet and a nine-member group called Hearing Voices. Then it was Freshmen time! This was the night Alan MacIntosh announced he was leaving the group, heading to New Hampshire to get married, and to do lots more things musical. Then Brian Eichenberger, Alan's replacement, came on stage and wowed everybody with the one song he had rehearsed with the group. He was warmly welcomed and Alan was sadly bid farewell by all of us.

On Saturday afternoon we filled the lounge room to hear the Metropolitan Jazz Orchestra of Chicago do Kentonesque arrangements very well! After dinner that evening, the Arbors did such a fine show before the Freshmen did theirs. The new guys called up the "Old Guys" (Bob, Ray, Rod and Ross). We did "Poinciana." Then all eight of us did "Day by Day" and "We'll Be Together Again."

On July 16th, Collectors' Choice Music released a CD with the *Five Trombones* and *Five Trumpets* albums on it.

The *Fresh News* for November/December carried the front page article about Bob Flanigan being honored by his hometown, Greencastle, Indiana. The city council adopted a resolution naming the band shell in Robe-Ann Park the "Bob Flanigan Band Shell." Bob graduated from Greencastle High School in 1944 and went to Germany with the Army. Then he went on the road - with a vocal group of all things - for 44 years! He made musical history and his hometown is proud of him.

Bob, Ken and Ross got together again on December 7th, but not to party. This time we wore dark suits and sat in a row quietly while Stan Freeburg did the eulogy for John Kraus, a masterful recording engineer who brought the Freshmen sounds and so many others to discs during his Capitol years.

On December 19th the Four Seasons Hotel Ballroom in Japan was full of Fresh fans who got their kicks from the Freshmen. Yasushi Ichiura was there to see that everything went right.

By this time the Vocal Group Hall of Fame in Sharon, Pennsylvania, had the trombone Bob played in the Army and my drums and the trumpet I learned on in the 8th grade. There are hundreds of photos and some old uniforms. The museum plans to rotate all the memorabilia so the display will continue to be different.

All through 1994, 1995 and 1996 Bob Baker and Chick Trafford hosted the weekly radio show called Freshmen and Friends on WHJB AM Greensburg, Pennsylvania. They made so many friends for the Freshmen. Thanks, guys!

1997

On January 19th, Orange Coast College's Moor Theater was a grand place for us to see and hear our Freshmen. Greg, Kevin and Bob Ferreira had taught Brian Eichenberger lots of tunes and they did just what the audience wanted - Freshmen stuff.

On January 20th I had lunch with Ken Albers. He has retired from the limousine business and is doing special projects for his son's manufacturing company. Ken does wiring and builds special work tables. He put a soundproof ceiling on the office so the shop sounds don't interrupt telephone orders.

January 31, 1997, my Sue retired from Rocketdyne and I stopped being a playground supervisor at our grade school down the street where I had been playing "grandpa" to the kids. We became footloose. . . no pool. . . no pets. Why stay at home? We went!

Hal Kratzsch was honored in his hometown of Warsaw, Indiana. The Historical Society there placed a sign in his memory in the downtown park where concerts are held.

The Four Freshmen Society Music Mart released another CD for members only. The two albums on this one were *Live in Tokyo* and *Mt. Freshmore.*

February 21st and 22nd found the Freshmen busy in Creston, Iowa, with shows, workshops and judging. They were long days full of rewarding experiences with very musical young people under the leadership of Steve Mattson, who has earned the respect of the Freshmen and lots of other people too. (Steve sent Brian Eichenberger to the Freshmen.) What a lucky group of students. If I could have interacted with real professional musicians at that age, I would have flipped!

Sunday, April 6, 1997, Greg, Brian, Kevin and Bob were back in California doing a concert in that beautiful hall at Mount San Antonio College. We missed them there, but we were at Fess Parker's Red Lion Inn, Santa Barbara, April 13th. Bob and Joan Magruder promoted the sold-out concert with some valuable help from 1390-AM, "KBOB," the "oldies" station there. It is owned by Bob Newhart, who did his first college appearance as the opening act for the Freshmen back in the stone age. In Santa Barbara the Freshmen did the new version of "Get Out of Town." As long as there are Cole Porter tunes like that, don't worry about the future of the Four Freshmen.

On May 8th the Freshmen did another benefit for Habitat for Humanity, this one in Buffalo's Center for the Arts. After the show the quartet met the University of Buffalo President, Bill Greiner and his wife, Carol, who knew the Freshmen Sound during their college years.

In June Sue and I flew back to Columbus, Indiana, for my 50th High School Reunion. All us kids spent the evening as if we were grown-ups. While I was there, the Mayor of Columbus, Fred Armstrong, gave me a wonderful surprise. It was the "Sagamore of the Wabash" award. (Years ago the Wabash Indian Chiefs relied on the "Sagamores," who were their hand-picked elders or advisors, for wisdom. Today, a Sagamore is the highest honor the Indiana Governor can give.) We also officially dedicated the sign west of town which you'll see in the photo section.

On July 17th, the 49th Anniversary Reunion was held at the Radisson Hotel in Sharon, Pennsylvania. This was the best yet. How do they keep getting better? Well, you hold it in a fine place like that and you invite 425 happy mellow people who mix well. Then you induct the Freshmen into the Vocal Group Hall of Fame and feature the current Freshmen in a fine hall on Saturday night. Add to that the Thursday and Friday appearances of the Lettermen. They charmed everybody. Toss in the Cleveland Jazz Orchestra on

Friday. Oh, and Bob Ferreira and Kevin Stout celebrated five years as Freshmen. That's the way to have a memorable occasion!

The *Fresh News* announced another new CD for FFS members only. The very rare album *Live at Penn State* is on this CD plus a few other recordings that had been equally hard to get - "Cape Cod," "I'll Be Seeing You" with Stan Kenton, our record of "Julie is Her Name" and Julie's response, a single she made of another Bobby Troup song called, "The Four Freshmen." Also featured is "Cry" and "Nowhere to Go." If you are not yet a Four Freshmen Society member, you have missed some very special CDs.

On October 4th, Ken and Nancy Albers and Ross and Sue Barbour were the dinner guests of Carmen Fangione and his wife, Sue Raney. We didn't have all the Freshmen there, but we had their records and fond memories of working with our "sister" Sue in the 1960s.

On November 1st the current Freshmen celebrated with Bob and Karen Cary and 250 of Bob's friends and relatives. It was Bob Cary's 60th birthday. He had dreamed of having a Freshmen evening for such a long time. The Visalia, California Country Club was the scene of his big soiree and the Freshmen sang "Happy Birthday" to a very happy man.

We saw the Freshmen again at the Glendale Theater, Glendale, California. The marquee called the afternoon show "Forever 50s Stage Show." The Freshmen didn't unpack their drums, keyboard, guitar or bass for this one because Nelson Riddle's son had an orchestra there to play behind all the acts. His musicians were mostly ex-Nelson Riddle Orchestra members. Tommy Sands sang some of his hits. Giselle McKenzie, in her knock-out blue dress, proved she can still please an audience. The Platters' voice trouble limited them, but the Freshmen had no limits at all.

Here are some numbers you might enjoy. As of December 1997 there were 2,051 Four Freshmen Society members, 20 of them in England, 75 in Japan, 8 in Denmark,

7 in Germany, 6 in Norway. There are members in 10 other countries. The crowd at the 50th Reunion in Las Vegas is expected to grow to almost 1000 people before September 17, 1998, when this Golden Anniversary Edition of *Now You Know* will go on sale.

1998

The Freshmen ushered in 1998 at the Holiday Inn in Ft. Walton Beach, Florida. Ray Brown, ex-Freshmen and friend-maker extraordinare, was the driving force who made the one-nighter happen.

January 10th marked the retirement of the quintessential morning man on Los Angeles radio. Robert W. Morgan was part of our landscape here for so many years, with his cleverness and his courage. He used "And So It's Over" as the last record he played on the air. I cried partly because I was so proud he would use my song from our record, and partly because we'll all miss him being there. Robert passed away May 26, 1998.

Also on January 10th Bob Ferreira married lovely Lisa Pritchard and they have settled down in Las Vegas.

The CD *Through the Years* was released by the Freshmen Music Mart for the FFS. This is music I never expected to be released at all. The "real fan" looks forward to this kind of inside information - songs from an old transcription - things Capitol didn't release. One is the Freshmen with the Airmen of Note in the background.

What would the Freshmen have done without Columbus, Ohio? January 24th, it was Columbus, Ohio, again, this time with the Four Aces and the Ink Spots. That great Columbus Jazz Orchestra did the backgrounds. Greg announced that the Freshmen quartet is not really a "nostalgia" group. Then they did the new arrangement of "Unforgettable." Wild applause prevailed! Of course - it's Columbus!

February 16th and 17th, Sue and I were in Ft. Walton Beach, Florida, with Ray Brown. He has a lot of irons in the fire, and keeps busy talking on the Internet with all you other computer junkies. We had come as far as New Orleans to see the Mardi Gras and stay with our good friend Ann Schroeder, who drove us to see Ray.

In March, Collectors' Choice Music released a CD of *Voices in Love* and *Love Lost,* my two favorite Freshmen albums. How sweet it is! The Four Freshmen Society Music Mart will have it for sale by 50th Anniversary time.

We four, who began doing that Freshmen Sound in 1948, had a need to hear chords sung that way. Evidently, you did too. *Happy 50th Anniversary everybody!*

EPILOGUE

I've never written a book before.

The only thing that made me think I could was my suitcase full of diaries of various shapes and sizes in which I had scribbled, in sleepy handwriting, the detailed report of what happened to us almost every day since high school.

I realized, as the story developed, that without any effort to do so I was shredding the press agent's glorified image of "show biz," but you'll note there were some glory and glamour days, too. We had some good times and some bad. Through it all, when we needed something good to happen, it happened.

As I look back now, it was almost as though God was a Freshmen fan and He wanted to keep us going so He could hear what we were going to do next. But we didn't sense that at the time. For all we knew, total defeat might have been waiting just around the next corner. Or total success. Fortunately we never met either of those two possibilities. I say "fortunately" because total failure could have sent us to other careers, and total success might have prompted us to cash in our chips and leave the game early.

Either way the fans would lose, and they needed us to satisfy their appetite for four-part harmony, because, at times, it seemed there was no other source.

If we continued to sing those four notes right, the fans could hear all those overtones - the harmonics that happen when four notes are sung right. It was the listeners' ears that turned the trick for us, and I'll always be thankful for the ears that made up the magic overtones.

We had enough success to keep us going, enough failure to keep us humble and enough fans to make it possible for the group to remain important from then to now. I feel very lucky to have been in the middle of all those good chords for the first 29 years.

Bringing pleasure to people was a fine way to make a living but we were worthwhile only because we were needed. Through all the personnel changes required by circumstances over the years, each man has tried to remain true to our quest.

That's why I say now to the overqualified over-achievers who are currently the Four Freshmen: It's an important thing you do. Along with countless others, I need your sound! Please do it well, and do it for a very long time, for the good of all of us out here who listen.

To you wonderfully supportive fans, I respectfully and gratefully say, "Thank You!" I wish I could mention each of your names in this paragraph and thank you individually. You made the Freshmen a permanent force for good in the music world. You came to the concerts and bought the recordings that kept us in the business. You have been making our dreams come true all along, and it's not over - not by a long shot. Heck, Capitol is even re-releasing our early songs on CDs! Today's Freshmen still thrive because of you fans.

If you have ever wondered how I feel about the Freshmen, then and now - and about you fans through it all, well - Now You Know!

Ross Barbour

APPENDIX 1

FOUR FRESHMEN ALBUMS

Voices in Modern
Capitol T522   8-2-54

Our very first album featured Bob, Don, Ross and Ken Errair. It was originally released as a 10-inch disc (H522, 8-2-54), then Capitol added "Stormy Weather," and "It's A Blue World," with Hal Kratzsch. We played the background sounds. The songs in this album are some of the strongest from our shows.

Four Freshmen and 5 Trombones
Capitol DT683   2-8-56

This has become the best known Freshmen album, featuring Bob, Don, Ross and Ken Errair. Pete Rugolo wrote the vocal and trombone arrangements, the first written charts we had used. The trombonists were all ex-Kenton players: Frank Rosolino, Harry Betts, Milt Bernhart, Tommy Pederson and George Roberts. Claude Williamson was pianist, Barney Kessel, guitar, Shelly Manne was on drums and Joe Mondragon played bass. This album was recorded in duo-phonic sound, a step toward stereo.

Freshmen Favorites
Capitol T743   7-30-56

Capitol liked to combine previously released single records into albums like this, and most Freshmen fans preferred albums rather than singles. Of the 12 songs, Hal Kratzsch, along with Bob, Don and Ross played and sang for "Poinciana," "The Day Isn't Long Enough," "Seems Like Old Times," and Bobby Troup's "Now You Know." The other eight songs were sung by Ken Errair, Bob, Don and Ross, but the backgrounds were provided by various musicians.

Four Freshmen and 5 Trumpets
Capitol T763   1-7-57

      Bob, Don, Ross and Ken Albers sang these Dick Reynolds' vocal and instrumental arrangements. The five trumpet players were Buddy Childers, Mannie Klein, Uan Rasey, and Joe and Ray Triscari. Milt Raskin played piano, Jack Marshall guitar, Frank Carlson drums and Don Simpson played bass. ("Easy Street" was recorded with four trumpets and Ken Errair, before Ken Albers joined us.)

Four Freshmen and Five Saxes
Capitol T844   9-2-57

      Instrumental arrangements for side one of this album were done by Pete Rugolo, those on side two by Dick Reynolds. The voices were those of Bob, Don, Ross and Ken Albers. These nine saxophone players were featured, but only five at a time: Georgie Auld, Gus Bivona, Chuck Gentry, Skeets Herfurt, Ted Nash, Willie Schwartz, Bob Cooper (solo on "Liza"), Dave Pell (solo on "I May Be Wrong") and Bud Shank (solo on "East of the Sun").

Voices in Latin
Capitol T922   2-3-58

      Pete Rugolo brought in a big band with Conrad Gozzo on trumpet, Laurindo Almeida on guitar and lots of Latin American drums by Chico Guerrero. Bob, Don, Ross and Ken Albers handled the vocals. The words on "Chelsea Bridge" were added to Billy Strayhorn's melody by Bill Comstock.

The Four Freshmen In Person
Capitol ST1008   5-5-58

      It was a rainy January 25, 1958, when Bob, Don, Ross and Ken Albers went out to Compton Junior College, just east of Los Angeles, to record this album. We accompanied ourselves as we sang all 14 numbers in a show punctuated with lots of Freshmen humor. (Note: if your album code begins with "T" it is a monaural record: "ST" indicates stereo.)

Voices In Love
Capitol ST1074   10-6-58

Bob, Don, Ross and Ken Albers sing the notes of this, my favorite Four Freshmen album. This is our first album with strings (violas and cellos). Bob Flanigan was heard on occasional trombone solos, as was Ken Albers on trumpet and flugelhorn. The album was arranged and conducted by Dick Reynolds.

Freshmen Favorites Vol. 2
Capitol T1103   1-5-59

Another combination of single records, except for "Till." I can't find any trace that it was released before this. Bob, Don and Ross are on all these vocals. Hal sang the low part and we played our own backgrounds on "Tuxedo Junction," "Baltimore Oriole" (Don's solo), "I Wanna Go Where You Go," and "Crazy Bones." (The drum sounds on "Crazy Bones" were played by Symphony Sid Garris.) You hear Ken Errair on the low part on "Please Remember." Walter Gross and Bobby Troup wrote this tune, accompanied by Nelson Riddle and his orchestra. Ken Albers is the low voice on "How Can I Begin To Tell," "What's It Gonna Be," (both arranged by Bob Enevoldsen); "You're So Far Above Me," "Whistle Me Some Blues," "Nights are Longer," and "That's the Way I Feel" (all arranged by Dick Reynolds). Ken and Bob did horn solos on "How Can I Begin To Tell" and "What's It Gonna Be," and Milt Bernhart soloed on "You're So Far Above Me."

Love Lost
Capitol ST1189   5-4-59

Here are more Dick Reynolds backgrounds, with vocal arrangements by Dick and Ken Albers. With this album we added violins to the violas and cellos, and Dick wrote the vocal interludes that Bob, Don, Ross and Ken Albers sang between the tunes. The horn solos are by Bob's trombone and Ken's trumpet and flugelhorn.

Four Freshmen and Five Guitars
Capitol ST1255   10-19-59

Dick Reynolds and Jack Marshall wrote single lines of notes for each guitar in most cases, so the guitarists were reading notes, not chord symbols. The guitar players included Al Hendrickson, Howard Roberts, Bobby Gibbons, Tommy Tedesco, Bill Pitman and George Van Epps. Shelly Manne and Jack Sperling played drums, Larry Bunker vibes, Red Mitchell bass. George Van Epps had a couple of guitar solos and Bob and Ken put in the brass solos. "Oh Lonely Winter" was written by Ken Albers and Bill Comstock when they were together as Stuarts. The Freshmen were Bob, Don, Ross and Ken Albers.

Road Show
Capitol TBO1327   1-18-60

This masterpiece two-record album features Stan Kenton and his Orchestra, June Christy and the Four Freshmen - Bob, Don, Ross and Ken Albers - live at Purdue University. We all spent 38 days between September 28th and November 4th on the Kenton band bus except to perform, to eat, and sometimes sleep. Saturday, October 10, 1959, the Capitol recording people, Lee Gillette and Johnny Palladino, met us at Purdue's Music Hall to record the show.

Voices and Brass
Capitol ST1295   2-1-60

Pete Rugolo wrote for ten trombones in this album, which provide the background for Bob, Don, Ross and Ken Albers. Dick Reynolds did the vocal arrangements. "Lonely For My Love," a Ken Albers/Bill Comstock song, is the sad, moody kind of thing trombones do so well. Don Barbour wrote "Never Again."

First Affair

Capitol ST1378   9-6-60

Ken Albers wrote the melody to the title song some-time before we started this album. We chose that title and decided we'd use harpsichord and woodwinds, but we didn't know of a song titled, "First Affair." I came to Ken with the idea, "Let me write the lyrics to that melody of yours and we'll have the title song." The Freshmen you hear are Bob, Don, Ross and Ken Albers. The idea for the album cover was a Capitol photographer's who photographed his children on some steps a block or so away from the Capitol Tower. It was just a vacant lot where a house had been torn down, but his photo technique made it look like a "secret garden." Buddy Cole and John Williams are heard on harpsichord. Buddy was well known the world over for his keyboard accompani-ment. John was just a newcomer on the Los Angeles scene who later went on to write movie scores and win so many Academy Awards, including for "E.T." and "Jurassic Park."

The Freshman Year

Capitol T1485   1-3-61

Through the years, Bob, Don, Ross and Ken Albers had been busily recording with orchestras and with five this-and-that. Some of the fans knew us as a vocal group, but they didn't know we played instruments as well. The Freshman Year returned us to the way we began, singing to our own accompaniments. Ken Albers and Bill Comstock came up with the title song. Bobby Troup calls "Their Hearts Were Full of Spring," his greatest achievement as a songwriter. Dick Reynolds wrote the arrangements we sang. My brother, Don, had been off the group four months when this was released. He is featured on three of the tunes. This is a very rare album. I think Capitol made very few because they wanted to promote the new group.

Voices In Fun
Capitol ST1543   5-1-61

This is the first Freshmen album with Bill Comstock on the second part (he replaced Don Barbour in September, 1960). Bob Flanigan is on lead, Ross Barbour on third, Ken Albers on fourth. To hear Billy May's writing and not hear his sense of humor is to be deaf! We had never used his rollicking good humor as our background before. He even sang a one-word solo on this album. Near the end of "Accentuate the Positive" we sang "Don't mess with mister in between," then he sang, "Yes!" Nobody will ever top Billy May at having fun with music!

Best of the Four Freshmen
Capitol ST1640   11-27-61

Capitol took eight songs from previous Freshmen albums, and ended each side with a single: "Day By Day" (Bob, Don, Ross and Ken Errair) and "Blue World" (Bob, Don, Ross, and Hal Kratzsch). The remaining songs feature Bob, Don, Ross and Ken Albers, except Bill Comstock sings second part on "Atchison, Topeka and the Santa Fe."

Stars In Our Eyes
Capitol ST1682   4-2-62

Here Bob, Bill, Ross and Ken Albers recorded songs other groups made famous. Their hit records made them "stars in our eyes." Dick Reynolds wrote for the band and some of the quartet arrangements, including "Tom Dooley." Ken Albers wrote the remaining quartet charts.

The Four Freshmen
Capitol Custom PB2503   1962

Here's an album that was never for sale - it was made for promotional purposes. The songs were primarily by Bob, Bill, Ross and Ken Albers. The album was packaged in a white, double-pocketed jacket with clean gold lettering on the front. Inside was a bio sheet on the group and its current members.

The Swingers
Capitol ST1753   9-4-62

Bill Holman wrote so many swinging, melodic arrangements for the Kenton band, Bob, Ken, Ross and Bill couldn't have done this album with anyone else. Dick Reynolds wrote some of the quartet arrangements, Ken Albers wrote the one for "Spring Isn't Spring Without You," a song Ken and Bill wrote together. Bill Comstock had been performing "Do Nothin' 'Till You Hear From Me," and Bill Holman enlarged that arrangement.

The Four Freshmen In Person Volume 2
Capitol ST1860   4-1-63

This album was taped live at Long Beach City College. Capitol recorded Bob, Bill, Ken and Ross, and took things from the two-hour concert that hadn't been recorded this way before. They left in some of our foolishness and the laughter.

Got That Feelin'
Capitol ST1950   9-3-63

Bob, Bill, Ken and Ross wanted Capitol to title this one "Folksy, Funky and Far Out" but the word "funky" wasn't considered acceptable then. Shorty Rogers wrote some spectacular things for his band, and we sang these as "dirty" as we could. Trumpets were Bud Brisbois, Al Porcino, Ray Triscari and Ollie Mitchell. Trombones were Lew McCreary, Tricky Lofton, Bobby Knight, and George Roberts. Earl Palmer played drums, Jimmy Bond bass, Ray Johnson keyboards, Bill Pitman bass guitar, Billy Strange tenor guitar, Glen Campbell 12-string guitar and Fats Blackstone played harmonica.

Funny How Time Slips Away
Capitol ST2067   3-30-64

Capitol put together a 10-tune album and tried to aim it at the "country" market with Willie Nelson's tune "Funny How Time Slips Away," as the lead-off hitter. "Do You Really Love Me" by Ken Albers had been released in the *Got That Feelin'* album. Bill Comstock wrote "Don't Make Me Sorry" and "Looking Over My Shoulder." Those fit right into the country-type background Jimmie Haskell and Shorty Rogers created. The same goes for my song "Tears In Our Eyes." Bob, Bill, Ross and Ken even did a country version of "Graduation Day." Here we are trying to do "country" and the previous album was supposed to be "funky." The record business was changing! We didn't know what would sell, and neither did Capitol.

More 4 Freshmen and 5 Trombones
Capitol ST2168   10-5-64

In Capitol's thinking and the thinking of many fans, the Freshmen and trombones fit together. We began the trend in 1956 and continued it in 1960 with *Voices and Brass*. Pete Rugolo did his thing again for Bob, Bill, Ken and Ross. Most of these songs were more contemporary hits.

Stan Kenton, June Christy, Four Freshmen
Capitol STCL575   1971

Capitol re-released our first in-person album as one of the three discs in boxed set. It's Bob Flanigan, Don and Ross Barbour and Ken Albers.

A Today Kind Of Thing
Liberty LST7542   1-2-68

This is the first album Bob, Bill, Ken and Ross did for Liberty after Jack Tracy got us together. He supervised the four studio albums we did for them. We had Dick Reynolds' backgrounds again, to make good things happen on songs of the '60s, as we'd already done on the songs of the '50s and '40s.

Today Is Tomorrow
Liberty LST7563   5-15-68

Bob, Bill, Ken and Ross recorded these tunes on April 2, 3, 4, and 5, 1968. Here again we tried to sing good chords, while the Dick Reynolds background reflected the times. The songs were recent hits by other people.

In A Class By Themselves
Liberty LST7590   1969

Three cheers for the very sensitive Ian Freebairn-Smith. His background treatment of the "Blue World/Phoenix" medley, "Misty Roses," "Old Friends," "Canadian Sunset" and "Girl Talk" won him our academy award. The background for "A Beautiful Friendship" is classic. I think this was our best Liberty album. Recorded by Bob, Bill, Ross and Ken in November, 1968.

Different Strokes
Liberty LST7   1969

Liberty released four of our albums, recorded in '68 and '69. They didn't hesitate. We were so eager to record music people would buy. But somehow we and Liberty couldn't come up with the winning combination, and this was the last studio album we recorded for them. Mike Melvoin and the Freshmen - Bob, Bill, Ken and Ross - gave it a good try with this LP.

My Special Angel
Sunset SUS5289   1969

Liberty re-packaged songs from two previous albums and released this on the Sunset label. "Canadian Sunset," "Cycles," "My Special Angel" and "Old Friends" came from the *Class By Themselves* album. "Glad To Be Unhappy," "Homeward Bound," "Love Is A Happy Thing," "Never My Love," "Fifty-Ninth Street Bridge Song" and "Wonderful World of Color" are out of the *Today Kind Of Thing* album. They were all recorded by Bob, Bill, Ken Albers and Ross.

Four Freshmen in Tokyo '68
Liberty LP8540   1969

As I remember, we imported 100 of these albums from Liberty of Japan and each Freshman - Bob, Bill, Ross and Ken - got ten to send to close friends. The other 60 were advertised in the *Fifth Freshman* newsletter on a first-come first-served basis and were sold in a day. Liberty of Japan recorded our live show at the Palace Hotel in 1968. It was a small room and a good audience. It was recorded on only two tracks, and some of the sounds that were not in balance could not be corrected.

That's My Desire
Coronet CXS279   1970

In 1951, film studios across the country were busily filming visual recordings, called "Telescriptions." They hoped TV show hosts would play these on television like disc jockeys played records on radio. We recorded "Poinciana" for Capitol in 1953, but the others, "That's My Desire," "Rockin' Chair" and "I Ain't Seen Nothin' Like You," recorded in Cleveland, are available only on this album. The other tunes in the album are by other groups. The "Telescription Disc Jockeys" didn't become a success. It was maybe 30 years later that MTV and others began using the telescription idea, calling them "videos."

The Fabulous Four Freshmen
Pickwick SPC3080   1970

Capitol released recordings from *Four Freshmen and 5 Trombones* and *Voices In Modern* in this package under the Pickwick label. Bob, Don, Ken Errair and Ross sang the songs.

Return to Romance
Stylist SA1900   1971

  The album cover also reads "The Greatest Hits of the Four Freshmen Sung for the 70s." Dick Reynolds put the backgrounds behind these songs. Some had strings, some trombones, some had both. Most of these tunes were first recorded long before "hi-fi" or stereo came into existence. This album has ten of our biggest hits, but with updated sound and backgrounds.

Four Freshmen Deluxe
Capitol Japan C80804   1971

  If you have the seven earlier albums - *Five Trombones, Freshmen Favorites, Voices in Love, Voices and Brass, Freshmen Year, Voices in Fun,* and *Swingers* - you have the music in this one. Freshmen voices include groups one through four.

Live At Butler University
Creative World ST1059   1972

  As this album shows, we didn't copy other vocal groups (we let them copy us!), we copied the Stan Kenton band. Through 17 songs, some with the band and some by ourselves, Bob, Bill, Ken and Ross spread the Four Freshmen sound all over everybody and we shared the thrill of Kenton with our listeners at our alma mater. Now that's fun!

Four Freshmen Story Volumes 1 & 2
Bovena Label 5C052   1973

  More re-releases of popular old singles and selections from earlier LPs. This is a double album and presumably very rare because I don't know that I've ever seen it! It is a collection of 28 songs, ranging all the way back to "Poinciana" and up to and including "Walk On By" from *Today is Tomorrow,* our 26th album.

A Taste Of Honey
Pickwick SPC3563   1977
    Under arrangement with Capitol, this Pickwick release is a package of nine songs from the *More 4 Freshmen and 5 Trombones album*. Freshmen voices are Bob, Bill, Ross and Ken.

Mt. Freshmore
Kahoots MRS8030   1977
    Before we got these songs played and sung, Ray Brown's wife. Nancy, and her brother, Jim Garrett, had the cover art ready: a rendering of the faces of Bob, Bill, Ross and Ray Brown superimposed over the faces of the four presidents on Mt. Rushmore! What an idea! The album contains some of the songs we did in our shows. We did some over-dubbing and multiple recording, so sometimes the four of us sound like ten. This is Ray's only album with the group.

Songs and Story of the Four Freshmen
Crystal 134EVC85   1978
(Germany)
    All re-issues.

Alive And Well In Nashville
Phonorama PR5563   1982
    This album features Group #6. These ten songs include some old Freshmen standards re-recorded, plus some new additions like "Carnival of Life," "Down Home Shangrila" and "Every Time You Touch Me." There's a unique bit of trivia on this album. The liner notes indicate the vocals are by Bob Flanigan, John Albers, William Goodman and Dennis Grillo. Is that the only time Ken and Autie used their legal names - John Kenneth Albers and William Austin Goodman - in the credits?

All Time Favorites
Capitol 4XL9170   1985
(cassette tape only)

Here again, Capitol has re-released the great hits of the Freshmen in a new package. The songs include "Blue World" and "Poinciana" from our earliest days, to more recent favorites like "Girl Talk" and "This Could Be The Start Of Something Big."

Fresh
Pausa PR7193   1986

Meet Group #8: Bob Flanigan on lead, Autie Goodman on second, Mike Beisner on third and Rod Henley on low voice, singing and playing their own backgrounds. The nine songs are "Do I Do," "IGY," "Route 66," "Sophisticated Suite" (the high spot of any evening!) "Sunshine Of My Life," "We're In This Love Together," "What is Life," "Sailing" and "Maxine."

Freshmas
Ranwood RCD 8239   1992

Bob Flanigan, Autie Goodman, Rod Henley and Mike Beisner put together the long-awaited Freshmen Christmas album. It's Autie's final recording and the last by Bob Flanigan before he retired after 44 years. The Dick Reynolds arrangements are the last before his untimely death.

APPENDIX II

ALBUMS OF SPECIAL INTEREST

Solo Session
Capitol T807   1957
    Features Ken Errair with instrumental backgrounds.

Togetherness
Capitol ST1957   10-63
    Veteran Freshmen lead singer Bob Flanigan joins
forces with the superb guitar styling of John Gray.

Here's the Solo Voice of Don Barbour
Capitol ST1716   1962
    There will never be a Freshmen voice mellower than
Don Barbour's. Don finished recording these tunes shortly
before his tragic death.

Thanks to You by Hal Kratzsch
Capitol   1955
    Recorded for Capitol's "Kenton Presents" series. This
is available on cassette from the Four Freshmen Society
Music Mart, 738 Monroe St., Oshkosh, WI 54901-4649.

APPENDIX III

FRESHMEN COMPACT DISCS

Collectors Series   Capitol   CDP7-93197-2

Road Show   Capitol   CDP7-96328-2
  Bob, Don, Ross and Ken Albers

Best Now   Capitol (Japan)   TOCP-9125
  various

**Four Freshmen and
5 Trombones**   Capitol (Japan)   TOCJ-5321
  Bob, Don, Ross & Ken Errair)

Live at Butler University   Creative World   STD-1059
  Bob, Bill, Ross & Ken Albers

Greatest Hits   Curb   D2-77612
  various

Graduation Day   Laserlight   12120
  Alive and Well in Nashville retitled

Fresh   Ranwood   RCD 8241
  Bob, Mike, Autie & Rod Henley

Freshmas   Ranwood   RCD 8239
  Bob, Mike, Autie and Rod

Voices in Standards   Hindsight   HCD 801
  Greg, Mike, Kevin Stout & Bob Ferreira

We Thought About You   MLB Records   MLB 1210
  Autie Goodman & Mike Beisner

Day by Day — Hindsight Jazz — HCD604
A Navy Swings radio show from 1962
Bob, Bill, Ross and Ken Albers

Angel Eyes — Viper's Nest — VN-159

**Spotlight on the
Four Freshmen** — Capitol — CDP 7243-8-31205-2-9
Part of Great Gentlemen of Song Series

It's a Blue World — Viper's Nest — VN-170
Part 2 of a never before released 1958 live concert
Part 1 is same as Angel Eyes (above)

Portrait of the Artists: 22 Legendary Hits
CEMA/Sound Exchange S21-18369

The Entertainers — Sarabandas — sri CD 383
Voices in Fun, coupled with 10 tracks by the
Billy May Orchestra

**5 Trombones and
5 Trumpets** — Collectors Choice Music — 72438-19175-2-7

Easy Street — Aero Space Records — RACD 1023
Soundtrack from a 1956 Ray Anthony TV show

**Voices in Love/
Love Lost** — Collector's Choice Music — 72438-19879-2-6

Live at Penn State — Four Freshmen Society — FFS 9701
Available only to Four Freshmen Society members

Four Freshmen Through the Years
Four Freshmen Society FFS 9702
Available only to Four Freshmen Society members

APPENDIX IV

FOUR FRESHMEN SINGLE RECORD DISCOGRAPHY

HAL

DON

BOB

ROSS

1. MR. B'S BLUES/
   THEN I'LL BE HAPPY 1293 2/51 CAPITOL
2. NOW YOU KNOW/PICK UP YOUR
   TEARS & GO HOME 1377 4/51 CAPITOL
3. IT'S A BLUE WORLD/
   TUXEDO JUNCTION 2152 7/52 CAPITOL
4. THE DAY ISN'T LONG ENOUGH/
   STORMY WEATHER 2286 11/52 CAPITOL
5. POINCIANA/
   BALTIMORE ORIOLE 2398 4/53 CAPITOL

**KEN
ERRAIR**

DON

BOB

ROSS

6. HOLIDAY 2564 8/53 CAPITOL
7. IT HAPPENED ONCE
   BEFORE 2564 8/53 CAPITOL
8. SEEMS LIKE OLD TIMES/
   CRAZY BONES 2745 2/54 CAPITOL
9. I'LL BE SEEING YOU/
   PLEASE REMEMBER 2832 6/54 CAPITOL
10. WE'LL BE TOGETHER AGAIN/MY HEART
    STOOD STILL 2898 8/54 CAPITOL
11. MOOD INDIGO/LOVE TURNS
    WINTER TO SPRING 2961 10/54 CAPITOL
12. IT NEVER OCCURRED TO ME/
    MALAYA 3070 3/55 CAPITOL
13. DAY BY DAY/
    HOW CAN I TELL HER 3154 6/55 CAPITOL
14. CHARMAINE/IN THIS WHOLE
    WIDE WORLD 3292 11/55 CAPITOL
15. ANGEL EYES/LOVE IS JUST AROUND
    THE CORNER 3359 2/56 CAPITOL
16. GRADUATION DAY/LONELY NIGHT
    IN PARIS 3410 4/56 CAPITOL

N.B. Numbers 6 and 7 are singles

KEN ALBERS **DON** **BOB** **ROSS**			

17. HE WHO LOVES AND RUNS AWAY/
    YOU'RE SO FAIR   3532   9/56 CAPITOL
18. THAT'S THE WAY I FEEL/
    WHAT'S IT GONNA BE 3652   2/57 CAPITOL
19. JULIE IS HER NAME/SOMETIMES
    I'M HAPPY   3779   8/57 CAPITOL
20. HOW CAN I BEGIN TO TELL/
    GRANADA   3832 11/57 CAPITOL
21. WHISTLE ME SOME BLUES/
    NIGHTS ARE LONGER 3930   3/58 CAPITOL
22. CANDY/ROUTE 66   4341   2/60 CAPITOL

23. TEACH ME TONIGHT/
    SHANGRI-LA   4749   6/62 CAPITOL
24. I'M GONNA GO FISHING/
    TAPS MILLER   4824   9/62 CAPITOL
25. SUMMERTIME/BABY WON'T YOU
    PLEASE COME HOME 5007   6/63 CAPITOL
26. FUNNY HOW TIME SLIPS AWAY/
    CHARADE   5083 11/63 CAPITOL

KEN ALBERS **BILL COM-STOCK** **BOB** **ROSS**			

27. MY BABY'S GONE/
    DON'T MAKE ME SORRY 5151   3/64 CAPITOL
28. WHEN I STOP LOVIN' YOU/
    NIGHTS ARE LONG   5401   4/65 CAPITOL
29. COLD CAPE COD/. . . MEN IN THEIR
    FLYING MACHINES   5471   8/65 CAPITOL
30. CRY/NOWHERE TO GO 32070 12/66   DECCA
31. CHERISH-WINDY/COME FLY WITH ME-
    UP,UP & AWAY   56047 6/68 LIBERTY
32. BLUE WORLD-PHOENIX/
    MY SPECIAL ANGEL   56099 4/69 LIBERTY
33. ACCENTUATE THE POSITIVE/
    I WANT TO BE HAPPY 1822   N/A CAPITOL*
34. HERE'S HOLLYWOOD/
    AND SO IT'S OVER   2402   N/A CAPITOL*

* Released as Capitol Special Products

APPENDIX V

FOUR FRESHMEN PERSONNEL

There have been 21 Freshmen in the 50 years between September, 1948 and September, 1998.

NAME	BEGAN	LEFT	YEARS	MONTHS
Bob Flanigan	9-20-48	9-92	44	
Ross Barbour	9-20-48	8-77	28	11
Don Barbour	9-20-48	9-60	12	
Hal Kratzsch	9-20-48	5-53	4	8
Ken Errair	5-53	4-56	2	11
Ken Albers	4-56	1-82	25	9
Bill Comstock	9-60	3-73	12	6
Ray Brown	3-73	8-77	4	5
Autie Goodman	8-77	9-92	15	
Dennis Grillo	8-77	4-82	4	8
Rod Henley	4-82	9-86	4	5*
Mike Beisner	4-82	10-94	12	6**
Dave Jennings	10-86	4-87	—	6
Newton Graber	4-87	7-87	—	3
Kirk Marcy	8-87	8-88	1	
Garry Lee Rosenberg	8-88	4-91	2	8
Greg Stegeman	8-89			current
Kevin Stout	9-92			current
Bob Ferreira	9-92			current
Alan MacIntosh	10-94	7-96	1	9
Brian Eichenberger	7-96			current

* plus July and August 1987
** minus August '89 to August '90

APPENDIX VI

THE FOUR FRESHMEN BY GROUPS

GROUP #	NAMES	FROM	TO
1.	Bob Flanigan, Don Barbour, Ross Barbour, Hal Kratzsch	9/48	5/53
2.	Bob, Don, Ross, Ken Errair	5/53	4/56
3.	Bob, Don, Ross, Ken Albers	4/56	9/60
4.	Bob, Bill Comstock, Ross, Ken (Albers)	9/60	3/73
5.	Bob, Ray Brown, Ross, Ken	3/73	8/77
6.	Bob, Autie Goodman, Ken, Dennis Grillo	8/77	1/82
7.	Bob, Autie, Mike Beisner, Dennis	1/82	4/82
8.	Bob, Autie, Mike, Rod Henley	4/82	8/86
9.	Bob, Autie, Mike, Dave Jennings	8/86	10/86
10.	Bob, Autie, Mike, Newton Graber	10/86	7/87
11.	Bob, Autie, Mike, Rod Henley (same as #8)	7/87	8/87
12.	Bob, Autie, Mike, Kirk Marcy	8/87	8/88
13.	Bob, Autie, Mike, Garry Lee Rosenberg	8/88	8/89
14.	Bob, Autie, Greg Stegeman, Garry Lee	8/89	8/90
15.	Greg, Autie, Mike, Garry Lee	8/90	10/90
16.	Bob, Autie, Greg, Gary Lee (same as 14)	10/90	4/91
17.	Bob, Autie, Greg, Mike Beisner	6/91	9/92
18.*	Greg, Mike, Kevin Stout, Bob Ferreira	9/92	10/94
19.	Greg, Alan MacIntosh, Kevin, Bob Ferreira	10/94	7/96
20.	Greg, Kevin, Bob, Brian Eichenberger	7/96	present

* This group is sometimes called the "New Four Freshmen," since none of the original members remained. Bob Flanigan toured with them for their first several weeks. Group #17 was briefly reactivated for a European tour in November, 1992.

THE FOUR FRESHMEN TODAY

Let me introduce you to the Four Freshmen as they are today. Greg Stegeman (clockwise from top) has been a Freshman since 1989. He sings the lead part and plays trumpet, flugelhorn and keyboards. Brian Eichenberger plays bass mostly, but you'll hear him on drums and keyboard, too. He has been with the group since summer, 1996, singing the second part. Bob Ferreira plays drums and flugelhorn. He has sung the fourth part since 1992. Kevin Stout also became a Freshman in 1992. He plays guitar, trombone and bass and sings the third part.

For booking information contact:

Bob Flanigan
P. O. Box 93534, Las Vegas, NV 89193-3534
Telephone: (702) 361-6132 • Fax: (702) 361-6132

Joel Rothman
27 Carmel Bay Drive, Corona Del Mar, CA 92625
Telephone: (714) 759-5003 • Fax: (714) 759-5421

You Can Keep Up With The Four Freshmen!
"Day In and Day Out"

738 *Monroe Street*
Oshkosh WI 54901-4649

The Society is dedicated to the support of The Four Freshmen, celebrating the historic contributions of the best vocal instrumental jazz quartet in the history of American Music . . . past, present and future!

We have over 2200 society members throughout the world, and our numbers are growing steadily because the organization provides so many services to members:

• FRESH NEWS, the official fanzine of the FFS is published six (6) times a year . . . with interesting articles and commentary by The Four Freshmen (current and alumni members of the group), plus contributions by members . . .

• The Freshmen Concert Itinerary

• Assistance in locating sources for historic records

• New compact discs, cassettes, videos,etc..

• Four Freshmen Reunions and society gatherings, etc.

First Y ear Membership Dues
Single (USA) @ $20.00
Couple (USA) @ $30.00
Single (Int'l) @ $25.00
Couple (Int'l) @ $35.00

For membership infor mation write, call or e-mail:
The Four Freshmen Society
P.O. Box 9804
McLean, VA 22102-0804
Voice: 1-703-471-4672
Fax: 1-703-471-6004
E-Mail: Lorrain4DB@aol.com

Visit the Four Freshmen Home Page on the World Wide Net:
http://www.opms.com/4fresh

The Early Years
1941 - 1947

BY EDWARD F. GABEL
Foreword by Pete Rugolo

STAN KENTON: THE EARLY YEARS
1941 1947
By Edward F Gabel
Foreword by Pete Rugolo

The Stan Kenton Orchestra was playing Chicago in January, 1942 when Ed Gabel went to hear the band. By the end of the day Kenton had offered the 17 year old Gabel a job!

For the next five years "Gabe" served as Stan Kenton's personal assistant and confidant. He chose and cleared the tunes the band played on live radio broadcasts. He made sure people got to the bus or train on time and that Stan didn't forget to eat dinner during those 16 hour days at the Paramount Theater in New York. Gabe was Kenton's sounding board about his plans and problems and the things he wanted to achieve in music.

Gabel recalls the endless road trips back and forth across the country, travels to military bases with the Bob Hope radio show, nerve-wracking wartime military flights, being stranded by a flood in Nebraska, flat tires miles from the nearest help, working in Canada's sub-zero temperatures. The book is filled with road stories and the endless progression of ballrooms and theaters.

Includes over 30 photos plus a reproduction of Bob Hope's radio monologue, aired on his D-Day broadcast. **STAN KENTON: THE EARLY YEARS** is a book every Kenton fan will want to own!

AND SO IT'S OVER

Words and Music by ROSS BARBOUR
Arrangement by KEN ALBERS

FOLLYWOOD PUBLISHING CO.
1386 Rio Vista Ct.
Simi Valley CA 93065